FOR SELF-EXAMINATION

AND

JUDGE FOR YOURSELVES!

AND

THREE DISCOURSES

1851

FOR SELF-EXAMINATION

AND

JUDGE FOR YOURSELVES!

AND

THREE DISCOURSES

1851

BY

SØREN KIERKEGAARD

TRANSLATED BY

WALTER LOWRIE, D.D.

PRINCETON
PRINCETON UNIVERSITY PRESS

First published in Great Britain, 1941

Reprinted by offset in the United States of America, 1944

ISBN 0-691-01952-5

Fourth Printing, 1974

PREFACE

THE accompanying volume, published on the same date, and entitled *Training in Christianity*, is introduced by an Introduction so adequate and by a Preface so inordinately long that I can spare the reader another introduction, which could only be a repetition of the first, and might spare myself the trouble of writing a preface. At this moment I am inclined almost to be resentful that another preface is required, for originally I proposed to publish in one big volume all the works which now, for the convenience of the purchaser, are presented in two.

However, there is pleasure to be found even in the writing of prefaces. Kierkegaard's prefaces were usually short, but they were always significant. Four of them are to be seen in this volume. However, one of his most amusing books (entitled *Prefaces*) consists of nothing but prefaces—eight of them in all, one on the heels of the other. He was reduced to this expedient because, as he pretended, his wife had exacted of him the promise that he would write no more 'books'.

This volume (which may be regarded as the second, because the works which it contains actually followed the others and are properly a sequel) appears on the same date as the other because the works contained in the twain belong intimately together, and therefore ought not to be far separated—in case someone may have an appetite prodigious enough to want both.

From the beginning of his 'authorship' it was S. K.'s custom to 'accompany' his 'aesthetic' works, which always were pseudonymous, with one or more 'Edifying Discourses', which were published over his own name, and therefore, to preserve the fiction of his anonymity, were often issued by another publisher. Although the principal works published in this volume were in themselves decisively religious, and now for the first time were no longer pseudonymous, S. K. continued the custom of accompanying them, when there was no longer the same reason for it. The first two Discourses in this volume were meant as an accompaniment of the longer work which follows. And it is well that they should not be separated; for the reader surely must feel a grateful sense of relief in passing from the more trenchant and closely reasoned works to the Discourses, which were really as well as ostensibly addressed to simple Christians.

The Discourse which concludes this volume may also be regarded as the conclusion of S. K.'s religious writing. It was published in 1855, introducing dramatically into the bitter conflict S. K. was waging against conventional Christianity a purely religious note, which dated, as he remarked, from an earlier time. This Discourse was in fact actually delivered in the Citadel Church on May 18, 1851, and the Preface is dated on S. K.'s forty-first birthday, May 5, 1854. He also meant it as a gesture of farewell to his deceased father, to whom in similar terms he had dedicated all of the earlier Edifying Discourses. This Discourse was not translated by me but by Professor David Swenson, who kindly contributes it to this volume—much to my satisfaction, not because it spares me a little labour, but because I am happy to be formally associated with him in the enterprise of making Kierkegaard known and understood, to which we have both of us contributed whole-heartedly.

The two larger works contained in this volume, although they were not published together, and although the second was not published at all in S. K.'s lifetime, evidently belong together, as the sub-title of the second suggests, as well as the characterization of it as 'Second Series'. Just as evidently they are the sequel of the work contained in the 'first' volume; and because of this close connexion it is not possible to deal with them separately in an introduction. The Introduction to the companion volume gives briefly an account of the *whole* 'production' dating from the years 1848–51, and it cannot be necessary to repeat it here if, as may be expected, the reader who will read only one of these works will prefer to read the first. In any case, for a fuller elucidation I have to refer to my book on *Kierkegaard*, especially to the chapters entitled 'Back to Christianity!' and 'Venturing Far Out'.

In these two later works, which are also the last of the sort, the polemical note becomes increasingly prominent, without becoming predominant as it was in the subsequent period. And the fact that such a book as *For Self-Examination*, the polemical point of which is so sharp, made no impression upon the Church—not even so much as to encourage the publication of the 'Second Series'—makes it evident, I think, that to make his voice heard

S. K. was compelled to shout as loudly and shrilly as he did in the open attack which followed tardily and reluctantly.

I take this occasion to say that, though I admire the courage and vigour with which the attack was conducted and sympathize with its aim, though I regard these tracts for the time as among the most virile documents that have ever been written, and though I revere the author of them as a witness for the truth who triumphed over great weakness to become a martyr, yet it is not for me to translate them. Some day they should be translated, but preferably not until S. K. has become well known and his deeply religious aim is understood. For the present, the works which are here presented supply us with all the buffeting we can bear or profit by. S. K. said that he regarded them as addressed 'solely' to himself. I cannot read them without feeling that they are addressed principally to me.

WALTER LOWRIE

PRINCETON

*June 10th, 1938**

*The date signifies that this volume and its companion were ready two years ago and only a year after I had finished my *Kierkegaard*. They are the first things I translated, and they were at once delivered to the printer. But publication has been so long deferred owing to Professor Swenson's insistence that these most incisive and trenchant works ought not to be set before a public which had not yet been made acquainted with the milder tone of S. K.'s Edifying Discourses. So I set to work to translate the numerous works which have been published under the titles *The Point of View* and the *Christian Discourses*. Others have made known *Fear and Trembling* and a discourse entitled *Purify your Heart!* My translation of the *Stages* will be published by the Princeton University Press at about the same time as this volume, and not much later Professor Swenson's translation of the *Concluding Unscientific Postscript* which I completed after his untimely death. But now (on July 26th, 1940) I am not sure whether I have done well to publish last these works which I translated first. I am sure only of this, that it is high time Kierkegaard were revealed to the English-speaking world through the books which most clearly reveal him.

CONTENTS

TWO DISCOURSES
AT THE COMMUNION ON FRIDAYS

by
S. Kierkegaard

Copenhagen
1851
[Aug. 7.]

At the end of 1849

NOTE BY THE TRANSLATOR. Regina of course is meant. This dedication is a reply to her husband's rejection of the suggestion of a *rapprochement*.

PREFACE

A gradually progressing work as a writer which had its beginning in *Either/Or* seeks here its definite point of rest at the foot of the altar, where the author, who personally knows best his imperfection and guilt, does not by any means call himself a witness for the truth, but only a peculiar sort of poet and thinker who, 'without authority', has nothing new to bring but would read the fundamental document of the individual, humane existence-relationship, the old, well-known, from the fathers handed down—would read it through yet once again, if possible in a more heartfelt way. (See the postscript to my 'Concluding Postscript'.)

In this direction I have nothing more to add. But let me give utterance to this which in a sense is my very life, the content of my life for me, its fullness, its happiness, its peace and contentment. There are various philosophies of life which deal with the question of human dignity and human equality—Christianly, every man (the individual), absolutely every man, once again, absolutely every man is equally near to God. And how is he near and equally near? Loved by Him. So there is equality, infinite equality between man and man. If there be any difference, O, this difference, if difference there be, is peaceableness itself, undisturbed it does not disturb the equality in the remotest degree. The difference is that one man bears in mind that he is loved, perhaps day in and day out, perhaps for seventy years day in and day out, perhaps having only one longing, the longing for eternity, impatient to lay hold of it and be off, he is busy with this blessed occupation of bearing in mind that he—ah, not for his virtue's sake—is loved. Another perhaps does not reflect upon the fact that he is loved, perhaps he is glad and thankful to be loved by his wife, by his children, by his friends, by his acquaintances, and does not reflect that he is loved by God; or perhaps he sighs at the thought that he is loved by nobody and does not reflect that he is loved by God. 'Yet', so might the first one say, 'I am guiltless, I cannot help it if another overlooks or disdains the love which is lavished as richly upon him as upon me.' Infinite divine love which makes no distinction! Ah—human ingratitude!—what if among us men there were likeness and equality in the sense that we are like one another, entirely alike, inasmuch as not one of us rightly reflects that he is loved.

Turning now to the other side, and expressing thanks for such sympathy and good will as have been showed me, I could wish that I might as it were present these works (as I now take the liberty of doing) and commend them to the nation whose language I am proud to have the honour of writing, feeling for it a filial devotion and an almost womanly tenderness, yet comforting myself also with the thought that it will not be disgraced by the fact that I have used it.

Copenhagen, late summer 1851.   S. K.

I

Luke 7 : 47

LORD JESUS CHRIST, though indeed Thou didst not come into the world to judge the world, yet as love which was not loved Thou wast a judgement upon the world. We call ourselves Christians, we say that we have none to turn to but to Thee—alas, where might we go when to us also, just because of Thy love, the condemnation applies that we love little? To whom (oh, disconsolate thought!) if not to Thee? To whom then (oh, counsel of despair!) if Thou really wouldst not receive us mercifully, forgiving us our great sin against Thee and against love, forgiving us who have sinned much because we loved little?

Luke 7: 47. BUT TO WHOM LITTLE IS FORGIVEN, THE SAME LOVETH LITTLE

MY hearer, at the altar the invitation is uttered: 'Come hither, all ye that labour and are heavy laden, and I will give you rest.' The individual responds to the invitation, he goes up to the altar—then there is another saying which might be inscribed above the church door, on the inside, not to be read by them that go into the church, but only by them that are going out: 'To whom little is forgiven, the same loveth little.' The first saying is the altar's invitation, the other is its vindication, as if it said, 'If at the altar thou wast not sensible of the forgiveness of thy sins, of every sin of thine, the fault lies in thee, the altar is blameless, because thou only lovest little.' Oh, how hard it is in praying to reach the Amen. For though to the man who never has prayed it looks easy enough, easy enough to get quickly through with it, yet to the man who had a longing to pray and began to pray the experience must have occurred that he constantly felt as if there were something more upon his heart, as if he could not get everything said, or get it said as he would like to say it, and so he does not reach the Amen—likewise how hard it is at the altar rightly to apprehend the forgiveness of sins. There thou art promised the gracious forgiveness of all thy sins. If thou dost rightly hear that promise, takest it quite literally as 'the forgiveness of all thy sins', then shalt thou leave the altar as light of heart, in a godly sense, as a newborn babe upon whom no anxiety weighs, even lighter in heart, forasmuch as much has weighed upon thy heart; at the altar there is no one who would retain even the least of thy sins—no one, unless it be thou. Then cast them all from thee, and the remembrance of them as well (lest in that way they be retained), and also the remembrance that thou didst cast them from thee (lest in that way they be retained by thee)—cast it all from thee, thou hast nothing whatever to do but to cast off, to cast off what weighs upon thee and oppresses thee. What could be easier? Commonly it is a heavy task to be bound by duty to assume burdens—but to dare, to be in duty bound to cast them off! And yet how difficult! Yes, rarer even than one who assumed all burdens, rarer even than that is one who has performed the apparently easy task of feeling himself, after receiving the assurance of the gracious pardon of his sins and the pledge of it, entirely lightened of every, even the least sin, and of every, even the greatest sin. If thou wert able to look into men's hearts, thou wouldst surely see how many there are who approach the altar oppressed and sighing under their heavy burden; and when they leave the altar, if thou couldst look into their hearts, possibly thou mightest see that substantially there was not a single one who went away entirely lightened of his burden, and sometimes perhaps thou mightest see that there was one who went away even more oppressed, oppressed now by the thought that he surely had not been a worthy guest at the altar, seeing that he found there no relief.

We will not conceal from one another that such is the case, we will not talk in such a way as to ignore how things are in reality and represent everything as so perfect that it does not fit the case of us real men. Oh, no, what help would such a discourse be? But, on the other hand, when the discourse makes us as imperfect as we are, it helps us to persevere in steady effort, neither being intoxicated by the vain dream that by the one effort everything was decided, nor losing heart in silent despondency because this effort did not succeed according to our wish, that what we had prayed for and desired did not come to pass.

In the brief time prescribed let us dwell upon this word: 'But to whom little is forgiven, the same loveth little'—a word of *condemnation*, but also a word of *comfort*.

And thou, my hearer, be not disturbed that I speak in this manner at the moment when thou art going up to the altar, perhaps expecting and exacting that he who is to speak at this moment should speak in another manner, employing every means to reassure the individual and render him confident, and then, if he learned subsequently that this holy ceremony had not been a joy and blessing to the individual, he could speak to him in a different manner. Ah, my friend, in part I make answer that in truth it is not the single individual who here fails to succeed entirely; no, it is only a single individual who succeeds entirely. In part I would say that there is a concern, a heart-felt concern, which perhaps assists a man better to succeed in the highest sense—better than too much confidence and too careless an intrepidity. There is a longing after God, a confidence in God, a comfort and hope in God, a love, a frankheartedness—but what most surely finds Him is perhaps a sorrow after God. Sorrow after God—that is no fleeting mood which promptly vanishes with a nearer approach to God; on the contrary, it is perhaps deepest when it draws nearest to God, as one who thus sorrows is more fearful for himself the nearer he comes to God.

To whom little is forgiven, the same loveth little. This is a word of condemnation.

Commonly the situation is conceived thus: justice means severe judgement; love is the gentle thing which does not judge, or if it does, love's judgement is a gentle judgement. No, no, love's judgement is the severest judgement. The severest judgement ever passed upon the world, more severe than the flood, more severe than the confusion of Babel or than the destruction of Sodom and Gomorrah—was it not Christ's innocent death, which yet was love's sacrifice? And what was this judgement? Surely this, that 'love' was not loved. So it is here. The word of judgement and condemnation does not say, the one to whom little was forgiven had sinned much, in the sense that the sins were too many or too great to be forgiven. No, the condemnation is, 'He loves little.' So it is not justice which sternly denies pardon and forgiveness to the sinner; it is love which says gently and compassionately, '*I* forgive thee all; if but little is forgiven thee, it is because thou dost love but little.' Justice sternly prescribes the limit and says, 'No farther, now the measure is full, for thee there is no more forgiveness', but there it stops. Love says, 'Everything is forgiven thee—if but little is forgiven, it is because thou dost love but little'; so that there is superadded a new sin, a new guilt, that of deserving condemnation, not for sins already committed, but for lack of love. Wouldst thou learn to fear, learn then to fear, not the severity of justice, but the gentleness of love.—Justice looks condemningly upon a man, and the sinner cannot endure its glance; but when love looks upon him, yea, though he withdraws from its glance, though he casts down his eyes, he nevertheless is aware that it looks upon him; for love pierces far more deeply into life, to the very issues of life, than does justice, which establishes a yawning gulf between the sinner and itself, whereas love stands beside him, accuses not, condemns not, pardons and forgives. The sinner cannot endure the condemning voice of justice, he seeks if possible to stop his ears; but even if he would, it is impossible for him to hear love, whose condemnation is (oh, frightful condemnation!), 'Thy sins are forgiven thee'. Frightful condemnation, in spite of the fact that the words in themselves are anything but terrifying; and this precisely is the reason why the sinner cannot close his ears to what nevertheless is a judgement of condemnation. Whither shall I flee from Justice, if I take the wings of the morning and flee to the uttermost sea, even there it is, and if I hide myself in the deep, it is there, and so it is in every place—yet, no, there is one place where I can flee: to love. But when love judges thee, and the judgement is (oh, horror!), 'Thy sins are forgiven thee'! Thy sins are forgiven thee—and yet there is something (and this something is in thee, for where else in all the world could it find foothold when love forgives all?), there is something in thee which makes thee sensible that they are not forgiven. What, then, is the horror of the sternest judgement in comparison with this horror? What is the stern sentence of wrath, calling down a curse, in comparison with this sentence: 'Thy sins are forgiven thee'? So justice indeed is almost gentler, which says as thou sayest, 'No, they are not forgiven'. What is the suffering of 'the fratricide' when he fled from place to place for fear of being recognized by the 'mark' of justice which condemned him—what is this suffering compared to the tortures of the unfortunate one who heard, 'Thy sins are forgiven thee', and heard it not as salvation but as condemnation? Thy sins are forgiven thee! Frightful severity! That love, that it is love, pardoning love, which, not censoriously, no, itself suffering thereby, is thus transformed into judgement and condemnation; that love, pardoning love, which would not, as justice does, reveal guilt, but on the contrary would hide it by pardoning and forgiving, that it is this nevertheless which, alas, itself suffering thereby, reveals guilt more frightfully than justice does!—Think of the thought expressed by 'self-condemned.' 'The man is self-condemned', says justice, 'there is no forgiveness for him'; and thereby it thinks of his many sins, for justice can hide nothing. Love says, 'The man is self-condemned'—thinking thereby not of his many sins, oh, no, it is willing to forget them all, it has forgotten them all, and yet, 'He is self-condemned', says love. Which is the more terrible? Surely the latter, which sounds indeed like the speech of madness; for he is not accused of his many sins, no, the accusation is that they are forgiven him, that everything is forgiven. Think of a sinner who is sinking into the abyss, listen to his anguished cry when with his last groan he justified the righteousness which his life had mocked, and says, 'The punishment is deserved, I am self-condemned'. Terrible! There is but one thing more terrible, if it is not justice he addresses but love, and says, 'I am self-condemned'. Justice will not be mocked, and love, verily, still less. Sterner than the sternest judgement against the greatest sinner is love's saying, 'To him but little is forgiven—because he loves but little'.

To whom little is forgiven, the same loveth little. This is a word of condemnation, but also a word of *comfort.*

I know not, my hearer, what evil thou didst do, what thy guilt, what thy sins are; but of one fault we are all guilty more or less: of loving too little. So comfort thyself with this word, as I comfort myself with it. And how do I comfort myself? I comfort myself with the thought that this word has nothing to say about the divine love, but only about mine. It does not say that now the divine love has grown weary of being love, that now it has changed, weary as it were of squandering indescribable compassion upon an ungrateful race or upon ungrateful me, and that now it has become something different, a lesser love, its heart cooled because love became cold in the ungrateful race of men or in ungrateful me. No, about this the Word says nothing whatever. And be comforted as I am—by what? By this, that the reason the Word does not say this is that the holy Word does not lie, so that it is not by accident or cruel design that the Word is silent about this, whereas in fact it is true that God's love has become weary of loving. No, if the Word does not say it, then it is not so; and even if the Word said it—nay, God's Word cannot say it, because the Word cannot lie. Oh, most blessed comfort in the deepest sorrow! If in truth God's love had changed, and thou not knowing of this, but concerned about thyself for the fact that hitherto thou hadst loved but little, wert to strive with pious resolution to kindle the love within thee to a flame, and with the same care wert to nourish the flame, and then, though with a feeling of shame for the imperfection of thy love, wouldst draw near to God to be reconciled with Him, as the Scripture expresses it, . . . but He had changed! Think of a maiden in love; she acknowledges to herself with deep concern how little she has loved hitherto—'Now', she says to herself, 'I will become sheer love'. And she succeeds; these tears of anguish which she sheds in concern about herself, these tears do not quench the fire, no, they are too hot for that; no, it is just these tears that bring the fire to a flame . . . but meanwhile the lover had changed, he was no longer loving. Oh, one deep concern for a man, just one may be enough—more than this no man can bear! If when a man in deep self-concern has to acknowledge how little he has loved, he then were to be afflicted by the anguishing thought that God might have changed—then, then indeed I should despair, and I should despair at once, for then there would be nothing to wait for either in time or in eternity. But therefore I comfort myself with this word, and I close every way of evasion, and I put aside all excuses and all palliations, and I lay bare my breast where I am to be wounded by the word which condemningly pierces me with the verdict, 'Thou has loved but little'. Oh, pierce even deeper, thou healing word, say, 'Thou hast not loved at all'— even if the verdict is pronounced in these terms, I feel, in one sense, no pain, I feel an indescribable bliss; for precisely this condemnation of me, this sentence of death upon me and my paltry love, implies at the same time something different: that God is unchanging love.[1]

Thus it is I comfort myself. And I find hidden in the word a

---

[1] In August 1855, in the midst of his attack upon the Established Church, S. K. issued his last Discourse, dedicated as usual to his father, and entitled 'God's Un-changeableness'. A preface dated May 5, 1854, which was his birthday, states that it had been delivered in the Citadel Church on May 18, 1851, i.e. shortly before the date of this sermon, and that it was a return to the text of his first Discourse, James 1: 17–21.

comfort which thou also, my hearer, must find precisely when
thou hearest the word in such a way that it wounds thee. For it
does not read, to whom little was forgiven, the same *loved* little;
no, it reads, '*loves* little'. Oh, when justice sits in judgement it
draws up the account, it closes it, it uses the past tense, it says,
'He *loved* little', and therewith pronounces that the case is for
ever decided, 'we two are separated and have nothing to do with
one another'. On the other hand, the Word, the Word of love,
reads, 'To whom little is forgiven, the same loves little'. He
loves little, yet he *loves*; that is to say, so it is now, at this present
instant—more than this love does not say. Oh, infinite Love!
that thou remainest true to Thyself even in Thy least utterance!
He loves little now, at this instant, and what is the Now? Swiftly,
swiftly it is past, and now, in the next instant, everything is
changed, now he loves, even if it be not much, yet he strives to
love much; now all is changed, except love, it is unchanged,
unchangeably the same love which lovingly has waited for him,
which lovingly could not bear to close the case for him, could
not bear to seek separation from him, but has remained with
him, and now it is not justice which pronounces conclusively,
'He loved little', now it is love which, rejoicing in heaven,
says, He loved little', meaning to say that it is different now, that
so it was once upon a time, but now he loves much.

But substantially is it not true then that the forgiveness of sins
is *merited*, if not by works, yet by love? When it is said that to
whom little is forgiven, the same loveth little, is it not implied that
it is love which determines whether and in how far one's sins are
to be forgiven—so that the forgiveness of sins is *merited*? Oh, no.
In the same passage of the Gospel, a bit earlier (v. 42 ff.), Christ
speaks about two debtors, one of whom was greatly in debt, the
other little, and both found forgiveness. He says, 'Which of them
will love him most?' and the answer is, 'He to whom he forgave
most'. Notice now how we do not enter the unblessed territory
of meritoriousness, but how everything remains within the sphere
of love! When thou dost love much, much is forgiven thee—and
when much is forgiven thee thou dost love much. Behold here the
blessed law of the progressive recurrence of salvation in love!
First thou dost love much, and much is forgiven thee—oh, but
see now how love exerts its influence more powerfully, the fact that
so much was forgiven elicits in turn more love, and thou lovest

much because much was forgiven thee! It is with love as it is with faith. Think of one of the unfortunates whom Christ healed by a miracle. In order to be healed he must believe—now he believes and is healed. Now he is healed—and then faith becomes twice as strong, now that he is saved. It is not as though he believed, and then the miracle occurred, and then it was all over; no, the accomplishment increases his faith as much again, after the accomplishment of the miracle his faith is doubly as strong as when he believed before being saved. And so, it is with this matter of loving much. Strong is the love, divinely strong in weakness, the love which loveth much and to which so much is forgiven; but still stronger is the second instance of love, when the same love loves a second time, and loves because much was forgiven.

My hearer, thou dost remember doubtless the beginning of this discourse. At this solemn moment it is possible to disturb the worshipper in two ways: either by talking about something inappropriate, even if the subject were important and the discourse weighty; or by talking disturbingly about that which in such a moment is one's most immediate concern. 'To whom little is forgiven, the same loveth little'—this might seem disturbing just at the moment when thou art on the point of going up to the altar where thou art to receive the forgiveness of all thy sins. Oh, but as the edifying in its first instance is always dismaying, and as all true love in the first instance is always disquietude, so also that which seems to be a disturbance is not always disturbing; that which is in truth tranquillizing is always disquieting. But is there any comparison between these two dangers: that of being tranquillized in deceitful security; and that of being disquieted by being reminded of a disquieting thought? Of what disquieting thought? Is it of *that* disquieting thought that also it can be forgiven if hitherto one has loved but little? It is a singular thing, this matter of disquietude. He who is thoroughly educated by it does not, it is true, appear so strong as he who has remained without knowledge of it. But at the last instant, just by his feebleness, it is he perhaps who is the strongest, in the last instant, just by feebleness, he perhaps succeeds when the strongest fails to succeed.

So may God bless this disquieting discourse, that it may have disquieted thee only for a good end, that tranquillized at the altar thou mightest be sensible that thou dost receive the gracious pardon of all thy sins.

II

1 Peter 4: 8

O Lord Jesus Christ, the birds have their nests, the foxes their holes, and Thou didst not have whereon to lay Thy head, homeless wast Thou upon earth—and yet a hiding-place, the only one, where a sinner could flee. And so to-day Thou art still the hiding-place; when the sinner flees to Thee, hides himself in Thee, is hidden in Thee—then he is eternally defended, then 'love' hides the multitude of sins.

1 Peter 4: 8. LOVE SHALL HIDE THE MULTITUDE OF SINS

THIS is true when it is a question of human love—and in a double sense, as we have shown in another place.[1] The loving man, he in whom there is love, hides the multitude of sins, sees not his neighbour's fault, or, if he sees, hides it from himself and from others; love makes him blind, in a sense far more beautiful than this can be said of a lover, blind to his neighbour's sins. On the other hand, the loving man, he in whom there is love, though he has his faults, his imperfections, yea, though they were a multitude of sins, yet love, the fact that there is love in him, hides the multitude of sins.

When it is a question of Christ's love, the word can be taken only in one sense; the fact that He was love did not serve to hide what imperfection there was in Him—in Him the holy One in whom there was no sin, neither was guile found in His mouth, this being inevitably so, because in Him there was only love, love in His heart and love only, in His every word, in all His work, in His whole life, in His death, until the very last. Ah, in a man love is not so perfect, and therefore, or rather nevertheless, he profits by his love: while he lovingly hides a multitude of sins, love does unto him as he unto others, it hides his sins. Thus he himself has need of the love which he shows to others, thus he profits by the love within him, which though it be directed outwardly to hide the multitude of sins, does not, however, like Christ's sacrificial love, embrace the whole world but only very few persons. Ah, though it is seldom enough a man is loving, yet 'what wonder', as a man might be tempted to say, 'what wonder a man endeavours to be loving, seeing that he himself is in need of love, and to that extent is really looking after his own interest by being loving'. But Christ was not in need of love. Suppose that He

[1] *The Works of Love*, Part II. v.

had not been love, suppose that unlovingly He would only be what He was, the holy One, suppose that instead of saving the world and hiding the multitude of sins He had come into the world to judge the world in holy wrath—imagine this in order to conceive the more vividly that precisely to Him it applies in a singular sense that His love covered the multitude of sins, that *this* is 'love', that (as the Scripture says) only one is good, namely, God, and that thus He was the only one who in love hid the multitude of sins, not of some individuals but of the whole world.

Let us then in the brief moment prescribed speak about this word:

Love (Christ's love) *hides the multitude of sins.*

And is it not true that thou hast felt the need, and to-day especially, of a love which is able to hide sins, to hide thy sins? For this reason it is thou art come to-day to the Lord's altar. For though it is only too true, as Luther says, that every man has a preacher with him, who eats with him, drinks with him, wakes with him, sleeps with him, is always with him wheresoever he may be, whatsoever he has in hand, a preacher called flesh and blood, lusts and passions, custom and inclination—yet it also is certain that every man has a confidant who is privy to his inmost thoughts, namely conscience. A man may succeed in hiding his sins from the world, he may perhaps rejoice foolishly in his success, or perhaps with a little more truthfulness he may acknowledge to himself that this is a pitiful weakness and cowardice, that he does not possess the courage to reveal himself—but a man cannot hide his sins from himself. That is impossible; for the sin which was hid absolutely even from the man himself would indeed not be sin, any more than if it were hid from God, a thing which cannot be, inasmuch as a man so soon as he is conscious of himself, and in everything in which he is conscious of himself, is also conscious of God, and God of him. And for this reason conscience is so mighty and so precise in its reckoning, so ever-present, and so incorruptible, because this privy confidant which follows man everywhere is in league with God, this preacher which is with man when he wakes and when he sleeps (ah, if only it does not make him sleepless with its sermon!), with him everywhere, in the noisy bustle of the world (ah, if only it does not with its voice transform the world's noise into stillness!), in loneliness (ah, if only it does not hinder him from feeling alone in the most solitary place!), in his daily work (ah, if only it does not estrange him from it and distract him!), in festal surroundings (ah, if only it does not make this seem to him a dismal prison!), in holy places (ah, if only it does not hold him back from going there!), this privy preacher which follows man, knowing privily what now, now at this instant, he does or leaves undone, and what long, long ago—I do not say was forgotten, for this privy confidant, having a frightful memory, takes care of that—but long, long ago was past. Man cannot escape from this confidant, any more than (according to the saying of the pagan poet[1]) he can ride away from the sorrow which sits behind him on horseback, or any more (if one would give a different turn to the comparison) than it 'helps the deer to rush forward to escape the arrow lodged in its breast—the more violently it moves forward, only the more deeply does it run the arrow into it'.

To-day, however, thou art far indeed from wishing to make the vain attempt to flee from or avoid this privy preacher, thou hast given him leave to speak. For in the pulpit it is doubtless the parson that preaches, yet the true preacher is the confidant of thine inmost thoughts. The parson can only preach in general terms—but the preacher within thee is exactly the opposite: he preaches solely and alone about thee, to thee, in thee.

I would make no attempt to dismay men, being myself only too much dismayed; but whosoever thou art, even if thou art, humanly speaking, almost pure and blameless, when this privy preacher preaches before thee in thine inward man, thou also dost feel, what others perhaps sense with more dismay, thou also dost feel a need to hide thyself, and though it had been told thee a thousand times, and a thousand times again, that it is impossible to find this hiding-place, thou yet art sensible of the need. Oh, would it were possible for me to flee to a desert isle where never any man had come or would come; oh, that there were a place of refuge whither I could flee far away from myself, that there were a hiding-place where I am so thoroughly hid that not even the consciousness of my sin could find me out, that there were a frontier line, which were it never so narrow, would yet be a separation between my sin and me, that on the farther side of the yawning abyss there were a spot never so small where I might stand while the consciousness of my sin must remain on the other

---

[1] Horace: *Odes*, iii. 1, 40.

side, that there were a pardon, a pardon which does not make me increasingly sensible of my sin, but truly takes my sin from me, and the consciousness of it as well, would that there were oblivion![1]

But such is actually the case, for love (Christ's love) hides the multitude of sins. Behold, all has become new! What in paganism was sought after and sought in vain, what under the dominance of the Law was and is a fruitless effort—that the Gospel made possible. At the altar the Saviour stretches out His arms, precisely for that fugitive who would flee from the consciousness of his sin, flee from that which is worse than pursuit, namely, gnawing remorse; He stretches out His arms, He says, 'Come hither', and the attitude of stretching out His arms is a way of saying, 'Come hither', and of saying at the same time, 'Love hides the multitude of sins'. Oh, believe Him! Couldst thou think that He who savingly opens His bosom for thee might be capable of playing upon words, capable of using a meaningless phrase, capable of deceiving thee, and at this precise instant—that He could say, 'Come hither', and the instant thou art come and He holds thee in His embrace it then might be as if thou wert entrapped, for here, just here there could be no forgetting, here . . . with the holy One! No, this thou couldst not believe, and if thou didst believe it, thou wouldst not come hither—but blessed is he who quite literally believes that love (Christ's love) hides the multitude of sins. For the loving man, yea, even the most loving, can only shut his eyes to thy sins—oh, but thine eye for them he cannot shut. A man can with loving speech and sympathy seek to mitigate thy guilt in thine eyes also, and so hide it as it were from thee, or at least up to a certain point almost as it were hide it in a way from thee—ah, but really to hide it from thee, literally to hide it from thee, so that it is hidden like what is hidden in the depths of the sea and which no one any more shall behold, hidden as when what was red as blood becomes whiter than snow, so hidden that sin is transformed to purity and thou canst dare to believe thyself justified and pure—that is something only one can do, the Lord Jesus Christ, who hides the multitude of sins. A man has no authority, he cannot command thee to believe and

<hr>

[1] The reader may need again to be apprised that it was only in the Easter experience of 1848 S. K. attained—after so many years of penance!—that his sins were 'forgotten' by God as well as forgiven, and that it was his duty as well as his privilege to forget them.

merely by commanding help thee to believe. But authority is required even if it be to teach, and what authority must that be (greater even than the authority which bade the troubled waves be still)—what authority is required to bid the despairing man, the man who in the tortures of repentance cannot and dare not forget, the contrite sinner who cannot and dare not cease to gaze upon his guilt, what authority is requisite to shut his eyes, and what authority to bid him open the eyes of faith so that he can see purity where he saw guilt and sin! This divine authority is possessed only by Him, Jesus Christ, whose love hides the multitude of sins.

He hides them quite literally. When a man places himself in front of another and covers him entirely with his body so that no one at all can get a sight of him who is hidden behind—so it is that Jesus Christ covers with his *holy body* thy sin. Though justice were to rage, what more can it want? For satisfaction has indeed been made. Though the repentance within thee be so contrite that it thinks it a duty to aid external justice to discover thy guilt—satisfaction indeed has been made, a satisfaction, a vicarious satisfaction, which covers thy sin entirely and makes it impossible to see it, impossible for justice, and therewith impossible for the repentance within thee or for thyself to see it, for repentance loses the sense of sight when justice to which it makes appeal says, 'I can see nothing'.

He hides them quite literally. As when the hen concerned for her brood gathers her chickens under her wing at the instant of danger, covering them completely and ready to give her life rather than deprive them of this shelter which makes it impossible for the enemy's eye to discover them—precisely thus does He hide thy sin. Precisely thus; for He too is concerned, infinitely concerned in love, ready to give His life rather than deprive thee of thy secure shelter under His love. Ready to give His life— yet, no, it was just for this He gave His life, to assure thee of shelter under His love. Therefore not just like the hen, concerned indeed in the same way, but infinitely more concerned than the hen when she hides her chickens, but otherwise unlike, for He hides by His death. Oh, eternally secure; oh, blessedly reassuring hiding-place! There is still one danger for the chickens; although hidden, they are constantly in danger: when the mother has done her utmost, when out of love she has given her life, then are they deprived of their shelter. But He on the contrary—true enough, if with His life He had covered thy sin, there would be possibility of the danger that He might be deprived of His life, and thou of thy shelter. It is quite different when with His death He covers thy sin. He would be ready (if such a thing were needful, if all had not been done decisively once for all)—He would be ready to give His life again to procure for thee a shelter by His death, rather than that thou shouldst be deprived of the shelter. It is to be taken quite literally: He covers over thy sin just by covering it with His death. Death may dispose of a living man, but a dead man cannot possibly be thus disposed of, and so it is impossible that thou mightest be deprived of thy shelter. Infinite love! They talk about works of love, and many such works can be enumerated. But when they say 'the work of love', then there is only one work, yea, only one work, and thou knowest at once (strange as it may seem) precisely about whom they are speaking, about Him, Jesus Christ, about His atoning death, about Him who hides the multitude of sins.

This is preached at the altar; for what is preached from the pulpit is essentially His life, but at the altar, His death. He died once for the sins of the whole world, and for thy sins; His death is not repeated, but *this* is repeated: that He died also for thee,[1] for thee who dost receive the pledge that He died also for thee, this is repeated at the altar where He gives *Himself* to thee for a shelter. Oh, sure hiding-place for sinners! Oh, blessed hiding-place!—especially if one has first learnt what it means when conscience accuses, and the Law condemns, and justice pursues with punishment, and then, when wearied unto despair, to find repose in the one shelter that is to be found! A man, even the most loving man, can at the most give thee extenuation and excuse, leaving it to thee to make what use of them thou art able; but himself he cannot give thee. That only Jesus Christ can do; He gives thee Himself as a shelter; it is not some comforting thought He gives thee, it is not a doctrine He communicates to thee; no, He gives thee Himself. As the night spreads concealment over everything, so did He give up His life and became a covering behind which lies a sinful world which He has saved.

---

[1] 'Also for me' expressed S. K.'s joyful experience at his first conversion in 1838—just after he had registered in his Journal the Hegelian reflection that 'Christ died for all', not for the single individual.

Through this covering justice does not break as the sun's rays break through coloured glass, merely softened by refraction; no, it impotently breaks against this covering, is reflected from it and does not pass through it. He gave Himself as a covering for the whole world, for thee as well, and for me.

Therefore Thou, my Lord and Saviour, Thou whose love covers and hides the multitude of sins, when I am thoroughly sensible of my sin and of the multitude of my sins, when before the justice of heaven only wrath is pronounced upon me and upon my life, when on earth there is only *one* man whom to escape I would flee were it to the end of the world, and that man myself—then I will not commence the vain attempt which leads only to despair or to madness, but at once I will flee unto Thee, and Thou wilt not deny me the shelter which Thou lovingly hast offered unto all, Thou wilt screen me from the eye of justice, save me from this man and from the memory with which he plagues me, Thou wilt help me as I become a transformed, another, a better man, to dare to abide in my shelter, forgotten by Justice and by that man I abhor.

My hearer, to-day thou art come to seek the love which hides the multitude of sins, seeking it at the altar. From the minister of the Church thou hast received assurance of the gracious pardon of thy sins; at the altar thou dost receive the pledge of it. Oh, not this only; for thou dost not merely receive this pledge as thou mightest receive from a man a pledge that he has such-and-such a feeling for thee or purpose towards thee; no, thou dost receive the pledge as a pledge that thou dost receive Him; in receiving the pledge thou dost receive Christ Himself, in and with the sensible sign He gives Himself to thee as a covering for thy sins. As He is the truth, thou dost not learn to know from Him what the truth is, to be left then to thine own devices, but thou dost remain in the truth only by remaining in Him; as He is the way, thou dost not learn from Him to know which way thou shalt go, and then being left to thine own devices canst go thine own way, but only by remaining in Him canst thou remain in the way; as He is life, thou dost not from Him have life given thee, and then canst shift for thyself, but only by remaining in Him hast thou life: so it is also that He is the covering; only by remaining in Him, only by living into Him, art thou in hiding, is there a cover over the multitude of thy sins. Hence the Lord's Supper is called Communion with Him; it is not merely in remembrance of Him, not merely a pledge that thou hast communion with Him, but it is the communion, the communion which thou shalt endeavour to maintain in thy daily life by more and more living thyself out of thyself and living thyself into Him, into His love who hides the multitude of sins.

FOR SELF-EXAMINATION
PROPOSED TO THIS AGE

by
S. Kierkegaard

Copenhagen
1851
[Sept. 10.]

'Since we have known the fear of the Lord, we seek to win men' (2 Cor. v. 11). For to begin at once, or as the *first* thing, to want to win men—that perhaps might even be called ungodliness, at all events worldliness, not Christianity, any more than it is fearing God. No, let thy striving *first* express, let it express first and foremost, thy fear of God.—This has been my striving.

But Thou, O God, let me never forget that though I were to win not a single person—if only my life expresses (for the protest of the mouth is deceitful!) that I fear Thee—this means that 'all is won!' And on the other hand, if my life (for the protest of the mouth is deceitful!) does not express that I fear Thee—this means that 'all is lost!'

In the summer of 1851

PREFACE

My dear reader:

If it be possible, read aloud! If thou art willing to do that, let me thank thee for it; if thou wilt not only do that thyself but wilt also prompt others to do it, let me thank each one severally and thank thee again and again! By reading aloud thou wilt receive the impression most strongly that thou hast to do here only with thyself, not with me, for I am without authority, and not with any other people at all, for that would be a distraction.

August 1851.   S. K.

CONTENTS

I

HOW TO DERIVE TRUE BENEDICTION
FROM BEHOLDING ONESELF
IN THE MIRROR OF THE WORD

James 1 : 22 to the end

Fifth Sunday after Easter

PRELIMINARY REMARKS

THERE is a saying which often comes into my mind, the saying of a man to whom I as a Christian cannot, it is true, be said to owe anything, for he indeed was a pagan, but to whom I personally owe much, a man who lived under conditions which, as I think, correspond exactly to the conditions of our age—I mean the simple wise man of olden time.[1] It is related of him that when he was accused before the people, there came to him an orator who handed him a carefully prepared speech of defence. The simple wise man took it and read it. Thereupon he gave it back to the orator and said, 'It is a fine and well-composed speech' (so it was not because the speech was a poor one that he gave it back), 'but,' he continued, 'I am now seventy years old, so I consider that it would not be becoming of me to make use of the art of an orator.' What did he mean by this? First of all he meant: my life is too serious to be profitably served by the art of an orator; I have staked my life; even if I am not eventually condemned to death, I have staked my life, and in the service of the Deity I have performed my mission—so I would not now, at the last moment, destroy the impression of myself and of my life by means of artful orators or oratorical arts. In the next place he meant: the thoughts, ideas, concepts, which in the course of twenty years (so long has the time been), when I was known to all, ridiculed by your comic poets, regarded as an eccentric, constantly attacked by 'nameless persons' (such are his very words),[2] I have developed in conversation with every sort of person in the market-place—these thoughts were my very life, they have been my concern early and late, if they have been of concern to no one else, at least they have concerned me infinitely, and at times (as you observed with wonder) when I have been capable of gazing steadily for a whole day at nothing, I was preoccupied with these thoughts—and so I think that, without the aid of artful orators or oratorical arts, if on the day of my trial I am inclined to say

[1] This of course is Socrates. The story which follows, about the orator Lysias, is derived from Cicero's *de Oratoria*.

[2] Plato's *Apology*, 18 c. S. K. thinks how aptly this applies to the anonymous attacks in the *Corsair* from which he had suffered.

anything at all, I shall be capable of uttering a few words; for the mere fact that presumably I shall be condemned to death does not essentially alter the situation, and what I shall say will naturally remain the same and about the same thing and in the same way as hitherto, just as yesterday I talked with the tanner in the market-place—these few words, it seems to me, I can say well enough without preparation or any man's assistance; of course I am not entirely without preparation, for I have been preparing myself for twenty years, nor am I entirely without assistance, since I count upon the assistance of the Deity. But, as I have said, these few words . . . as for that, I do not deny that 'these few words' may become more prolix, but if I were to live twenty more years I should continue to talk about the same things I have constantly talked about, in any case artful orators and oratorical arts are not for me.—Oh, thou most serious of men! Misunderstood, thou wast obliged to drain the poisoned goblet. Thou wast not understood. Then for over two thousand years thou hast been admired —'but have I been understood?' is a true word.

And now about preaching! Ought it not also to be as serious? He who is to preach ought to live in the thoughts and conceptions of Christianity; this should be his daily life—if such is the case, then (as Christianity teaches) thou also shalt have eloquence enough, and just what is needed, when thou dost speak straight-forwardly without special preparation. On the other hand, it is a false eloquence, if without being concerned with these thoughts or living in them, one sits down from time to time to make a collection of such thoughts, culling them perhaps in the field of literature, and working them up together into a well-developed discourse, which then is learned perfectly by rote and is admirably delivered, both with respect to elocution and with respect to the movements of the arms. No, just as in a well-appointed house one is not obliged to go downstairs to fetch water, but by pressure already has it on the upper floors merely by turning the tap, so too is with the real Christian orator, who, just because Christianity is his life, has eloquence, and precisely the right eloquence, close at hand, immediately present to him—however, it goes without saying that the intent of this is not to allot a place of honour to twaddlers, certain as it is that it is without preparation the twadd-lers twaddle. Moreover, the Scripture saith, 'Swear not at all, let your speech be Yea and Nay, whatsoever is more than this is of the evil one.' So also there is an art of oratory which is of the evil one, when it is treated as the higher, when in fact it is the lower. For the sermon ought not to establish an invidious distinction between the talented and the untalented, it ought rather in the unity of the Holy Ghost to fix attention exclusively upon the requirement that actions must correspond with words. Thou simple man, even if thou wert of all men the most limited—in case thy life expresses the little thou hast understood, thou dost speak more potently than the eloquence of all orators! And thou woman, although thou art entirely mute in gracious silence—in case thy life expresses what thou hast heard, thine eloquence is more potent than the art of all orators!

Such is the case. But let us beware of grasping at what is too high; for because it is true, it does not follow that we are able to do it. And thou, my hearer, wilt reflect that the more lofty the conception of religion is, the more stern it is; but from this it does not follow that thou canst bear it, it would perhaps be to thee an occasion of offence and of perdition. Perhaps thou art still in need of this lower form of the religious, requiring a certain art in the presentation of it to render it more attractive. The strictly religious man is one whose life is essentially action—and his presentation of religion is far more impertinent and more lenten than the more perfectly composed oration. If thou, my hearer, art of this mind, then accept this book and read it for edification. It is not to be ascribed to my perfection, nor to thine, that this discourse is composed as it is; on the contrary, it is (from a godly standpoint) an imperfection and a weakness. I acknowledge—and thou too, wilt thou not?—my imperfection; and so thou wilt acknowledge thine—not to me, no, that is not required, but to thyself and to God. Alas, we who call ourselves Christians are, Christianly understood, so coddled, so far from being what Christianity requires of them that call themselves Christians, men who have died to the world; we have hardly even a notion of that sort of seriousness, we cannot yet dispense with or renounce the artistic presentation and its soothing effect, cannot endure the true impression of reality—well then, let us at least be honest and admit it. If some one does not straightway understand what I say here and what is intended by it, let him be slow to judge, let him take his time, we shall soon get closer to the subject. Ah, but whoever thou art, have confidence, surrender thyself. There is no question of any force I might employ—I the most powerless of men—but there shall not even be employed the least persuasion or craft or guile or allurement to draw thee so far out that thou mightest (as nevertheless for all that thou surely oughtest not, and surely wouldst not if thy faith were great)—thou mightest regret that thou didst surrender thyself; believe me (I say it to my own shame), I also am too much coddled.

But be ye doers of the Word, and not hearers only, deceiving your own selves. For if any be a hearer of the Word and not a doer, he is like unto a man beholding his natural face in a mirror: for he beholdeth himself, and goeth away, and straightway forgetteth what manner of man he was. But he that looketh into the perfect law, the law of liberty, and continueth therein, he being not a forgetful hearer but a doer of the work, this man shall be blessed in his deed. If any man among you seems to be religious, and bridleth not his tongue, but deceiveth his own heart, this man's religion is vain. Pure religion and undefiled before God and the Father, is this, To visit the fatherless and widows in their affliction, and to keep himself unspotted from the world.

PRAYER

Father in heaven, what is man that Thou visitest him, and the son of man that Thou art mindful of him?—and in every way, in every respect! Verily, Thou didst never leave Thyself without a witness; and at last Thou didst give to man Thy Word. More thou couldst not do; to compel him to make use of it, to hear it or read it, to compel him to act according to it, Thou couldst not wish. Ah, and yet Thou didst do more. For Thou art not like a man—rarely does he do anything for nothing, and if he does, he at least would not be put to inconvenience by it. Thou, on the contrary, O God, bestowest Thy Word as a gift—and we men have nothing to give in return. And if only Thou dost find some willingness on the part of the single individual, Thou art prompt to help, and first of all Thou art the one who with more than human, yea, with divine patience, dost sit and spell it out with the individual, that he may be able rightly to understand the Word; and next Thou art the one who, again with more than human, yea, with divine patience, dost take him as it were by the hand and help him when he strives to do accordingly—Thou our Father in heaven.

TIMES differ and even though it often is the case with 'times' as with a man who is completely changed—but remains as mad as ever, only in a new form—nevertheless it is perfectly true that times differ, and different times demand different things.

There was a time when the Gospel, the Gospel of grace, was transformed into a new law, more severe towards man than the old law. Everything had become in a way torturing, laborious, and reluctant, almost as if (in spite of the angels' song at the first introduction of Christianity) there was no joy either in heaven or on earth. By their narrow-minded self-torture, people had (in revenge!) made God just as narrow-minded. They went into monasteries and stayed there—oh, yes, it is true, this was voluntary, and yet it was bondage, for it was not truly voluntary, they were not content, not glad to be there, not free, and yet they had not frankheartedness enough to let the thing alone or to leave the monastery again and become free. Good works had become everything.[1] And like unwholesome excrescences, upon trees, so were these works spoiled by unwholesome excrescences, which often were merely hypocrisy, the vain conceit of meritoriousness, or simply idleness. Precisely here is where the fault lay, not so much in the works. For let us not exaggerate, let us not use the error of another age as the occasion of a new error. No, take away from works this unwholesomeness and untruth, and let us then merely retain good works in sincerity, in humility, and in serviceable activity. That is to say, with these works it should be as when, for example, a bellicose youth, in view of a dangerous undertaking, comes voluntarily to the commander and begs, 'Oh, may I not have leave to get into it?' If in this wise a man were to say to God, 'Oh, may I not have leave to give all my goods to the poor? That there might be anything meritorious in it—oh, no! I recognize in deep humility that if ever I am to become blessed, it is by grace I shall be saved, just like the robber on the cross; but may I not have leave to do it, so that I can work solely for the extension of God's kingdom among my fellow men?' Then, yes (to speak in a Lutheran way), in defiance of Satan, of the newspapers, of 'the highly esteemed public' (for the Pope is no longer a menace), in defiance of the sensible ecclesiastical or worldly objections of all shrewd men and women, in spite of all this it is well pleasing to God. But it was not thus at the time of which we were speaking.

Then there stepped forth a man, Martin Luther, from God and with faith. With faith (for verily faith was needed for the task)

---

[1] The reader may need to be reminded that S. K. hesitated to publish his *Works of Love* for fear of scandalizing the Lutheran orthodoxy which insisted upon the doctrine of 'faith alone'. It may be remarked also that, in spite of the tone of this passage, the monastic life had a powerful attraction for him.

or by faith he reinstated faith in its rights. His life was an expression of works—let us not forget that—but he said, 'A man is saved by faith alone.' The danger was great. How great it was in Luther's eyes is shown most conspicuously by the conclusion he came to, that in order to put things to rights the Apostle James must be shoved aside. Just think of Luther's reverence for an Apostle!—and then that he must venture to do such a thing as this to get faith reinstated in its rights![1]

In the meantime, what came to pass? There is always with us a worldliness which would have the name of being Christian, but would have it at a price as cheap as possible. This worldliness became observant of Luther. It listened, and it took the precaution to listen a second time for fear it might have heard amiss, and thereupon it said, 'Capital! That suits us exactly. Luther says, 'It is faith alone that matters'; the fact that his life expresses works he does not himself say, and now he is dead, so that this is no longer an actuality. Let us take then his word, his doctrine—and we are liberated from all works. Long live Luther!

> Wer nicht liebt Weiber, Wein, Gesang,
> der bleibt ein Narr sein Leben lang.[2]

'This is the significance of Luther's life, that man of God who so opportunely reformed Christianity.' And although all did not take Luther in vain quite in so worldly a way—yet every man has a disposition *either* to want to have merit from works when they are to be done; *or*, when faith and grace are to be stressed, to want to be as far as possible liberated entirely from works. 'Man', this rational creation of God, verily will not suffer himself to be hoaxed; he is not like a rustic who comes to the fair; no, he has his eyes about him. 'No, either the one thing or the other', says man. 'If it is to be *works*, very well, but I beg you to take into consideration the lawful profit which accrues to me from my work, as meritorious work. If it is to be *grace*, very well, but then I would beg to be exempted from works, otherwise it is not grace. If it is to be works and grace at the same time, it is nothing but

[1] As early as 1519 Luther inveighed against the Epistle of St. James. He called it 'an epistle of straw'. It is significant that S. K. found in this Epistle his favourite texts.

[2] 'Who loves not woman, wine, and song remains a fool his whole life long.' These verses were first attributed to Luther (perhaps falsely) in 1775, in *Wandsbecker Bothe*, No. 75.

madness.' Yes, indeed, it is madness, so was true Lutheranism also, and so was Christianity. Christianity's requirement is: Thy life shall as strenuously as possible give expression to works— and then one thing more is required: that thou humble thyself and admit, 'But none the less I am saved by grace.' People abhorred the medieval error of merit. When one looks deeper into the matter, one will readily perceive that they had perhaps even a greater conception of the meritoriousness of works than the Middle Ages had; but they applied 'grace' in such a way as to exempt them from works. When they had done away with works, they could not very well be tempted to regard the works they didn't do as meritorious. Luther wanted to take away the meritoriousness from works and apply it in a somewhat different place, namely, to witnessing for the truth. Worldliness, which understood Luther radically, did away entirely with meritoriousness—and with works along with it.

And where are we now? I am 'without authority'; far be it from me to condemn anybody at all. But since I want to have light thrown on this matter, I will take myself and test my life by a purely Lutheran definition of faith: 'Faith is a perturbing thing'.[1] I assume here that Luther has risen from his grave. He has been among us, though unrecognized, for several years, has watched the life we lead, has been observant of all the others, and also of me. I assume that one day he addresses me and says, 'Art thou a believer? Hast thou faith?' Everyone who knows me as an author will recognize that I after all am the one who might come out best from such an examination; for I have constantly said, 'I have not faith'—like a bird's anxious flight before the approaching tempest, so have I expressed the presentiment of stormy confusion, 'I have not faith.' This therefore I might say to Luther. I might say, 'No, my dear Luther, at least I have shown thee this deference, that I declare I have not faith.' However, I will not lay stress upon this; but as all the others call themselves Christians and believers, I also will say, 'Yes, I am a believer', for otherwise I shall be throwing no light upon the matter I want to see illuminated. So I answer, 'Yes, I am a believer.' 'How is that?' replies Luther, 'for I have not noticed anything in thee, and yet I have watched thy life; and thou knowest, faith is a perturbing thing. To what effect has faith, which thou sayest

[1] Luther, *Werke*, Erlangen ed., xiv, pp. 42 ff.

thou hast, perturbed thee? Where hast thou witnessed for the truth, and where against untruth? What sacrifices hast thou made, what persecutions hast thou endured for Christianity? And at home, in the family life, how has thy self-sacrifice and abnegation been observable? My reply: 'I can protest to you that I have faith.' 'Protest, protest—what sort of talk is that? With respect to having faith, no protestation is needed, if one has it (for faith is a perturbing thing which is at once observable), and no protestation is of any avail, if one does not have it.' 'Yes, but if only thou wilt believe me, I can protest as solemnly as possible. . . .' 'Bah, an end to this nonsense! What avails thy protestation?' 'Yes, but if thou wouldst read some of my books, thou wilt see how I describe faith, so I know therefore that I must have it.' 'I believe the fellow is mad! If it is true that thou dost know how to describe faith, it only proves that thou art a poet, and if thou canst do it well, it proves that thou art a good poet; but this is very far from proving that thou art a believer. Perhaps thou canst also weep in describing faith, that would prove then that thou art a good actor. Thou dost remember surely the story of the actor of olden times who was able to impersonate the moving roles to such a degree that he was still weeping when he came home from the theatre and wept for several days afterwards— that only proves that he was a good actor. No, my friend, faith is a perturbing thing; it is health, and yet it is stronger and more violent than the hottest fever, and it is useless for a sick man to asseverate that he has no fever when the physician feels his pulse, or for a well man to say that he has a fever when the physician by feeling his pulse feels that it is not true—so also when one feels no pulse of faith in thy life, it means that thou hast no faith. When on the other hand, one is sensible of the perturbation of faith as the pulse of thy life, then thou canst be said to have faith and to 'witness' in behalf of faith. And this in turn is what preaching really is. For to preach does not mean to describe faith in books, nor to describe it in 'quiet hours in church'. As I have said in one of my sermons, 'Properly, one ought not to preach in churches, but in the street',[1] and the preacher should not be an actor but a witness—that is, faith, this perturbing thing, ought to be recognizable in his life.'

[1] *Kirchenpostille, Epistelpredigten, Werke,* Erlangen ed., vii, p. 212. Note that Bishop Mynster was famous for his 'quiet hours in church'.

Yes, faith is a perturbing thing. In order to direct a little attention to this trait, let me describe the perturbation of faith in the case of such a hero of faith or witness for the truth. So then there is a given reality; this there is indeed every instant. These thousands and thousands and millions, all of them tending to their own business, the public official to his, the artist to his, the tradesman to his, the scandalmonger to his, the idler not less busily to his, and so forth, everyone tending to his own business in this intersecting play of manifold interests which constitutes reality. At the same time, there sits, in a cloister cell like Luther, or in a remote chamber, a solitary man in fear and trembling and much trial of temptation. A solitary man! There indeed lies the truth. For it is falsehood these times of ours have discovered when they conceive that reforms issue from numbers (the numerical), the crowd, or from the 'highly esteemed' and 'highly esteemed cultured public'—I mean religious reforms, for in the matter of street-lighting and the service of transportation the reform most likely issues from the public; but that a religious reformation might issue from the public is a falsehood, a seditious falsehood. So there sits a solitary man in temptation. Perhaps I enjoy some recognition in my day for my knowledge of souls (psychology); I can testify that I have seen men of whom I venture to say that they had doubtless been much exposed to alluring temptations (*Fristelse*); but never have I seen anyone of whom I could venture to say that he was assaulted by trials of deterrent temptation (*Anfægtelse*). And yet to be exposed for a year to alluring temptations is nothing in comparison with one hour in the assault of deterrent temptation. So there sits that solitary man—or perhaps, if you prefer it, he walks back and forth on the floor like a captive beast in a cage; and yet what he is caught in is marvellous, he is by God, or at God's instigation, caught in himself.—Now what he has beforehand suffered in the trial of faith must be put into terms of real life. Dost thou imagine he is eager for it? Verily, everyone who comes jubilantly along this path is not one of the 'called', you may be sure. Of the called there is none that would not prefer to be exempted, none that would not beg and beseech for himself like a child, and who has not begged; but it was of no avail, he must go on.—So he knows that now when he takes the step the terror erects itself. He who is not called—the moment the terror erects itself he flees. But he who is called—oh, my friend, more than willingly would he flee, shuddering before the terror; but when he has already turned to flee he sees behind him —he sees the still greater horror, the horror of the trial of faith, he must go on—so on he goes, he is now quite calm, for ah, the horror of the trial of temptation is a terrible task-master, it bestows courage.--The terror erects itself. Everything which belongs entirely to the given reality arms itself against this man of trials whom no one can make afraid, for the strange reason that he is so much afraid—before God. They attack him, hate him, curse him. The few who are devoted to him cry out, 'Oh, spare thyself, thou dost make thyself unhappy and all of us; oh, hold up, do not arouse the terror more strongly, check the word which is upon thy lips, or rather recall the last word.' Oh, my hearer, faith is a perturbing thing. So it is to be supposed perhaps that I preach riot, the overturning of everything, disorder? No—every one who is acquainted with my literary works must be content with this assertion. Every one who knows my literary works must know that I have laboured in the opposite direction.

But from the Christian point of view there are two kinds of disorder. The one is rioting, exterior hubbub. The other is the stillness of death, dissolution, and this perhaps is the most dangerous.

Against this latter I have worked, and I have worked to awaken disquietude with the aim of effecting inward change. Let me define exactly where I am, so to speak. Among us is a very reverend old man, the primate of the clergy of this Church.[1] What he, or his 'sermons', have wanted to effect is the same thing that I want, only with a stronger emphasis, which is accounted for by my personal difference and what the difference of the time demands. Among us there are some who[2] require that to be Christians in the strictest sense they must be such in contrast to the rest of us. I have not been able to join them. In part my objection is that their lives do not come up to the measure they themselves suggest or even compel one to apply when they emphasize so strongly that they are Christians. To me, however, this is the less important consideration. In part I am not enough of a Christian to dare to join those who make such a requirement. If it be that I am perhaps a little (yea, even if I were perhaps not

[1] Mynster.
[2] The followers of Grundtvig—S. K.'s brother Peter among them.

merely a little) more advanced than sundry of the average persons among us—it is only poetically that I am in advance, that is to say, I know better what Christianity is, and know better how to present it—ah, but this (remember what Luther said to me!) is a very unessential difference. Essentially I belong to the average. And here it is I have laboured for disquietude in the direction of inwardness.

For from the Christian point of view there are two kinds of true disquietude. The disquietude in the heroes of the faith and the witnesses for the truth who aim to reform the established order. So far as that I have never ventured out, that is not my affair.[1] And whenever anyone in our time might seem to want to venture so far out, I was not disinclined to enter into a polemic against him,[2] by way of contributing to reveal whether he was the legitimate reformer. The other kind of disquietude has to do with inward reformation. A true love-affair also is a disquieting thing, but it does not occur to the lover to want to change the established order.

For this disquietude in the direction of inward change I have laboured. But 'without authority'. Instead of being emptily puffed up to the point of giving myself out to be a witness for the truth and encouraging others to wish rashly to be the same, I am an unauthoritative poet who moves people by means of the ideals. As such then, that I may give example of it at once, and at the same time show, among other things, how I employ the heroes of the faith. . . . Thou, my hearer, callest thyself surely a Christian. Well then, thou knowest that what is the most certain of all things and at the same time the most uncertain, that is, death, will some day approach thee also, and it will be the death of thee. Thou, however, art a Christian, hoping and believing that thou art to be blessed, just as blessed as any witness for the truth[3] or any hero of the faith, in spite of the fact that he had to

[1] It must be remembered that after the lapse of a few years he had the courage to venture so far out and attack the 'established order'.

[2] S. K. has here especially in mind his polemic against Dr. Rudelbach, who had appealed to his works in support of a revolutionary movement in the Church. This was a welcome assistance to Bishop Mynster.

[3] When Professor Martensen, in his panegyric upon Bishop Mynster, proclaimed that he was 'a genuine witness for the truth, one of that long line of witnesses which stretches from the Apostles' age to ours', he could not have been unaware of the exalted significance S. K. attached to this title. S. K. naturally regarded it as a

purchase the title of Christian at a far higher price. Perhaps in consideration of this one who is equipped with authority might speak to thee in a different way, terrifying thee by saying that it was a vain fancy on thy part that thou art a Christian, that thou art on the path to hell. Far be it from me to represent this as an exaggeration on the part of the authoritative teacher; no, I understand only too well what effort is required in order to dare to venture to apply such an either/or to another man. But I, the unauthoritative poet, dare not speak thus; I suppose that thou art to be just as blessed as any of the witnesses for the truth, any of the heroes of the faith. But in view of this I say to thee: Just think now of thy life in contrast with the life of such a one. Think what he had to sacrifice, he that sacrificed his all: that which in the first instance seemed hardest to sacrifice; and that which in the long run seemed the hardest to have sacrificed.[1] Think what he has suffered, how bitter it was, and how long drawn out! Oh, if thou art living happily in a beloved home, where thy wife is devoted to thee with all her heart and with all her might, and where thou hast delight in thy children—consider what it means to live on day after day in this peace and repose which is so beneficial to a man's soul, more beneficial than is the subdued light of evening to weak eyes, and that such is thy daily life. And then think of the witness for the truth! And if thou art living, not in idleness, far from it, but in such circumstances that thy labour which takes thy time, thy diligence, thy strength, yet takes only so much of it that not only is there sufficient repose from labour, but the labour itself is often as refreshing as a pastime; and if thou art living, if not in opulence, yet with an ample competence, and hast time for the many enjoyments which refreshingly occupy the time and give a new zest for life, in short, if thy daily life is serene enjoyment—ah, his life was painful suffering—then you both

challenge, and he promptly accepted it as the signal he was waiting for to begin the open attack upon the Established Church. S. K. denied to the very last that he accounted himself 'a witness for the truth', and yet what he did with an assured air of authority, and died in doing, corresponds perfectly to the picture he had formed of the 'witness', and already in this paragraph there are evident reflections upon the hardships of his own life which suggest that at this time, when he was on the point of 'venturing so far out', he had begun to think of himself as one who might become a 'witness'.

[1] Phrasing this thought as he does here, I have no doubt that S. K. was thinking of his sacrifice of Regina.

die and become equally blessed! Ah, if it so be that in happy obscurity thou canst rejoice in life, and art allowed undisturbed and unobserved to be thyself; and if, just by reason of thine obscurity, thou hast often opportunity to learn to know men from their better, their favourable, their lovable side; and if in moving in the swarm thou dost encounter, either strangers who know thee not, or the kindly and sympathetic glances of those who know thee;[1] and if when thou findest opportunity to do another a service, a good turn, thou art then rewarded by so much joy that it is a question whether thou hast not done a service, a good turn, to thyself; and if, thine own life being easily understood by thee, thou dost easily understand others and art easily understood— ah, he must day in and day out (as a thing inseparable from this work of his) be devoured as it were and eaten up by this human gossip which with insatiable hunger is always craving something to chatter about; he must daily, year after year, learn to know men from (to speak in the mildest terms) their bestial side, and sometimes from the side of the deepest depravity; again and again he must be made conscious that he is known to every one, as he can ascertain by the fact that in everybody's glance he encountered ill-will, opposition, bitterness, scorn, &c. He did well by his whole generation and was rewarded by the curses of the whole generation; amidst the tortures of his trial of temptation he must laboriously acquire an understanding of his own life, and then he must laboriously, day after day, work his way through all the misunderstandings of his contemporaries, and through all the tortures of misunderstanding—then you both die, and you become equally blessed! Reflect upon this, and surely thou wilt then say

---

[1] One unacquainted with the Journal may be in redu ous of the assertion that one of the hardships S. K. most bitterly complained of was his notoriety—not merely the humiliating notoriety which the lampoons of the *Corsair* inflicted upon him, but also the favourable notoriety he had won as an author. He complained that in the street there was no stranger who did not recognize him, and too often he suspected a hostile or envious intention in the glances of acquaintances. So he longed for obscurity—such obscurity as he had enjoyed as a youth in Copenhagen. Goldschmidt recognized sagaciously that he died opportunely at the moment when his attack upon the Established Church had made him again a popular figure, for the last thing he could endure was popularity.—What follows in the text, about the 'misunderstanding' the witness for the truth must encounter, describes again his own case—perhaps better than that of the 'witness'—and one cannot but reflect that this misfortune was in part his own fault.

to thyself what I say to myself: 'Whether it be that I shall venture so far out, or whether I shall pamper myself and not venture out at all, one thing I will do, I shall find the time, however much business I have in hand, to remember this glorious one every single day. Oh, it seems to me an injustice which cries to heaven, that we two should become equally blessed! But my life, in any case, shall be a memento of him!'—And behold, here thou hast at once an example of a movement which is disquietude in the direction of inward reformation.

And this disquietude is the least, the mildest, the lowest form of godliness. And yet dost thou think that we are so perfect that there is no need for anyone to labour for this? Remember how I fared with Luther. If others would fare like me were Luther to come to them, I do not know.

But imagine Luther in our age, observant of our situation. Dost thou not believe that he would say, as he says in one of his sermons, 'The world is like a drunken peasant: when you help him up on one side of the horse, he falls off on the other.'[1] Dost thou not believe he would say: 'The Apostle James must be dragged a little into prominence—not in behalf of works *against* faith; no, no, that was not at all the Apostle's meaning, but in behalf of faith, in order to bring it about if possible that the need of "grace" be deeply felt with genuine, humble sincerity, and to hinder if possible that "grace", grace and truth, the only thing which saves, the only thing which insures blessedness, be taken quite in vain and become a false pretext for a more refined worldliness.' Luther—that man of God, that upright soul!— overlooked perhaps, or forgot, a certain something which a later age, and our age especially, only too strongly inculcates. He forgot—oh, upright man! I repeat—he forgot what he himself was too upright to know, upright soul that he was, and which I (not for my virtue's sake but for truth's sake), must emphasize. The Lutheran doctrine is excellent, it is truth; I have only one misgiving about this excellent Lutheran doctrine. That does not apply to the Lutheran doctrine, but it applies to me: I have reason to know that I am not an upright soul, but a crafty fellow. So it doubtless would be well to examine a little more carefully the subordinate clauses (works, existence, witnessing and suffering for the truth, works of love, &c.), the subordinate clauses of

[1] Not in a sermon but in the *Tischreden, Werke,* lxii, p. 470.

E

Lutheranism. Not that the subordinate clauses should be made the principal clauses, faith and grace be done away with or disparaged—God forbid; no, it is just for the sake of the principal clauses, and then because I am such as I am, that it doubtless would be well to examine a little more carefully the subordinate clauses of Lutheranism—for so far as 'upright souls' are concerned nothing needs to be done.[1]

And James says: 'Be not hearers only of the Word but doers of it.'

However, to become doers of it, one must first be a hearer or a reader of it, as James also says.

And now we have reached our text.

So we will speak about

WHAT IS REQUIRED IN ORDER TO DERIVE TRUE BENEDICTION FROM BEHOLDING ONESELF IN THE MIRROR OF THE WORD?

First of all, what is required is, that thou must not look at the mirror, not behold the mirror, but must see thyself in the mirror.

This seems so evident that one might think it was hardly necessary to say it. And yet it most certainly is necessary; and what confirms me in this opinion is that it is not a remark of mine, nor of what we nowadays call a pious man, a man who now and then has pious moods, but of a witness for the truth, a blood-witness, and such glorious ones are well informed. He warns against the illusion of getting into the habit of beholding the mirror instead of seeing oneself in the mirror. I merely make use of his observation and ask thee, my hearer, is it not as though it were coined expressly for our age and for our situation, and in general for the later ages of Christianity?

For 'God's Word' indeed is the mirror. But, but—oh, the limitless horizons of prolixity! How much belongs in a stricter sense to God's Word? which books are genuine? are they also Apostolic? and are these also authentic? have the authors themselves seen everything? or in some instances perhaps have they merely reported what they heard from others? And then the

---

[1] Even this qualified praise of Luther and Lutheranism must be regarded as a measure of 'economy' designed to win some sympathy if possible for the polemic he was chiefly intent upon pressing. For in the later Journals the comments upon Luther are generally disparaging and often terribly sharp.

various readings—30,000 various readings. And then this throng or crowd of scholars and opinions, learned opinions and unlearned opinions, about how the particular passage is to be interpreted . . . you must confess that this seems rather prolix. God's Word is the mirror—by reading or hearing it I am to see myself in the mirror; but, lo, all this about the mirror is so confusing that I never come to the point of seeing my own reflection —at least not if I take that path. One might be tempted almost to suppose that there is a lot of human craftiness in play here (ah, and that is true, we men are so crafty in relation to God and things divine and godfearing truth, it is by no means true as we like to say to one another, that we should be so willing to do God's will, if only we could learn what it is), one might be tempted almost to suppose that this is craftiness, that we men are far from willing to see ourselves in that mirror, and that it is for this reason we have hit upon all this which threatens to make reflection from the mirror impossible, all this which we glorify by the laudatory name of learned and profound and serious research and investigation.

My hearer, how highly dost thou esteem God's Word? Do not say now that thou dost esteem it more highly than words can express; for one may speak so highly that one says nothing. Let us therefore, in order to get somewhere, take a simple human relationship. If thou dost esteem God's Word higher, so much the better.

Think of a lover who has now received a letter from his beloved—as precious as this letter is to the lover, just so precious to thee, I assume, is God's Word; in the way the lover reads this letter, just so, I assume, dost thou read God's Word and conceive that God's Word ought to be read.

But perhaps thou wilt say, 'Yes, but the Holy Scripture is written in a foreign tongue.' It is indeed more properly the learned who have the obligation to read the Holy Scriptures in the original tongues; but if thou dost insist, if thou wouldst stick to it that thou must read the Holy Scriptures in the original tongues— all right, we can very well retain the picture of the lover, only we add a little qualification to it.

I assume then that this letter from the beloved was written in a language which the lover did not understand; and there is no one at hand who can translate it for him, and perhaps he did not even desire any aid of that sort, which would initiate a third person into his secrets. What does he do? He takes a dictionary and sits down to spell out the letter, looking up every word so as to get at the translation. Let us suppose that while he is sitting employed in this labour there comes in an acquaintance of his. The friend knows that he has received this letter, and, looking at the table and seeing it lying there, exclaims, 'Oho! There you sit reading the letter you got from your lady-love.' What dost thou think the other will say? He replies, 'Are you out of your senses? Is this what you call reading a letter from a lady-love? No, my friend, I sit here toiling and drudging to make a translation of it by the help of the dictionary; at times I am on the point of bursting with impatience, the blood rushes to my head so that I want to fling the dictionary down on the floor—and that's what you call reading! You are mocking me. No, thank God, I shall soon be through with the translation, and then, ah, then I shall get to the point of reading the letter from my lady-love—that is an entirely different thing.—But to whom am I speaking . . . stupid man, get out of my sight, I don't want to look at you. Oh, that you could think of insulting my lady-love and me by speaking of this as reading her letter! Yet stay, stay, it is only a jest on my part; indeed I should be glad to have you stay, but honestly I have no time, there still remains something to translate, and I am so impatient to get to the point of reading—therefore don't be angry, but go away so that I may finish.'

Thus the lover made a distinction between reading and reading, between reading with the dictionary and reading the letter from his lady-love. The blood rushes to his head for impatience while he sits and conjures out the meaning with the dictionary; he is furious with his friend for speaking of this erudite reading as a reading of the letter from his lady-love. He regarded all this (if I may so call it) erudite preparation as a necessary evil, that he might get to the point of . . . reading the letter from his lady-love.

Let us not dismiss this picture too soon. Let us suppose that this letter from the lady-love not only contained, as such letters generally do, the declaration of an emotion, but that there was contained in it a desire, something which the beloved desired the lover to do. There was, let us suppose, a great deal required of him, a very great deal, there was good reason, as every third person would say, to hesitate about doing it; but the lover—he was off in a second to accomplish the desire of the beloved. Let us suppose that in the course of time the lovers met, and the lady said, 'But my dear, I didn't think of requiring that of thee; thou must have misunderstood the word or translated it wrong.' Dost thou believe that the lover now would regret that instead of hastening at once to fulfil the desire of his beloved he had not first entertained some misgivings, and then perhaps had obtained a few more dictionaries to help him out, and then had many misgivings, and then perhaps got the word rightly translated, and so was exempted from the task—dost thou believe that he regrets this misapprehension? Dost thou believe that he is less in favour with the beloved? Take the case of a child, one whom we might well call a clever and diligent pupil. When the teacher had appointed the lesson for the next day he says, 'Let me see to-morrow that you know your lesson well.' This made a deep impression upon our clever pupil. He comes home from school and at once sets to work. But he had not heard quite exactly how far the lesson extended. What does he do? It was this exhortation of the teacher which impressed him, and he reads double the amount actually required of him, as it afterwards proved. Dost thou believe that the teacher will be the less pleased with him because he can recite admirably a lesson double the prescribed length? Imagine another pupil. He also had heard the teacher's exhortation; nor had he heard exactly how far the lesson extended. Then when he came home he said, 'First I have got to find out how much I have to study.' So he went to one of his companions, then to another, he was not at home at all, on the contrary he fell to chatting with an elder brother of his—and then at last he came home, and the time for study was past, and he got nothing at all read.

So the lover made a distinction, as regards this letter from his beloved, between reading and reading; moreover, he understood how to read in such a way that, if there was a desire contained in the letter, one ought to begin at once to fulfil it, without wasting a second.

Think now of God's Word. When thou readest God's Word eruditely—we do not disparage erudition, far from it—but remember that when thou dost read God's Word eruditely, with a dictionary, &c., thou art not reading God's Word—remember the lover who said, 'This is not to read the letter from the beloved.' If thou art a learned man, then take care lest with all thy erudite

reading (which is not reading God's Word) thou forgettest per-
chance to read God's Word. If thou art not learned—ah, envy
the other man not, rejoice that thou canst at once get to the
point of reading God's Word! And if there is a desire, a commandment, an order, then (remember the lover!), then be off at
once to do accordingly. 'But', thou perhaps wouldst say, 'there
are so many obscure passages in the Holy Scriptures, whole books
which are almost riddles.' To this I would reply: 'I see no need
of considering this objection unless it comes from one whose life
gives expression to the fact that he has punctually complied with
all the passages which are easy to understand.' Is this the case
with thee? Yet thus it is the lover would deal with the letter;
if there were obscure passages, but also clearly expressed desires,
he would say, 'I must at once comply with the desire, then I will
see what can be made of the obscure passages. Oh, but how could
I sit down to puzzle over the obscure passages and leave the
desire unfulfilled, the desire which I clearly understood?' That
is to say: when thou readest God's Word, it is not the obscure
passages which impose a duty upon thee, but that which thou
understandest; and with that thou must instantly comply. If
there were only a single passage thou didst understand in Holy
Scripture—well, the first thing is to do that; but thou dost not
first have to sit down and puzzle over the obscure passages.
God's Word is given in order that thou shalt act in accordance
with it, not in order that thou shalt practise the art of interpreting
obscure passages. If thou dost not read God's word so as to bear
in mind that the very least bit that thou dost understand instantly
obliges thee to do accordingly, thou dost not read God's Word.
So the lover thought: 'If instead of hastening to fulfil instantly
the desire which I understood, I wish to sit down and puzzle
over what I don't understand, I am not reading the letter from
the beloved. I can appear before my beloved with a good conscience and say, "There were some obscure passages in thy letter,
with regard to which I said, sufficient unto the day is the evil;
but there was a desire which I understood, and that I instantly
fulfilled." But I could not appear before her with a good conscience and say, "There were some obscure passages in thy letter
which I did understand, so I sat down and puzzled over them,
and with regard to thy desire which I did understand I said,
sufficient unto the day is the evil thereof."' But perhaps thou

art afraid that with thee it might turn out as it did with the lover, that (but surely this fear is groundless in relation to God's requirement), that thou mightest be doing too much, that by thumbing the pages of still another dictionary it might prove that not so much was required. Oh, my friend, was the lady-love displeased that the lover had been doing too much? and what would she say about entertaining such a fear? She would say, 'He who entertains such a fear of doing too much is not really reading the letter from his beloved.' And so I would say: 'He does not read God's Word.'

Let us not even yet dismiss this picture of the lover and his letter. While he was busily engaged translating with the aid of a dictionary, he was disturbed by the visit of an acquaintance. He became impatient—'But', he likely would have said, 'that was only because I was retarded in my work, for otherwise it would have been of no importance. I wasn't reading the letter then. Of course, if someone had come to see me when I was reading the letter, it would have been quite another matter—that would have been a disturbance. Against that danger, however, I shall ensure myself; before beginning a thing like that I lock my door tight and am not at home. For I would be alone with the letter, alone and undisturbed; if I am not alone, I am not reading the letter from the beloved.'

He would be alone with the letter, alone and undisturbed— 'otherwise', says he, 'I am not reading the letter from the beloved'.

And so it is with God's Word: he who is not alone with God's Word is not reading God's Word.

Alone with God's Word! My hearer, permit me to make an admission about myself: I am not yet bold enough to be so entirely alone with God's Word that no illusion surreptitiously intrudes. And allow me to say one thing more: I have never seen anyone of whom I could venture to believe that he had sincerity and courage enough to be so completely alone with God's Word that absolutely no illusion surreptitiously intruded.

How strange it is! When in our day a man who is deeply moved comes forward and sets the price of what it is to be a Christian only one-fifth as high as the Gospel fixes it, they cry out, 'Beware of that man! Do not read what he writes, least of all in solitude; do not converse with him, least of all in solitude, he is a dangerous man.' But the Holy Scriptures! In fact, almost every man possesses them; one does not hesitate to present this book to a young person about to be confirmed—that is, at the most perilous age. In truth, many an illusion must accompany it; one must be inured to the fact that after all such a book does exist; one must read it in a very special way—least of all in such a way that one finds oneself alone with it.

To be alone with the Holy Scriptures! I dare not! When I turn up a passage in it, whatever comes to hand—it catches me instantly, it questions me (indeed it is as if it were God Himself that questioned me), 'Hast thou done what thou readest there?' And then, then . . . yes, then I am caught. So then it is action at once, or instantly a humiliating admission.

Oh, to be alone with the Holy Scriptures!—and if thou art not, then thou art not reading the Holy Scriptures.

That this thing of being alone with God's Word, that this is a dangerous business, is tacitly admitted precisely by the more efficient sort of people. There was perhaps one (a peculiarly efficient and serious man, even though we cannot approve the decision he came to) who said, 'I am no good at doing anything by halves—and this book, God's Word, is an exceedingly dangerous book for me, and it is a domineering book. Give it a finger, and it takes the whole hand, give it the whole hand, and it takes the whole man, suddenly transforming perhaps my whole life on a huge scale. No, without permitting myself to utter a single word of mockery or disparagement of that book (which is a thing I abhor) I remove it to an out-of-the-way place; I don't want to be alone with it.' We do not approve of this, but there is something we can approve of, a certain honesty.

But there is also an entirely different way of defending oneself against God's Word, while boasting defiantly that one is quite capable of daring to be alone with God's Word, though this is far from the truth. For take the Holy Scriptures—shut thy door; but take also ten dictionaries, twenty commentaries, and then thou canst read it just as tranquilly and unembarrassed as thou dost read a newspaper column. If perhaps, while thou art sitting comfortably and reading, it should occur to thee, strangely enough, to raise the question, 'Have I done this? do I act accordingly?'—it is of course only in a moment of distraction that such a thing could occur to thee, at a moment when thou art not self-collected in true seriousness—the danger after all is not great. For, look you, there are perhaps a number of various readings, and perhaps there has just been discovered a new manuscript—good gracious! . . . and perhaps the prospect of another various reading, and perhaps there are five commentators of one opinion, and seven of another, and two who maintain singular opinions, and three who are vacillating or have no opinion, and 'I myself have not quite made up my mind about this passage, or, if I must express my opinion, I am of the same opinion as the three vacillating commentators who have no opinion', &c. So such a man does not fall into the same embarrassment as I, who am compelled either to act at once in accordance with the text, or to make a humiliating admission. No, he is tranquil and says, 'There is on my part nothing to hinder me from doing accordingly—if only the correct reading is established and the commentators arrive at some sort of an agreement.' Aha! it will be a long time before that comes about. The man, however, has succeeded in obscuring the fact that the fault lay in himself, that it is he who has no inclination to deny flesh and blood and act in accordance with God's Word. Ah, pitiable misuse of erudition! Alas, that it is so easy for men to deceive themselves!

For if it was not for illusion and self-deception, no doubt every man would acknowledge as I do, that I hardly dare to be alone with God's Word.

Alone with God's Word—so it is one must be, just as the lover desired to be alone with the letter, for otherwise it would not be reading the letter from the beloved—and otherwise it would not be reading God's Word and beholding oneself in the mirror. And this indeed is what we should do, and what we should do first; if with true benediction we are to behold ourselves in the mirror of the Word, we should not look at the mirror but see ourselves in the mirror. Art thou learned, remember then that if thou dost not read God's Word in a different fashion, it may be said of thee that after having devoted many hours every blessed day throughout a long life to reading God's Word, thou hast nevertheless never read . . . God's Word. Then make the distinction, so that (over and above the erudite reading) thou mayest get to the point of reading God's Word—or at least of acknowledging to thyself that in spite of the daily learned reading in God's Word thou dost not read God's Word, that thou art not willing to have anything at all to do with it. Art thou unlearned, then thou hast the less occasion to read amiss—so get to work straightway, do not behold the mirror, but straightway behold thyself in the mirror.

But how in fact is God's Word read in Christendom? If we were to distinguish two classes (for we cannot here concern ourselves with individual exceptions), one might say that the greater part never read God's Word, and that a smaller part read it learnedly in one fashion or another, that is to say, do not really read God's Word, but behold the mirror. Or, to say the same thing in another way, the greater part regard God's Word as an antiquated document of olden time which one puts aside, and a smaller part regards God's Word as an exceedingly notable document of olden time upon which one expends an astonishing amount of diligence and acumen, &c. . . . beholding the mirror.

Imagine a country. A royal command is issued to all the office-bearers and subjects, in short, to the whole population. A remarkable change comes over them all: they all become interpreters, the office-bearers become authors, every blessed day there comes out an interpretation more learned than the last, more acute, more elegant, more profound, more ingenious, more wonderful, more charming, and more wonderfully charming. Criticism which ought to survey the whole can hardly attain survey of this prodigious literature, indeed criticism itself has become a literature so prolix that it is impossible to attain a survey of the criticism. Everything became interpretation—but no one read the royal command with a view to acting in accordance with it. And it was not only that everything became interpretation, but at the same time the point of view for determining what seriousness is was altered, and to be busy about interpretation became real seriousness. Suppose that this king was not a human king—for though a human king would understand well enough that they were making a fool of him by giving the affair this turn, yet as a human king he is dependent, especially when he encounters the united front of office-bearers and subjects, and so would be compelled to put the best face on a bad game, to let it seem as if all this were a matter of course, so that the most elegant interpreter would be rewarded by elevation to the peerage, the most acute would be knighted, &c.—Suppose that this king was almighty, one therefore who is not put to embarrassment though all the office-bearers and all the subjects play him false. What do you suppose this almighty king would think about such a thing? Surely he would say, 'The fact that they do not comply with the commandment, even that I might forgive; moreover, if they united in a petition that I might have patience with them, or perhaps relieve them entirely of this commandment which seemed to them too hard—that I could forgive them. But this I cannot forgive, that they entirely alter the point of view for determining what seriousness is.'

And now as to God's Word! 'My house shall be a house of prayer, but ye have made it a den of thieves.' And God's Word— what is it intended to be, and what have we made of it? All this interpretation and interpretation and science and newer science which is introduced with the solemn and serious claim that this is the way rightly to understand God's Word—look more closely and thou wilt perceive that this is with the intent of defending oneself against God's Word. It is only too easy to understand the requirements contained in God's Word—'give all thy goods to the poor', 'when a man smites thee upon the right cheek, turn to him also the left', 'when a man take away thy coat, let him have thy cloak also', 'rejoice always', 'count it all joy when ye fall into divers temptations', &c.—all this is just as easy to understand as the remark, 'It is a good day to-day', a remark which only in one way might become difficult to understand, namely, if there grew up a whole literature to interpret it; therefore no poor wretch of the most limited intelligence can truly say that he is unable to understand the requirement—but flesh and blood are reluctant to understand and be obliged to do accordingly. And to my thinking it is only human that a man shrinks from letting the Word really get the mastery of him—if no one else will admit it, I admit that I do. It is human to beg God to have patience if one cannot at once do what one ought to do, and yet promises to strive; it is human to beg God to have compassion, seeing that the re-quirement is too exalted for one—if no one else will admit this of himself, I admit that I do it. It is not human, however, to give the matter an entirely different turn—that I insert layer upon layer, interpretation and science and more science (pretty much as a boy inserts a napkin, or several of them, under his pants when he is about to get a thrashing), that I insert all this between the Word and myself, and then bestow upon this commentating and scientific method the name of seriousness and zeal for the truth, and then let this busy occupation swell to such proportions that I never come to the point of getting an impression of God's Word, never come to the point of beholding myself in the mirror. It seems as if all this investigating and inquiring and pondering and reflecting would bring God's Word quite close to me—the truth is that precisely thus, in the slyest way, I remove God's Word to the farthest possible distance from me, infinitely farther than it is from him who never saw God's Word, infinitely farther than from him who was so much in dread and fear of God's Word that he cast it as far away from him as possible.

For it is a still greater distance from the requirement (of beholding oneself in the mirror), a still greater distance from it than never to have seen the mirror, a still greater distance is that of sitting year after year, every blessed day, sitting quite tranquilly . . . and beholding the mirror.

In the second place, it is required that when thou readest God's Word in order to see thyself in the mirror, thou must remember (so as really to get to the point of seeing thyself in the mirror), *thou must remember to say to thyself continually, 'It is I that am here addressed, it is about me this is said.'*

Let not thyself be deceived—or be not thyself crafty. For in relation to God and God's Word we men are, oh, so sly, even the stupidest amongst us is so sly—yea, flesh and blood and self-love are very sly.

So then we have made the discovery (for we do not say that this is done to defend ourselves against God's Word, we are not so crazy as all that, for if we were to say as much, we should reap no advantage from our shrewd discovery), we have made the discovery that to think about oneself is (as in fact it may be in many cases, only not when it is a question of letting God's Word get the mastery of us), that this is—observe the slyness of it!—this is vanity, morbid vanity! 'Fie! how could I be so vain? For to think about oneself and to say, "It is I", we learned people call subjectivity, and subjectivity is vanity, the vanity of not being able to read a book—God's Word!—without having the notion that it refers to me. Should I not detest vanity, and could I be stupid enough not to, seeing that thereby I at the same time ensure myself against God's Word getting a grip on me? I am ensured against this danger just because I do not put myself into **any** personal (subjective) relation to God's Word, but on **the** contrary, with the seriousness for which people so highly commend me, I transform the Word into an impersonal entity (the objective, an objective doctrine, &c.), to which I, a man not only serious but cultured, relate myself objectively, so that I am not so uncultivated and vain as to bring my personality into play, and to suppose it was I who was addressed, I and constantly I who was being spoken about. Ah, far be from me such vanity and lack of culture—and far be from me also what otherwise might so easily occur, that the Word might get a grip on me, on me precisely, might get me in its power so that I could not defend myself, so that it would continue to persecute me until I either acted in accordance with it or admitted that I did not—the well-deserved punishment incurred by everyone who permits himself to have dealings with God's Word in an uncultivated way.'

No, no, no! True seriousness is this: when thou readest God's Word, then in everything that thou readest, constantly to say to thyself, 'It is I that am addressed, to me this is spoken', precisely that is seriousness. Among those to whom the cause of Christianity was entrusted in a more exalted sense, there is not one who has forgotten to emphasize this again and again as the most decisive, the most unconditional condition of coming to see oneself in the mirror. So it is this thou shalt do, thou shalt as thou readest say continually to thyself, 'It is to me it is said, about me it is spoken.'

Of that mighty emperor in the Orient,[1] whose wrath the renowned little nation had brought down upon itself, it is related that he had a slave who every day said to him, 'Remember to take vengeance!' So this was something to be remembered; it seems to me it would have been better to have a slave who every day reminded him to forget—which, however, is not a good suggestion, for if one were every day to be reminded to forget, it would not be a serious way of forgetting. But in any case, that ruler understood very well, just because he was wroth (and wrath is a trait of personality, though not a laudable trait), what one must do to make a personal impression upon a person.

But better still than this ruler was King David served—sure enough it was a sort of service a man himself seldom desires by free inclination, which he is tempted rather to regard as one of

[1] Darius, whose slave daily said to him, 'Remember the Athenians!' Herodotus, v. 105.

life's greatest inconveniences. The story I refer to is well known.[1]
King David saw Bathsheba. To see her, and to see that her husband stood in his way, was one and the same thing. So he must
be got rid of. And this also came to pass. One did not know
exactly how it happened, it may have been providential, he fell in
battle, yet 'Such is war', said the king; presumably he himself
had chosen with foolhardiness a post so dangerous that it was
certain death—I merely remark that if there was anybody who
wanted him out of the way and was in a position to command,
he could not have done better than to assign him to that post
which was certain death. Now he is out of the way. The thing
went off very smoothly. And now also there is nothing to hinder
the king from getting lawful possession of his wife. 'Nothing
to hinder'—art thou queer in the head? Why, it was even noble
in a high degree, magnanimous, genuine kingly behaviour,
which will arouse enthusiasm in the whole army, that the king
marries the widow of a soldier who had died for the fatherland.

Then one day there came a prophet to King David. Let us
make the situation vivid to us and modernize it a little. The one
is the king, the man who has the highest rank in the nation; the
other a prophet, a man much esteemed in the nation—both of
them of course men of culture, and one may be sure that their
intercourse with one another, their conversation, will bear un-
mistakably the marks of culture. Besides, they were both, and
one of them more especially, celebrated authors. King David was
the renowned poet, and, as a natural consequence of this, a
connoisseur, an elegant arbiter of good taste, who knew how
to appreciate the form of presentation, the choice of expressions, and the construction of a poem, the linguistic form and
the cadence, and whether it was favourable or prejudicial to
morals, &c.

And it is a lucky meeting, just the right man to come to; for the
prophet had composed a *novella*, a story which he would fain have
the honour of reciting before his Majesty, the crowned poet and
connoisseur of poetry.

'There dwelt two men in one city; the one rich, and the other
poor. The rich man had exceeding many flocks and herds: but
the poor man had nothing save one little ewe lamb, which he had
bought and nourished up; and it grew up together with him and

[1] II Sam. 11 and 12.

with his children; it did eat of his own meat, and drank of his own cup, and lay in his bosom, and was unto him as a daughter. And there came a traveller unto the rich man, and he spared to take of his own flock and of his own herd to dress for the wayfaring man that was come unto him: but took the poor man's lamb and dressed it for the man that was come to him.'

I imagine that David has listened to this attentively, has given expression to his opinion, of course without intruding his personality (subjectively), but impersonally (objectively) has duly appreciated this charming little work. There was perhaps a particular trait which he thought might have been different, he perhaps proposed an expression more happily chosen, perhaps also pointed out a little fault in the plan, praised the prophet's masterly delivery of the story, his voice, the play of his features, expressed himself, in short, as we cultured people are accustomed to do when we criticize a sermon delivered before a cultured congregation, that is, a sermon which itself also is objective.

Then says the prophet to him, 'Thou art the man.'

Behold, this tale which the prophet recited was a story, but this, 'Thou art the man', was another story—it was a transition to the subjective.

But dost thou not believe that David himself already knew perfectly well how abominable it was to let a woman's husband be slain in order that he might marry her? Dost thou not believe that David, the great poet, was quite capable of describing it—eloquently, awefully, movingly? And, moreover, dost thou not believe that David knew within himself what he was guilty of and how guilty? And yet, yet, yet there was needed one from without who said to him, 'Thou'.

From this thou canst perceive how little one is helped by the impersonal (the objective), a doctrine, a history, science, &c., when even one who in other respects was so god-fearing a man as David was (and piety and godly fear are in fact aspects of personality—the subjective side), when even he, in the perpetration of such an abominable misdeed (and beforehand he found—objectively enough—no obstacle, not the obstacle of conscience to letting Uriah be slain, not the obstacle of conscience to marrying Bathsheba), when even he, after the thing has come to pass, can preserve so much impersonality (objectivity) that he can live on as if it was nothing, that he can listen to the prophet as if it was nothing—until the prophet, weary of this impersonality or objectivity which in our century is so much lauded as culture and seriousness, assumes authority and says, 'Thou art the man.'

From this likewise thou canst perceive what a depth of slyness and cunning there is in Christendom when world culture, taking advantage of what undeniably is true, that selfishly to intrude one's own personality, one's ego, is vanity, that taking advantage of this they have made out *that* to be vanity which in relation to God's Word is just seriousness, so that they may be exempted from seriousness and its strenuous exertion, and just by this means assure themselves of being esteemed as serious and cultured men. Oh, depth of cunning! They make God's Word something impersonal, objective, a doctrine—whereas instead it is as God's voice thou shouldst hear it. Thus it is the fathers heard it, God's dreadful voice—now it sounds as objective as printed calico! And people relate themselves impersonally (objectively) to this impersonal thing; and at the apex of world culture, in the forefront of the cultured public, is science, upon which they defiantly rely as true seriousness and culture, while that unfortunate wretch the personal (the subjective) is obliged, like a naughty schoolboy, to occupy with shame a place in the corner. Oh, depth of cunning! For we men find it only too easy to preserve in relation to God's Word this attitude of impersonality (subjectivity), it is in fact an inborn quality of genius which we all of us possess, something we obtain gratis . . . along with original sin, inasmuch as this much lauded impersonality (objectivity) is neither more nor less than want of conscientiousness. And of course want of conscientiousness naturally does not express itself in actions which are foolish, stupid, or imprudent, like the perpetration of a punishable crime; no, no, in moderation, up to a certain point, and so with good taste and refinement it makes life easy and pleasurable—and yet is it not going too far when they regard this as seriousness and culture?

No, if thou art to read God's Word so as to see thyself in the mirror, thou must while reading it say to thyself continually, 'It is I that am addressed, it is about me this is said.'

A certain man went down from Jerusalem to Jericho and fell among thieves, who stripped him of his raiment, and wounded him, and departed, leaving him half dead—and now when thou readest, 'and by chance there came down a certain priest that way, and when he saw him, he passed by', then thou shalt say to thyself, 'That is I.' Thou shalt not seek evasions, and still less shalt thou become witty (for though it is true enough that in the worldly world a witticism may atone for the deepest baseness, such is not the case when thou readest God's Word), thou shalt not say, 'It is not I, in fact it is a priest, and I am not a priest; I consider, however, that the Gospel has most appropriately represented this man as a priest, for the priests are a thoroughly bad lot.' No, when thou readest God's Word, it must be in all seriousness, and thou shalt say, 'This priest is me. Alas, that I could be so uncompassionate—I who call myself a Christian— and in a way I also am a priest, at least we know well how to make that claim when it is a question of liberating ourselves from the priests, for we say that in a Christian sense all men are priests. Alas, that I could be so uncompassionate, that I could see such a sight (and I saw it, it is written in the Gospel, "when he saw him, he passed by") and see it unmoved!'—'And likewise a Levite, when he was at the place, came and looked on him, and passed by.' Here thou shalt say, 'It is I, oh, that I could be so hard-hearted, and that what had occurred once before could occur now again, and that I have not become any better!' —And along the same road there came a practical man, and when he came near, he said to himself, 'What have we here? There lies a man half dead; it is not worth while to go that way, it might well become an affair for the police, or perhaps the police might come along this very instant and take me for the perpetrator of the deed'—then thou shalt say to thyself, 'It is I, oh, that I could be so shabbily shrewd, and not only this, but that later I could take pleasure in my shrewdness, and that when I recounted it to one of my acquaintances, I could take pleasure in hearing him praise this as so shrewd and practical of me!'—And along the same road there came along a man deep in thought, thinking of nothing, and he saw nothing whatever and passed by—then thou shalt say to thyself, 'It was I, what an ass I am, that I could walk along so like a fool without seeing that a man half dead was lying there!' So thou wouldst say to thyself at least if a great treasure had been lying beside that road, and thou hadst gone by without seeing it. —'But a certain Samaritan, as he journeyed, came where he was.' In order not to become weary with saying continually, 'It is I', thou canst here say for a change, 'It was not I; alas, no, I am not like that.'—Then when the parable ends and Christ says to the Pharisee, 'Go and do thou likewise', then thou shalt say to thyself, 'It is to me this is addressed. Off then at once!' Thou shalt not seek evasions, still less try thy hand at witticisms (for from a godly point of view witticisms do not atone for anything but only aggravate the condemnation), thou shalt not say, 'I can protest on my honour that never in my life have I chanced to go along a road where there lay a man half dead who had been attacked by thieves; in fact thieves are a rarity in our parts.' No, in this fashion thou shalt not talk, thou shalt say, 'It is to me the word is addressed, "Go and do thou likewise."' For thou dost understand the saying very well, and if in thy parts thou didst never encounter one who was attacked by thieves, yet on thy path and mine there are wretched people enough. Or, to take an example which bears a good deal of likeness to that in the Gospel, hast thou never followed a road where (if not literally, yet nevertheless truly) there lay one whom slander and calumny had attacked and stripped naked and left half dead? And a priest came the same way, and passed him by—that is, he first listened to what slander recounted about the man, and then went on farther . . . and recounted the story further. 'And this priest', thou shalt say—yea, even if it was a bishop or a dean, thou shalt nevertheless say to thyself, 'This priest was me!' And a Levite came the same way, and he passed by—that is, after first gleaning the news as he went by, he passed by and carried it with him. 'And this Levite', thou shalt say to thyself, 'was me!' And then there came along a respectable citizen; he also heard the story and went off with it and said, 'It is really a shame the way people—as I do now!—recount this and that about the man.' 'And this Levite', thou shalt say to thyself, 'was me—ah, this is indeed worse than that story in the Gospel, for there neither the priest nor the Levite were on hand to beat the man half dead, but here they are the accomplices of the thieves.'

Thou art reading about that ruler, a member of the Sanhedrim, who came to Christ by night. Thou shalt not divert thy attention, not even by making the possibly just remark that it was strange for him to choose that time, for when one would be hid, what use is it after all to choose to go by night when one is going to Him who is the light, as it is written in the Psalm (139: 11), 'If I say, Surely the darkness shall cover me; even the night shall be light about me; yea the darkness hideth not from thee, but the night shineth as the day.' No, in this fashion thou shalt not talk—for, alas, thou understandest only too well why he chose the night, thou knowest that though Christ is the way, yet in contemporaneousness He was, and if He were to come again, He would be . . . the forbidden path.

When thou readest about this, about the man upon whom Christ had made an impression, but only such an impression that he neither could quite surrender himself, not quite tear himself loose, and hence chose the night time, chose to steal to Him by night—then thou shalt say to thyself, 'It is I.' Thou shalt not seek evasions, not mix up with this things that are irrelevant; thou shalt sit quite still during the lesson hour; thou shalt not say, 'This was one of those people of rank (*Fornemme*), and that's the way such people are, great for their rank, and so cowardly and faithless. How could the Gospel which is meant for the poor be for people of rank?' No, thus thou shalt not talk. When thou readest God's Word, thou hast nothing to do with people of rank, nor with rank in general, neither hast thou to arraign them; for even if thou wert one of these people of rank, thou hast only thyself to do with. No, thou shalt say, 'It is I', and if thou hast at the same time to admit that thou wast actually on the point of making this observation about people of rank, then thou shalt not say merely, 'It was I', but adjoin, 'It was I who would moreover seek an evasion, would once again (however little it avails when I am before Him who is the light) hide myself in the darkness of night, in evasion or excuse, as if I did not understand God's Word, as if it were only about people of rank the passage speaks. No, it was I, ah, that I could be so paltry, such a contemptible fellow, neither cold nor hot, neither one thing nor the other!'

Thus it is (these are merely a few examples) that thou shouldest read God's Word; and just as, according to the report of superstition, one can conjure up spirits by reading formulae of incantation, so shalt thou, if only thou wilt continue for some time to read God's Word thus (and this is the first requisite), thou shalt read fear and trembling into thy soul, so that by God's help thou shalt succeed in becoming a man, a personality, saved from being this dreadful absurdity into which we men—created in God's image! —have become changed by evil enchantment, into an impersonal, an objective something. Thou shalt, if thou wilt read God's

Word in this way, thou shalt (even though it prove terrible to thee —but remember that this is the condition of salvation)—thou shalt succeed in the thing required, in beholding thyself in the mirror. And only thus is success possible.

For if to thee God's Word is merely a doctrine, an impersonal, objective something, then there is no mirror—for an objective doctrine cannot be called a mirror; it is just as impossible to be mirrored in an objective doctrine as to be mirrored in a wall. And if thou dost assume an impersonal (objective) relationship to God's Word, there can be no question of beholding thyself in a mirror; for to look in a mirror surely implies a personality, an ego; a wall can be seen in a mirror but cannot see itself or behold itself in the mirror. No, in reading God's Word thou must continually say to thyself, 'It is to me this is addressed, it is about me it speaks.'

Finally, if with true benediction thou art to behold thyself in the mirror of the Word, thou must not straightway forget what manner of man thou art, not be the forgetful hearer (or reader) about whom the Apostle speaks: '*He beheld his natural face in the mirror, and straightway forgot what manner of man he was.*'

This is obvious enough, for to see oneself in a mirror and then at once to forget is like writing upon the sand or upon the water, or like drawing a picture in the air.

Therefore the most expedient thing is to say to thyself immediately, 'I will begin immediately to keep myself from forgetting; immediately, this very instant, I promise it to myself and to God, if it be only for the next hour or for this present day; so long at least it will be certain that I shall not forget.' Believe me, this is the most expedient thing, and thou knowest well enough that I am reputed to be something of a psychologist, and what thou knowest not, alas, I know, through how much suffering, through what bitter experiences, I have become such, if in fact I have become such. So to do is far better than immediately to bite off more than thou canst chew, and say immediately, 'I shall never forget.' Ah, my friend, it is much better never to forget to remember it *immediately*, than to say immediately, I shall *never* forget. Seriousness consists precisely in having this honest suspicion of thyself, treating thyself as a suspicious character, as a capitalist treats an insolvent person, to whom he says, 'Very well, but these great promises are of no use, I would rather have a small part of the sum immediately.' And so it is also here. Ah, how poor a showing it makes, when one has promised never to forget—then to have to begin immediately, the very next hour, to try to remember! And yet this next hour perhaps decides everything; the next hour after what we call 'a quiet hour' is the critical hour. If thou dost let this hour pass and say, 'I have promised never to forget, so my whole life is consecrated to remembering, how petty a thing it is then to be precise about the very next hour.' If thou dost say this, then it is substantially decided that thou wilt be the forgetful hearer or reader. Imagine a man who has been and still is addicted to a bad habit. Then there comes an instant (it comes thus to every man, perhaps many times, alas, many times in vain) when he is brought to a standstill, a good resolution is awakened in him. Imagine that he (let him be, for example, a gambler) said to himself in the morning, 'So I solemnly vow by all that is holy that I shall nevermore have anything to do with gambling, nevermore—to-night shall be the last time.' Ah, my friend, he is lost! Strange as it may seem, I would venture to bet rather on the opposite, supposing that there was a gambler who at such a moment said to himself, 'Very well, thou shalt be allowed to gamble all the rest of thy life, every blessed day—but to-night thou shalt let it alone', and so he did. Ah, my friend, he is certainly saved! For the resolution of the first man was a knavish trick of lust, but that of the other is a way of hoaxing lust; the one is hoaxed by lust, the other hoaxes lust. Lust is strong merely in the instant, if only it gets its own way instantly, there will be no objection on its part to making promises for the whole life. But to reverse the situation so as to say, 'No, only not to-day, but to-morrow and the day after, &c.', that is to hoax lust. For if it has to wait, lust loses its lust; if it is not invited to enter the instant it announces itself, and before everyone else, if it is told that it will not be granted admittance until to-morrow, then lust understands (more quickly that the most ingratiating and wily courtier or the most artful woman understands what it signifies to meet with such a reception in the antechamber), lust understands that it is no longer the one and all, that is to say, it is no longer 'lust'. So it is with this thing of being on the watch not to forget immediately. Do not promise never to forget, only for the sake of being exempted from the necessity of remembering immediately, the very next hour. No, the whole situation is to be reversed, thou art to say, 'This indeed is not something to be remembered all my life, but I promise to remember it immediately, the next hour, and this resolution I shall keep.' And now when thou goest hence (for we may imagine that this is a speech which is being delivered), be not then busy about the speech or the speaker. For though doubtless thou canst not be said in this case to have forgotten the speech, yet to remember it in this way is to be a forgetful hearer. No—yet, for the matter of that, forget the speech and the speaker, but when thou hast returned home, read for thyself, aloud if possible, the whole Epistle for the day—oh, but do it immediately! This thou wilt do, wilt thou not? I thank thee for it. And if there might be one who after the lapse of ten years should happen, quite by chance, to read this discourse, and were to read it to the end— oh, this is what I beseech thee, read then to thyself, aloud if possible, the Epistle for the day, oh, but do it immediately! This thou wilt do, wilt thou not? I thank thee for it.

And thou, O woman, to thee at least it is reserved to be the hearer and reader of the word who is not forgetful. Thou dost comply becomingly with the Apostle's injunction that women must keep silent in the Church. That is becoming. For her to go out and preach, without concerning herself at all about the home—that is unseemly. No, let her be silent, let her treasure the Word in silence; her silence will express how deeply she treasures it. Dost thou not believe in silence? I do. When Cain slew Abel, Abel was silent. But Abel's blood cries to heaven; it 'cries' (not cried), it cries to heaven; dreadful eloquence, which never becomes mute! Oh, the power of silence! That kingly man who bears the name of the Silent[1]—did not his silence mean anything? The others no doubt had talked loudly enough about the salvation of the State, and perhaps about what they would do —he only was silent. What did this silence signify? That he was the man for the task, that he saved the State. Oh, the power of silence!

So it is with woman. Let me describe such a woman, a hearer of the Word who does not forget the Word; but in listening to this description do not forget to become thyself such a one. As has been said, she does not speak in the Church, nor does she talk at home about religion, she keeps silent. Neither is she like an absent-minded person, far away in other regions. Thou dost sit

[1] William the Silent, Prince of Orange.

talking to her, and sitting there for all thou art worth, thou dost say to thyself, 'She is silent. What does this silence mean?' She tends to her house, she is perfectly alert and attentive, as if with her whole soul, to even the least little insignificant thing; she is joyful, sometimes full of jest and merriment, almost more than the children she is the joy of the home—and as thou dost sit with all thy might looking at her, thou wilt say to thyself, 'What does this silence mean?' And so too, in case he who is closest to her, to whom she is bound by an indissoluble tie, whom she loves with all her soul, and who has claim to her confidence—in case it could be supposed that he might say to her directly, 'What does this silence mean? What art thou thinking about?' For there is something behind all the rest, something thou must always be thinking about, tell me what it is.' She does not tell it directly; at the most she might perhaps say evasively, 'Come along then to Church next Sunday'—and then she talks of other things. Or she says, 'Promise me to read a sermon aloud to me on Sunday'— and then she talks of other things. What does this silence mean?

What does it mean? Well, let us not probe farther into that; if she does not tell anything directly to her husband, how could we outsiders expect to get to know anything? No, let us not probe farther into that, but let us bear in mind that this silence is precisely what we have need of if God's Word is to acquire a little power over men.

Oh, if one might (as surely one is justified in doing from a Christian point of view), if, in view of the present situation of the world, of life as a whole, one might Christianly say, 'It is a sickness'—and if I were a physician, and someone asked me, 'What dost thou think must be done?', I should answer, 'The first, the unconditional condition of doing anything, and therefore the first thing to be done is, procure silence, introduce silence, God's Word cannot be heard, and if, served by noisy expedients, it is to be shouted out clamorously so as to be heard in the midst of the din, it is no longer God's Word. Procure silence! Everything contributes to the noise; and as it is said of a hot drink that it stirs the blood, so in our times, every event, even the most insignificant, every communication, even the most fatuous, is calculated merely to harrow the senses or to stir up the masses, the crowd, the public, to make a noise. And man, the shrewd pate, has become sleepless in the effort to find out new, ever new means

for increasing the noise, for spreading abroad, with the greatest
possible speed, and on the greatest possible scale, the meaningless
racket. Indeed, the apogee has almost been attained: communication has just about reached the lowest point, with respect to its
importance; and contemporaneously the means of communication have pretty nearly attained the highest point, with respect
to quick and overwhelming distribution. For what is in such
haste to get out, and on the other hand what has such widespread
distribution as . . . twaddle?[1] Oh, procure silence!

And this is what woman can do. A very extraordinary superiority is required if a man by his presence would impose silence
upon men—but, on the other hand, every woman can do it;
within her limits, in her own circle, provided she desires to do it,
not selfishly, but serving humbly a higher aim.

Truly nature has not showed partiality for women, no, nor
Christianity either. Well, after all, it is only human, and therefore womanly, within one's own limit and becomingly, to desire
to have one's own significance, to be—well what?—well, to be a
power. So there are various ways for a woman to exercise power:
by her beauty, by her charm, by her talents, by her active imagination, by her happy temper—she may also try in a noisy way to
become a power. The last is ungraceful and untrue, the first is
frail and uncertain. But if thou wouldst be a power, O woman,
let me confide to thee how. Learn silence; oh, learn silence from
thyself! Oh, thou didst know it indeed—yes, when but narrow
means were thy lot, thou nevertheless didst know how to arrange
thy house, thy home, pleasantly, agreeably, invitingly, not without
fascination, in spite of its frugality; and if more ample means were
thy lot, thou didst know how to arrange thy house, thy home,
tastefully, cosily, invitingly, not without fascination; and if
opulence were thy lot, thou didst know with ingenious tact
almost concealing wealth how by these very means to spread a
certain fascination over thy house, thy home, uniting wealth and
frugality. Mine eye is not blind to this, I have perhaps only too
much of the poetical in me; but for this let others praise thee. On

---

[1] It is to be remembered that the means of communication S. K. was thinking of
were only the newspaper (his special abhorrence) and the telegraph (which was just
coming into use)—and yet from this passage one might suppose that he had in view
the telephone, wireless telegraphy, the radio, the news reel, not to speak of other
modern means of making a noise.

the other hand, there is one thing, which if thou didst forget to introduce it into thy house, thy home, the most important matter is lacking—that is, Silence! Silence! Silence is not a definite something, for it does not consist simply in not speaking. No, silence is like the subdued light in the cosy room, like friendliness in the humble chamber—it is not a thing one remarks upon, but it is there, and it exercises its beneficent influence. Silence is like the note, the ground-note, which is not made conspicuous; it is called the ground-note just because it is underlying.

But this silence thou canst not introduce into the house as thou dost summon, for example, a man to hang the curtains; no, if silence is to be introduced, it has to do with thy presence, or with the way in which thou art present in thy house, thy home. And when thus by thy presence year after year thou hast steadily introduced silence into thy house, in time this silence will remain there also in thine absence as a witness unto thee, finally, alas, as a memento of thee.

There is an adjective which characterizes the trait which is decisive for women. Great as the differences may be between one woman and another, this one thing is required of every woman, no opulence conceals, no poverty excuses the lack of this; it is like the badge of authority worn by civil officials—there are personal distinctions, one man being in command, as a person highly esteemed in the community, the other being the most inconsiderable, a very subordinate person in the community; but one thing they have in common, the badge of authority. This trait is homeliness—'wifely homeliness', in the best and most favourable sense of the word. It is woman's character, just as it is regarded as man's character to be a character. The countless hosts of women, with all these manifold and manifoldly diversified diversities, all of them should have in common one thing, as all have this in common that they are women—they should have homeliness. Take, for example, a poor plain woman—if it can truly be said of her that in this fine sense she is homely, all honour to her, I bow to her as profoundly as to a queen. And on the other hand, in case the queen does not possess homeliness, she is but a mediocre madam. Take a young girl of whom it might be said that it would be a sin to say she was anything of a beauty— in case she, so far as a young girl can be such, is homely, all honour to her. And on the other hand, a beaming beauty, and for that matter we may bestow upon her in addition all sorts of talents, and for that matter let her be a celebrity—but she is not homely, indeed she has not even a respect for this trait, so with all her talents, beauty, and celebrity, she is but a mediocre wench. Homeliness! With this word we make to woman the great concession that really it is she who creates the home. The young girl, even if she were never to be married, we nevertheless rank in accordance with the measure of her feminine worth: homeliness. But silence introduced into the house is the homeliness of eternity.

However, if thou, O woman, art to introduce this silence, learn it from thyself, and then thou mayest school others in it. Thou must take good care, must find time for thyself, and though thou hast so much to attend to, ah (here we have it again), thou art a homely body, and when one has a homely way of dealing with time, one can find time enough. This thou must be careful about. Man has so much to attend to, so much to do with noisy things, all too much; if thou dost not attend to it that everything is as it should be, that silence is there, never will silence enter thy house.

Attend well to this! For in these times a young girl learns so much in the Institute, not only French and German but drawing —the question is whether in these times she learns what is most important, that which later she will have to learn by herself (for there are only a few individuals who later learn French and German by themselves), if indeed she learns it, namely, silence. Whether she will learn it I do not know. But be attentive thou to this, it is indeed thy task to introduce silence. Remember the words of the Apostle about beholding thyself in the mirror of the Word. For a woman who looks much at her reflection in the mirror becomes vain and vainly talkative! And alas, a woman who looks at her reflection in the mirror of the age becomes loudly vociferous! Oh, but a woman who looks at her reflection in the mirror of the Word becomes silent! And if she becomes silent, this is perhaps the strongest expression of the fact that she is not a forgetful hearer or reader. One who after beholding herself in the mirror of the Word became talkative—that may be an indication that she has not forgotten, perhaps; but if she became silent, then it is sure. Thou knowest it indeed: one fell in love—and became talkative ... maybe! But to become silent—that is surer.

II
CHRIST IS THE WAY

Acts 1 : 1—12

Ascension Day

The first account I wrote, O Theophilus, about all that Jesus undertook both to do and to teach, until the day when He was taken up, after He had through the Holy Ghost given commandment to the Apostles whom He had chosen, before whom He also showed Himself alive after His passion, by many infallible proofs, being seen of them forty days and speaking of the things pertaining to the kingdom of God. And when He had assembled them together, He commanded them not to depart from Jerusalem, but to wait for the promise of the Father, which, saith He, ye have heard from me. For John truly baptized with water, but ye shall be baptized with the Holy Ghost not many days hence. When they therefore were assembled, they asked of Him, saying, 'Lord, wilt thou at this time restore again the kingdom to Israel?' But He said unto them, 'It is not for you to know the times or the seasons, which the Father hath put in His own power. But ye shall receive the power of the Holy Ghost which shall come upon you; and ye shall be my witnesses, both in Jerusalem, and in all Judaea, and in Samaria, and unto the uttermost part of the earth.' And when He had spoken these things, while they beheld, He was taken up, and a cloud received Him out of their sight. And while they gazed towards heaven as he went up, behold, two men stood by them in white apparel, which also said, 'Ye men of Galilee, why stand ye gazing up to heaven? This same Jesus who is taken up from you into heaven, shall so come in like manner as ye have seen Him go into heaven.'

PRAYER

O Lord Jesus Christ, who didst behold Thy fate in advance and yet didst not draw back; Thou who didst suffer Thyself to be born in poverty and lowliness, and thereafter in poverty and lowliness didst bear the sin of the world, being ever a sufferer, until, hated, forsaken, mocked, and spat upon, in the end deserted even by God, Thou didst bow Thy head in the death of shame—oh, but Thou didst yet lift it up again, Thou eternal victor, Thou who wast not, it is true, victorious over Thine enemies in this life, but in death wast victorious even over death; Thou didst lift up Thy head, for ever victorious, Thou who art ascended to heaven! Would that we might follow Thee!

CHRIST IS THE WAY

CHRIST is the way. This is His own word, so it surely must be truth.

And this way is narrow. This is His own word, so it surely must be truth. Indeed, even if He had not said it, it would still be truth. Here thou hast an example of what it is in the highest sense of the word to 'preach'. For if Christ never had said, 'Strait is the gate and narrow is the way that leadeth unto life', thou hast only to look at Him, and at once thou dost see that the way is narrow. But this is a much more solid and a much more forcible proclamation that the way is narrow—this fact that His life, every blessed day, every hour, every instant, expresses the truth that the way is narrow—than if His life had not expressed it, and then on several occasions He had proclaimed, 'The way is narrow.' Thou canst see here also that it is at the farthest possible remove from the genuine preaching of Christianity when a man whose life every day, every hour of the day, every instant, expresses the very opposite, then preaches Christianity for half an hour. Such preaching transforms Christianity into its exact opposite. In that ancient hymn ('We praise Thee, O God') which enumerates the various sorts of preachers of the Word no mention is made of this sort of preaching, which is the invention of a later age—'when Christianity is completely victorious'. In the hymn it is said, 'The Prophets praise Thee' O God—they were the first in point of time. Next, 'The Apostles praise Thee'. These are the extraordinary ministers: Prophets and Apostles. Then there comes a whole army, a swarm of men—thou and I come along with them, I can imagine—well, but just hear now: 'And the noble army of Martyrs praise Thee solemnly in the hour of death.' And then it is over. This is the preaching of the doctrine that the way is narrow; the preacher does not mock himself, as is the case when the way he himself follows is easy, whereas (perhaps movingly, persuasively, perhaps not without tears—but perhaps, too, weeping comes easy to him) he preaches that 'the way' is narrow—that is to say, not the way he himself follows. No, the preacher's life expresses the doctrine: the way is narrow; there is only one way, that which the preacher follows as he preaches that 'the way' is narrow. There are not two ways, one of them being easy, a beaten path, along which the preacher goes, preaching that 'the way' is narrow, that is, the true way, the way in which the preacher does not walk, so that his preaching invites men to follow Christ in the narrow way, whereas his life (and that naturally exercises far more influence) invites them to follow the preacher in the easy way, the beaten path. Is this Christianity? No, life and preaching should express the same thing, that 'the way' is narrow.

And this way, which is Christ, this narrow way, *is narrow at the very beginning.*

He is born in poverty and wretchedness—one is almost tempted to think that it is not a human being that here is born—He is born in a stable, wrapped in rags, laid in a manger, yet, strangely enough, He was plotted against by the mighty while He was still an infant, so that His poor parents were obliged to flee with Him. That in truth is already a very narrow way. For when one is born in an exalted position, for example as heir apparent, it well may chance that one becomes the object of the plots of the mighty; but to be born in a stable and be swaddled in rags—there we have poverty and indigence which may be narrow enough; but in such circumstances one is commonly exempted at least from the plots of the mighty.

But as He did not seem by His birth to be designated for high position, so in fact things remained about as they were at the beginning; He lives in poverty and lowliness, not having whereon to lay His head.

This already would surely be about enough to justify one, humanly speaking, in saying about a way that it is narrow. And yet in fact this is the easiest part of the narrow way.

In a very different sense from this the way is narrow, and that from the very beginning. For from the very beginning His life is a story of temptation; it is not only a single period of His life, the forty days, which is the story of temptation; no, His life (just as it is also all of it the story of the Passion) is a story of temptation. He is tempted every instant of His life—that is to say, He has in his power the possibility of taking His calling, His task, in vain. In the desert it is Satan who is the tempter; in later instances it is the other people who play the role of the tempter, now it is the populace, now the disciples, perhaps also at one time, more especially at the beginning, the mighty made an effort to tempt Him to secularize His calling, His task—and then, in one way or another, He would have become something great in the world, a king and despot, in conformity with the dearest wish of His beloved disciples, so that He might have been tempted for their sake to give in a little, instead of being obliged, humanly speaking, to make them as unhappy as possible. Whereas other men struggle from the very beginning with prodigious effort to become kings and despots, He with infinitely greater effort from the very beginning had to defend Himself against being made king and despot. Oh, narrow way! Narrow enough when suffering is inevitable, when there is no way out of it—a still narrower way when in every instant of suffering (alas, every instant was suffering!) there is this—frightful!—possibility which is almost forced upon Him, this possibility of being able so easily to procure, not relief only, but victory and all that an earthly heart could crave. Oh, narrow way, which many true followers, however, have had to travel, though on a lesser scale! It is the universal human trait to aspire to be regarded as something great, and the universal forgery is to give oneself out to be more than one truly is. Religious suffering begins differently. By reason of his relationship to God, the man who is called feels himself so mighty that he is not in the least tempted to aspire to be regarded as more. No, but in the same instant he is pierced through and through by a mortal dread; for he understands that this sort of endowment is usually certain destruction. And so his temptation is to affirm of himself less than he truly is. No one shall know this along with him, no one but God; and if he carries this out, then peace awaits him, and exultation, and glory, for thus he conquers—he has to endeavour precisely to defend himself against conquering. Narrow way!

The way is narrow from the very beginning; for from the very beginning He knows His fate. Oh, frightful weight of suffering, from the very beginning! There have been many, many who buoyantly, almost exultantly, went forth to war with the world, hoping that they should conquer. It did not come to pass as they hoped, things took another turn; but even at the instant when it seemed most like inevitable destruction, even at that instant there was in them perhaps a human hope that the situation might turn to victory, or a godly hope that even yet it might turn to victory, since all things are possible with God. But Christ knew His fate from the beginning, knew that it was inevitable—He Himself indeed would have it so, He Himself went freely into it! Frightful knowledge, from the very beginning! When the populace at the beginning of His life acclaimed Him, He knew at that instant what it meant, that it was the same populace which would cry out, 'Crucify him!' 'Why does He want to have anything to do with the populace?' Presumptuous man! Dost thou dare to speak thus to the Saviour of mankind? Now he performs again a work of love towards this people (and His whole life was nothing else but this), but He knew at the same instant what it means, that also this work of love contributes to bring Him to the cross; had He in this instance loved Himself and refrained from performing a work of love, His crucifixion perhaps would have been doubtful. 'But then He could have left the work undone!' Presumptuous man! Dost thou dare to speak thus to the Saviour of the world? Oh, narrow way! A narrow way which nevertheless many a true follower has had to travel, though on a lesser scale! A human heart finds joy in apprehending how much is granted to one. So at the beginning there is an instant when the man with a 'call' tries his muscles as it were, happy and grateful as a child for what is granted to him, and like a child he perhaps craves more, yet humbly, and it is granted to him. And still more, which is granted. He himself is almost overwhelmed, he says, 'No, now I crave nothing more.' But it is as if there was a voice which said to him, 'Oh, my friend, this is only a small part of what is granted thee.' At that the man with a call sinks almost impotently to the ground, and says, 'O my God, I understand it, so then my fate is already decided, my life consecrated to suffering, it is sacrificed. And to think that now, already, I should be able to understand this!'[1]

Yes, the way is narrow, from the very beginning; for He knows from the very beginning that His work is to work against Himself. Ah, the way can well be narrow even where thou art at liberty to employ all thy powers to press through, where the opposition is

[1] I wonder if the reader needs to be apprised that this passage is autobiographical.

without thee; but when thou must employ all thy powers to work against thyself—that is if it were far too little to say that the way is narrow, rather it is impassable, barred, impossible, crazy! And yet it is the way to which applies the saying that Christ is the way, it is just as narrow as this. For the True and the Good which He wills—if he does not relinquish them, if He labours for them with all His might, He labours Himself into certain destruction. And on the other hand, if He too quickly stakes the whole truth, His destruction will come too early; so He must work against Himself, must for a long while seem to indulge in illusions, in order the more thoroughly to ensure His destruction. Narrow way! To walk in that way is at once, even at the beginning, like dying! Almightily to exert the powers of omnipotence, to be at the same time a man, and therefore with the capacity to suffer every human suffering—and then to have to use these powers of omnipotence to work against Himself, to know this from the very beginning—oh, from the very beginning how narrow a way!

And this way which is Christ, this narrow way, becomes, as it goes on, narrower and narrower, until the very last, until death.

It becomes narrower; so it does not little by little become easier. No, the way which little by little becomes easier cannot be said to be the way in the sense that Christ is the way. Such is the way human shrewdness and human understanding takes. One man perhaps has more shrewdness, greater understanding, than another, and is capable therefore of venturing more and holding out longer than another, but understanding and shrewdness can constantly reckon upon the expectation that when for a longer or shorter time suffering has been endured and effort expended, the way will become easier and at the last one triumphs in this life. On the other hand, a way which becomes narrower and narrower up to the very last—such a way shrewdness and understanding never take—'it would be madness'.

However, whether it be madness or shrewdness, so it is: the narrow way becomes narrower.

'I am come to cast fire upon the earth, and how I would that it were already kindled!' This is a sigh—the way is narrow. A sigh! What is a sigh? A sigh signifies that there is something imprisoned within, something that would out, but cannot or must not, something that would have air; so a man sighs and gives himself air (so as not to perish), while he is struggling for air so as not to perish. 'I am come to cast fire upon the earth, and how I would that it were already kindled!' How shall I describe this suffering? Let me attempt it—but let me at once retract the attempt beforehand and say that it is only an impotent nothing if it were to be taken to describe the suffering. Imagine then a ship, but thou canst well imagine it infinitely bigger than anything that is to be seen in reality; suppose, to mention a figure at random, that it could contain one hundred thousand men. It is a warship, engaged in battle—and the strategy of the battle requires that it be blown up. Think of the commander who has to kindle this fire! And yet this is but a wretched, insignificant picture. For what are one hundred thousand men compared with the whole race! and what is it to be blown up together compared with the fire which Christ was to kindle, which on exploding would separate in dissension father and son, son and father, mother and daughter, daughter and mother, the mother-in-law and the daughter-in-law, the daughter-in-law and the mother-in-law—and where the danger is not that of death but the loss of eternal blessedness! 'I am come to cast fire upon the earth, and how I would that it were already kindled!' However, the moment has not yet come, the terrible moment, though the not less terrible moment is the moment before, when a man sighs, 'Oh, would it were come to pass!'

'O faithless and perverse generation! how long shall I be with you? how long shall I suffer you?' This is a sigh. It is as when a sick man—not on a sick-bed, but on a death-bed, for this is no light sickness, his life is despaired of—raises his head from the pillow and says, 'What time is it?'—death being a certainty, the question only is, How long will it be? What time is it? However, the moment is not yet come, the terrible moment, although the not less terrible moment is the moment before, when a man sighs, 'How long have I still to hold out?'

So then for the last time He is assembled with His disciples at the supper which He has earnestly desired to eat with them before He died. Defenceless He is as ever. Defenceless. Yes, for in one respect He might have defended Himself. He might (and that would have been on his part a mildness which men might have admired endlessly), He might have said to Judas, 'Stay away, come not to the supper, the sight of thee affects me painfully.' Or He might have charged one of the Apostles (without telling him what He knew about Judas) to say to him not to come. But no! They were all assembled together. Then He said to Judas, 'What thou doest, do quickly.' This is a sigh. Only quickly! Even the most frightful thing is less frightful than this—only do it quickly! A sigh which draws breath deeply and slowly—only quickly! It is as when a man has a prodigious task to perform; although the effort almost exceeds his power, he yet has strength left for the next instant—'one instant longer and my strength may be sapped, I may be no longer myself—hence, quickly!' 'What thou doest, do quickly!'

Then He rises from the table and goes out to the Garden of Gethsemane. Here He sinks to the ground—oh, that it might quickly come to pass! He sinks as in a death-swoon. Was He indeed more a dying man on the cross than in Gethsemane? If the suffering upon the cross was a death-struggle—oh, this struggle in prayer was a struggle also for life, and not without blood, for His sweat fell like drops of blood upon the ground.

Then He rises with strength renewed: 'Father in heaven, Thy will be done.'

Then Judas kisses Him—hast thou heard the like of it!— then He is apprehended, accused, condemned! It was in the regular course of law, it was human justice! This was a people He had done good to; verily He had wanted nothing for Himself, every day of His life and every thought was sacrificed to it—and this people cried, 'Crucify him, crucify him!' There was then a ruler of the land who feared the Emperor, a man of culture who as such did not neglect the most important matter, 'of washing his hands'—so He was condemned! Oh, human justice! Yes, in quiet weather, when all goes smoothly, a little bit of some sort of justice is done; but whenever the situation is extraordinary— oh, human justice! O human culture, what really distinguishes thee from that which thou dost most abhor: from lack of culture, the vulgarity of the crowd? It is the fact that thou doest the same as they, only with attention to the form, not to do it with un- washed hands—oh, human culture!

Then He was nailed to the cross—and then only one sigh more, then it is over. One sigh more, the deepest, the most terrifying: 'My God, my God, why hast Thou forsaken Me?' This humiliation is the last extreme of suffering. Among those who were followers in the strictest sense, the blood-witnesses, thou wilt find faint intimations of this same experience. They have relied upon God and upon God's assistance, then there comes a moment at the last when the sigh is to this effect: 'God hath forsaken me, so ye are right, ye mine enemies, exult not, for all that I have said was not true, it was a delusion, now it is shown to be such—God is no more with me, He hath forsaken me.' O my God! And now He—He had said that He was the only begotten Son of the Father, one with the Father—but if they are one, how can the Father for an instant forsake Him? And yet He says, 'My God, my God, why hast Thou forsaken Me?' So then it was not true that He was one with the Father. Oh, extremest limit of superhuman suffering! A human heart would have broken a little sooner, only the God-Man has to suffer this last clean through.—Then He dies.

My hearer, remember now what it was we said at the beginning: this way is narrow—is it not?

However, we go on farther; *and Christ is the way.* Christ is the way, He goes up unto the mountain, a cloud receives Him out of the sight of the disciples, He ascends into heaven—and He is the way.

Perhaps thou sayest, 'Yes, and it was about this thou shouldst have spoken to-day, not as thou hast been speaking, almost as though it were Good Friday.' Oh, my friend, art thou one of those who, punctually at the stroke of the clock and by the date of the calendar is able to put himself into a definite mood? Or dost thou suppose that it is Christianity's intention that we should be like that, and not rather that we should combine together as far as possible the various factors of Christianity? Precisely on Ascension Day it ought to be remembered that the way is narrow, for otherwise we easily might take the Ascension in vain. Remember, the way was narrow up to the last, death comes in between—then follows the Ascension. It was not midway that He goes to heaven, it was not even at the end of the way, for the way ended at the cross and in the grave. The Ascension is not a direct continuation of the foregoing, verily no! And a narrow way which even in this life becomes easier and easier never leads so high, even when it leads to its highest goal, to victory, never so high that it becomes an ascension into heaven. But every living man is indeed—if he is in the right way and not on a byway

—is indeed in the narrow way. Therefore doubtless the Ascension should be talked about, and about Christ as the way to it— oh, but as for the Ascension, that is so easy to go through with, if only we reach that point, and the last way in the world to reach it is by wanting merely to think about the Ascension, even if thou also dost let thyself be uplifted by the thought of the Ascension.

He ascends into heaven—no one ever conquered thus! A cloud received Him out of their sight—no triumphator was ever thus raised above the earth! They saw Him no more—in no other case was triumph the last experience for anyone! He sits at the right hand of the Power—so the triumph did not end with the Ascension? No, that was only the end of the beginning. O eternal Conqueror!

My hearer, in which way art thou walking? Remember (as I also tell myself) that it is not true of every narrow way that Christ is that way, neither that it leads to heaven.

A pious man has said that it costs a man just as much trouble, or even more, to go to hell as to get into heaven. That also is a narrow way, the way of perdition; but Christ is not that way, neither does it lead to heaven. There is anguish and torment enough upon this way, and to that extent the way is truly narrow, the way of perdition, the way which, in contrast to the other ways about which we have been speaking (the way which at the beginning is narrow and becomes easier and easier, and the narrow way which becomes narrower and narrower), is recognizable by the fact that at the beginning it seems so easy, and becomes more and more terrible. For it goes so easily to join in the dance of pleasure; but when it has gone on apace, and it is pleasure which dances with man against his will—that is a heavy dance! And it is so easy to give rein to the passions—audacious speed, one scarcely can follow it with the eye!—until passion, having taken the bit in its teeth, goes with a still more audacious speed—the man himself is not audacious enough to look where they are going!—carries him forcibly along with it! And it is so easy to permit a sinful thought to slip into the heart—no seducer is so adroit as a sinful thought!—it is so easy, it does not here apply as in other instances that it is the first step which costs, oh, no, it costs nothing whatever, on the contrary, the sinful thought pays for itself at an exorbitant rate, it costs nothing—until at the conclusion, when thou must pay dear for this first which did not cost anything; for when the sinful thought has gained entrance, it exacts a fearful price. Sin usually enters into a man as a flatterer; but then when a man has become a slave of sin—that is a frightful servitude, a narrow, a prodigiously narrow way to perdition!

There are moreover other narrow ways of which it cannot absolutely be said that Christ is the way or that they lead to heaven. There are human sufferings enough, only too many of them, sickness, and poverty, and misunderstanding, and who can enumerate all of these sufferings! Everyone who walks in such a way walks also in a narrow way. Verily we should not speak loftily, as though these sufferings were to be counted as nothing —but, oh, my friend, thou knowest indeed what Christianity is, let me merely remind thee of it. That which distinguishes the Christian narrow way from the common human narrow way is willingness. Christ was not one who sought after earthly possessions but had to be content with poverty; no, He chose poverty. He was not one who aspired after human honour and repute but had to be content to live in lowliness, or to be misjudged and slandered; no, He chose humiliation. This in a stricter sense is the narrow way. The common human sufferings are not in a stricter sense the narrow way, yet verily the way may be narrow enough, and thou mayest strive also to walk Christianly in this narrow way of human suffering. If thou dost walk in it Christianly, it leads to heaven, where He entered, the ascended Christ.

It is true, however, that people have doubted about the Ascension. Yes, but who is it that has doubted? Surely not any one of those whose life bore the marks of a 'follower'? Surely not any one of those who forsook everything to follow Christ? Surely not any one of those who were marked by persecution—which follows as a consequence when 'following' is posited? No, by none of them. But when they did away with 'following' and thereby made persecution an impossibility (which in the thieves' Latin we men speak among ourselves did not sound like an indictment of a perplexed century for its defection from Christianity—O gracious, no, it sounded like a eulogy of the enlightened century's progress in tolerance); when they so abated the price of being a Christian that to be a Christian almost meant nothing, so that there was nothing left to persecute—then in idleness and self-indulgence there arose all sorts of doubt. And doubt assumed an air of importance (who could doubt it?), and people became self-important by doubting—just as once upon a time (as we can better understand, though we do not approve of it) they became self-important by giving all their goods to the poor, so now (presumably in order to establish the true concept of 'merit' instead of the medieval misunderstanding which they abhorred) people became self-important by doubting. And while they doubted everything, there was yet one thing beyond all doubt, that by this ('one must doubt everything')[1] they assured for themselves anything but a doubtful, nay, an exceedingly sure position in society, along with great honour and repute among men.

So some doubted. But then again there were some who sought by reasons to refute doubt. Really, however, the situation is this: the first thing was that they sought by reasons to prove the truth of Christianity, or to adduce reason in support of it. And these reasons—they begat doubt, and doubt became the stronger. For the proof of Christianity really consists in 'following'. That they did away with. So they felt the need of reasons; but these reasons, or the fact that there are reasons, is already a sort of doubt—and so doubt arose and thrived upon the reasons. They did not observe that the more reasons one adduces, the more one nourished doubt and the stronger it becomes, that to present doubt with reasons with the intent of slaying it is like giving to a hungry monster one wants to be rid of the delicious food it likes best. No, doubt—at least if one intends to slay it—must not be presented with reasons, but one must do like Luther, command it to keep its mouth shut,[2] and to the same end keep one's own mouth clean and bring forth no reasons.

Those, on the other hand, whose lives were marked by 'following' had no doubt about the Ascension. And why not? First of all, because their lives were too full of effort, too much sacrificed in daily suffering, to be able to sit in idleness and deal with reasons and doubts, odds or evens. The Ascension was a sure thing to them, but they were accustomed perhaps even more rarely to think about it or to dwell upon it—because their life

---

[1] One of S. K.'s earliest philosophical works (left unfinished and unpublished) was *Johannes Climacus, or de omnibus dubitandum est* (1842-3), ridiculing, not Descartes, but the followers who blindly exalted this maxim.

[2] e.g. *Werke,* xlvii. 337 f.

was so laborious and in the narrow way. It is like a warrior who possesses a gorgeous robe; he knows well that he has it, but he almost never looks at it, for his whole life is passed in daily combat and peril, and therefore he wears an everyday dress which gives him freedom of movement. So it was that those whose lives were marked by 'following' were convinced that their Lord and Master had ascended into heaven. And what contributed to this was again 'following'. All these daily torments of suffering which they had to bear, all these sacrifices they had to make, all this human opposition, scorn and mockery and grins and bloody cruelty, all this painfully prompted in the 'follower' the need which, like the Ascension, breaks or defies natural law (such in fact is the objection doubt raises), breaks in pieces the purely human reasons of comfort (how could these give comfort to men who must suffer because they have done well?), and presses for another sort of comfort, pressingly needs the Ascension of their Lord and Master, and believingly presses through to the Ascension. So it always is with human need, 'from the eater cometh forth meat': where the need is, it produces as it were that which it needs. And the 'followers' verily had need of His Ascension in order to hold out in such a life as they led—so therefore it was a certainty to them. But one who sits in idleness enjoying 'good days', or is busily engaged in bustle from morning till night, but never has suffered anything for the truth's sake, he really has no need, it is rather something he imagines, or something he lets himself be persuaded of for money. It almost might be said that he interests himself in it rather as a curiosity, this thing of the Ascension—and so he doubts, naturally enough, for he has no need; or else he discovers several reasons, or another man is so kind as to present him with three reasons for . . . oh, well, it is evident at any rate that his need is not singularly great!

And now as to thee, my hearer, how is it with thee? Dost thou doubt the Ascension? If so, do as I do; say to thyself, 'Well one need not make a great fuss about such a doubt; I know very well whence it comes and what it is due to, namely, to the fact that in respect to "following" I must have been sparing of myself, that in this respect my life has not been strenuous enough, that I have too easy a life, that I have spared myself the danger of witnessing for the truth and against falsehood.' Only do thus! But above all, do not become important in thine own eyes by doubting. There is no justification for that, I assure thee, since all such doubt is really self-betrayal. No, make this admission to thyself and before God, and thou shalt see that one of two things will come to pass: either thou wilt be moved to venture farther out with respect to 'following'—and then certainty about the Ascension comes at once; or else thou dost humble thyself for having spared thyself, for having become a 'parlour-priest', and then at least thou wilt not permit thyself to doubt, but wilt say humbly, 'Will God be so gracious as to treat me as a child which is spared almost entirely the sufferings of a "follower", and then at least I will not be a naughty boy who on top of everything else doubts the Ascension.' Oh, when thou art living in opulence, admired, flattered, highly esteemed—thou art tempted to say so many a word and to take part in so much which had better have been left alone, and for which—remember this!—thou shalt give an account—and at the same time the Ascension is taken so lightly, perhaps in chancing to think of it thou art even in doubt and sayest, 'An ascension to heaven, that surely conflicts with all the laws of nature and with the "spirit in nature"[1] (meaning, I suppose, world soul). But when it is for a good cause (for otherwise it is unavailing, and even in a good cause it does indeed conflict with all merely human conceptions—that one should suffer because one does well, because one is in the right, because one is loving), when it is for a good cause thou livest in poverty, forsaken, persecuted, ridiculed—thou shalt see that thou wilt have no doubt about the Ascension . . . because thou hast need of it. And indeed not even so much as this is needed to stop doubt, for if thou wilt humble thyself before God with the confession that thy life is not distinguished as that of a 'follower' in the strictest sense, when thou dost humble thyself under this confession, thou wilt not presume to doubt. How might it be possible for thee to present thyself with a doubt when the answer might be, 'First go and become a follower in the strictest sense—only such are permitted to speak on this subject—and of them none has doubted.'

[1] Alluding to a book by H. C. Ørsted entitled *The Spirit in Nature*.

III

IT IS THE SPIRIT THAT GIVETH LIFE

Acts 2: 1—12

Pentecost

And when the day of Pentecost was come, they were all with one accord in one place. And suddenly there came a sound from heaven as of a rushing mighty wind, and it filled all the house where they were sitting. And there appeared unto them tongues like as of fire, which divided and sat upon each of them. And they were all filled with the Holy Spirit and began to speak with other tongues as the Spirit gave them utterance. And there were dwelling at Jerusalem, Jews, devout men, out of every nation under heaven. Now when this was noised abroad, the multitude came together and were confounded, because that every man heard them speak in his own language. And they were all amazed, and marvelled, saying one to another, 'Behold, are not all these which speak Galilaeans? And how hear we every man in our own tongue in which we were born? Parthians, and Medes, and Elamites, and the dwellers in Mesopotamia, and in Judaea, and Cappadocia, in Pontus and Asia, in Phrygia and Pamphilia, in Egypt, and in the parts of Libya about Cyrene, and strangers of Rome, Jews and proselytes, Cretes and Arabians, we do hear them speak in our tongues the wonderful works of God.' And they were all amazed, and were in doubt, saying one to another, 'What meaneth this?'

PRAYER

Thou Holy Ghost, Thou makest alive, bless also this our gathering, the speaker and the hearer; fresh from the heart it shall come, by Thine aid, do Thou let it also go to the heart.

My hearer. If thou wilt give heed, not to the way one talks on holy days in our churches, but to the way they talk on week-days, and for the matter of that also on Sundays outside of church, thou wilt scarcely find anyone who does not believe in—let us say, for example, the spirit of the age, the *Zeitgeist*. Even he who has taken leave of higher things and is rendered blissful by mediocrity, yea, even he who toils slavishly for paltry ends or in the contemptible servitude of ill-gotten gain, even he believes, firmly and fully too, in the spirit of the age. Well, that is natural enough, it is by no means anything very lofty he believes in, for the spirit of the age is after all no higher than the age, it keeps close to the ground, so that it is the sort of spirit which is most like will-o'-the-wisp; but yet he believes in spirit. Or he believes in the world-spirit (*Weltgeist*), that strong spirit (for allurements, yes), that powerful spirit (for delusions, yes), that ingenious spirit (for deceits, yes); that spirit which Christianity calls an evil spirit—so that, in consideration of this, it is by no means anything very lofty he believes in when he believes in the world-spirit; but yet he believes in spirit. Or he believes in 'the spirit of humanity', not spirit in the individual, but in the race, that spirit which, when it is god-forsaken by having forsaken God, is again, according to Christianity's teaching, an evil spirit—so that in view of this it is by no means anything very lofty he believes in when he believes in this spirit; but yet he believes in spirit.

On the other hand, as soon as the talk is about a holy spirit—how many, dost thou think, believe in it? Or when the talk is about an evil spirit which is to be renounced—how many, dost thou think, believe in such a thing?

How does this come about? Is it perhaps because the situation becomes too serious when it is a holy spirit? For the spirit of the age, the world-spirit, and such-like, I can talk about, believe in, and thereby I do not exactly need to think of anything definite, it is a sort of a spirit, but I am by no means bound by what I say; and not to be bound by what one says is something people set store by: how often one hears, 'I will say this or that, but I will not be bound by my word.' But when it is a question of a Holy Spirit, and of believing in a Holy Spirit, one cannot talk without binding oneself, and then not without binding oneself to this Holy Spirit and renouncing the evil spirit—this is too serious, that there is a Holy Spirit—oh, seriousness!—and also (to render seriousness secure) that there is an evil spirit—how serious! Yes, he who believes in the spirit of the age and in the world-spirit, he to be sure, according to Christianity's opinion, believes in an evil spirit;

but this is not his opinion, and in so far he does not believe in an evil spirit. For him, in a deeper sense, the opposition between good and evil does not really exist; slack or loose as he is—in a literal sense, dissolute—doubting in his faith, unstable in all his ways, pliant to every slightest wind of the age, the object of his faith is of the same sort, something airy, the spirit of the age—or, worldly as he has become in his every thought, the object of his faith is concordant—the world-spirit.

But Christianity, which requires renunciation of the evil spirit, teaches that there is a Holy Spirit. And to-day in the Church we celebrate the festival of the Holy Spirit, Pentecost, in remembrance of that day when the Spirit was first poured out upon the Apostles. So to-day it is the Holy Spirit one must speak about, as we will now do, speaking upon the text:

IT IS THE SPIRIT WHICH GIVETH LIFE.

My hearer. With regard to Christianity, there is nothing to which every man is by nature more inclined than to take it in vain. There is nothing whatsoever in Christianity, not one solitary Christian definition, which may not, by undergoing a little alteration, merely by leaving out a subordinate determinant, become something entirely different, something of which it can be said that 'it has entered into the heart of man to believe' —and so it is taken in vain. On the other hand, there is nothing which Christianity has secured itself against with greater vigilance and zeal than against being taken in vain. There is absolutely no definition of Christian truth given without the subordinate determinant which is posited at the outset by Christianity, namely, death, this thing of dying—by which it would secure Christian truth against being taken in vain. They say, 'Christianity is gentle consolation, this is the gentle teaching of the grounds of consolation'—yes, that cannot be denied, if only one first will die, die from (*afdøe*); but that is not so gentle! They picture Christ, they say, 'Hear His voice, how invitingly He calls all unto Him, all who suffer, and promises to give them rest for their souls'— and verily so it is, God forbid that I should say anything else; and yet, and yet, before this rest for the soul becomes thy portion, it is required (as the Inviter also says, and as His whole life here upon earth expresses, every blessed day and every blessed hour of the day) that thou must first die, die from—is this so inviting?

So it is also with this Christian truth: it is the Spirit which giveth life. To what feeling does a man cling tighter than to the vital feeling? What does he more strongly crave and more vehemently than to feel keenly the pulse of life in himself? What does he shudder at more than at dying? But here is preached a life-giving Spirit. So let us grasp at it. Who will hesitate? Give us life, more life, that the vital feeling may expand in me, as though all of life were gathered together in my breast!

But might this be what Christianity is, this dreadful error? No, no! This bestowing of life in the Spirit is not a *direct* increment of the natural life of man, *immediately* continuous with this—oh, blasphemy, oh, horror, thus to take Christianity in vain!—it is a new life. A new life, yes, and this is no mere phrase, as when the word is used for this or that, whenever something new begins to stir in us; no, a new life, literally a new life—for (observe this well!) death comes in between, this thing of being dead; and a life on the other side of death, yes, that is a new life.

Death comes in between, that is Christ's teaching, thou must die, precisely the life-giving Spirit is that which slays thee, this is the first expression of the life-giving Spirit, that thou must depart in death, that thou must die from (*afdøe*)[1]—this is in order that thou mayest not take Christianity in vain. A life-giving Spirit—that is the invitation. Who would not grasp at it? But die first—that gives us pause!

It is the Spirit which giveth life. Yes, it giveth life through death. For as it is said in an old hymn which would comfort the survivors for the loss of the deceased, 'With death we began to live', so in a spiritual sense it is true that the communication of the life-giving Spirit begins with death. Think of to-day's festival! It was indeed a Spirit which makes alive which on this day was poured out upon the Apostles—and verily it was also a life-giving Spirit, as is shown by their life, by their death, whereof we have witness in the history of the Church, which came into existence precisely by the fact that the Spirit which giveth life was communicated to the Apostles. But what was their condition before this? Ah, who like the Apostles could teach what it is to

---

[1] It is time to remark that, although *dø* and *afdø* both mean simply to die, the latter (literally, 'to die from') can be used metaphorically, as S. K. does here, in the sense of dying to self and to the world. An English translation is necessarily imperfect.

die unto the world and unto themselves? For who has ever cherished such great expectations as for some time the Apostles were in a certain sense prompted to entertain? And whose expectations ever were so disappointed? Then came Easter morning, it is true, and Christ rose from the grave, and then came the Ascension—but then what further? Yes, He then was carried up to glory—but what then further? Oh, dost thou believe that any human, even the most audacious human hope could dare in the remotest way to engage in the task which was set the Apostles? No, here every merely human hope must despair. Then came the Spirit which made alive. So then the Apostles were dead, dead to every merely earthly hope, to every human confidence in their own power or in human assistance.

Therefore, first death, first thou must die to every merely earthly hope, to every merely human confidence, thou must die to thy selfishness or to the world; for it is only through thy selfishness that the world has power over thee; if thou hast died to thy selfishness, thou hast died also to the world. But, naturally, there is nothing a man clings to so tight as to his selfishness—which he clings to with his whole self! Ah, when in the hour of death soul and body are separated, it is not so painful as to be obliged to separate in one's lifetime from one's own soul! And a man does not cling so tight to his physical body as a man's selfishness clings to his selfishness! Let me take an example modelled after those old tales about what a man in more ancient times has experienced in the way of heart-felt sufferings, which these untried, sagacious times of ours will regard as a fable, possessing at most a little poetical value. Let us take an example, and to this end let me choose a subject about which we men talk so much and which employs us so much, I mean love. For love precisely is one of the strongest and deepest expressions of selfishness. So then think of a lover![1] He saw the object, and thereupon he fell in love. And this object then became his eyes' delight and his heart's desire. And he grasped after it—it was his eyes' delight and his heart's desire! And he grasped it, he held it in his hand—it was his eyes' delight and his heart's desire! Then (so it goes in these old tales)

[1] The 'lover' is S. K., and Regina is 'the object'. Anyone who knows S. K. from his Journals will recognize (as his contemporaries could not) how intimately personal this whole paragraph is. In one of his earliest books, *Fear and Trembling*, he had likened his sacrifice of Regina to Abraham's sacrifice of Isaac.

a command was issued to him, 'Let go of this object!'—ah, and it was his eyes' delight and his heart's desire! My hearer, let us take pains to apprehend rightly how deep this shaft must penetrate if selfishness is really to be slain. For in his misery he cried, 'No, I will not let go, I cannot let go of this object; oh, have compassion upon me; if I may not retain it, well then, kill me, or at least let it be taken from me!' Thou canst well understand him; his selfishness would be wounded very deeply indeed by being deprived of the object, but he recognized justly that his selfishness would be still more deeply wounded if the requirement was that he should deprive himself of it. My hearer, let us go farther in order to follow the suffering into its deeper recesses when selfishness must be killed even more completely. Let us take the 'object' also into account. So then this object, which he had desired, which he grasped, of which he is in possession, his eyes' delight and his heart's desire, this object which he must let go, ah, his eyes' delight and his heart's desire, this object, let us assume for the sake of illuminating more strongly the pain of dying to it, this object is of the same opinion as he, that it would be cruel to sunder it from him—and it is he who must do this! He is to let go of that which no earthly power thinks of depriving him of, which now he finds it doubly difficult to let go, for (thou canst well imagine this) the object resorts to tears and prayers, invokes the living and the dead, both men and God, to prevent him—and he it is who must let go of this object! Here we have (if indeed he manages to get round that sharp corner without losing his senses)—here we have an example of what it is to die (*afdø*). For not to see his wish, his hope, fulfilled, to be deprived of the object of his desire, his beloved—that may be very painful, selfishness is wounded, but that does not necessarily mean to die. No, but to be obliged to deprive oneself of the object of desire of which one is in possession—that is to wound selfishness at the root, as in the case of Abraham, when God required that Abraham himself, that he himself—frightful!—with his own hand—oh, horror of madness!—must sacrifice Isaac, Isaac, the gift so long and so lovingly expected, and the gift of God, for which Abraham conceived that he must give thanks his whole life long and would never be able to give thanks enough—Isaac, his only son, the son of his old age, and the son of promise. Dost thou believe that death can smart so painfully? I do not. And in any case, when it is a question of death, it is then all over with, but with this thing of 'dying from' it is by no means all over with, for he does not die, there lies perhaps a long life before him . . . the deceased (*afdøde*).

This is what it means to die. But before the Spirit can come which giveth life thou must first die. Ah, sometimes when for a day or for a longer period I have felt so indisposed, so weary, so incapacitated, so (this indeed is the way we express it) almost as if I were dead, then I too sighed within myself, 'Oh bring me life, life is what I need!' Or when perhaps I am taxed beyond my strength and discover, so I think, that I can hold out no longer; or when for a while it has been as if I had only misfortune in everything, and I sank down in despondency—then I have sighed within myself, 'Life, bring me life!' But from this it does not follow that Christianity is of the opinion that this is what I need. Suppose it held another opinion and said, 'No, first die completely; this is thy misfortune, that thou dost yet cling to life, to thy life which thou callest a torment and a burden, die completely!' I have seen a man sink almost into despair, I have also heard him cry out, 'Bring me life, life, this is worse than death which puts an end to life, whereas I am as dead and yet not dead!' I am not a severe man; if I knew any assuaging word, I should be very willing to comfort and cheer the man. And yet, and yet it is perfectly possible that what the sufferer had need of was really something else, that he needed harder sufferings. Harder sufferings! Who is the cruel one who ventures to say such a thing? My hearer, it is Christianity, the teaching which is offered at a selling-out price under the name of gentle comfort, whereas it—yes, verily, it is the comfort of eternity and for ever, but indeed it must take a rather hard hold. For Christianity is not what we men, both thou and I, are only too prone to make of it, it is not a quack. A quack is at your service right away, and right away applies the remedy, and bungles everything. Christianity waits before applying its remedy, it does not heal every wretched little ailment by means of eternity—this clearly is an impossibility as well as a self-contradiction—it heals by means of eternity and for ever when the sickness is such that eternity can be applied—that is to say, to this end thou must first die. Hence the severity of Christianity, in order that it may not itself become twaddle (into which we men are so prone to transform it), and in order that it may not

confirm thee in twaddle. And the rightness of this thou surely
hast experienced in relation to smaller matters. Hast thou never
had the experience—I have—that when perhaps thou hadst
begun to moan and already to say, 'I can't endure it any longer',
then, the following day, when thou wast treated rather more
sternly than ever—and then what? Then thou wast able to do it!
When the horses groan and pant, thinking that they are jaded
and that therefore a handful of hay is what they need—but when
on the other hand, even with the halt of an instant the heavily
loaded wagon would roll back to the brink and perhaps drag
horse and driver and all with it into the abyss—is it then so cruel
of the driver that the blows fall frightfully, frightfully, as he never
had had the heart to beat that team of horses especially, which
were to him (such a thing may well be true) like the apple of his
eye—is that cruel, or is it loving? Is it cruel to be (if one will)
cruel when this is absolutely the only thing that can save from
destruction or help one through? So it is with dying (*at afdøe*).

My hearer. Then, then cometh the life-giving Spirit. When?
Why, when this has come to pass, when thou art deceased (*afdød*);
for as it is said, 'If we be dead with Christ, we shall also live with
Him', so also it may be said, 'If we are to live with Him, we must
also die with Him.' First death, then life. But when? Well, when
the first has come to pass; for with the coming of the life-giving
Spirit it is as with the coming of the 'Comforter' which Christ
promises the disciples. When comes the Comforter? He comes
when all the dreadful things which Christ predicted of His own
life have come first, and the like horrors which He predicted
concerning the lives of the disciples—then comes the Comforter.
And that He comes precisely at that same instant is not said; it is
said only that it is when the first has come to pass, when this
dying has occurred. Thus it is with the coming of the life-giving
Spirit.

But it comes, it does not disappoint by failure to appear. Did it
not come to the Apostles, did it disappoint them? Did it not come
later to the true believers, did it disappoint them by failing to make
an appearance?

No, it comes, and it brings the gifts of the Spirit: life and
spirit.

It brings *faith*, 'faith', that only being in the strictest sense
faith which is the gift of the Holy Spirit after death has come be-

tween. For we men are not so precise in the use of words, we often speak of faith when in the strictest Christian sense it is not faith. In every man, with differences due to natural endowment, a stronger or weaker spontaneity (immediacy) is inborn. The stronger, the more vitally powerful it is, the longer it can hold out against opposition. And this power of resistance, this vital confidence in oneself, in the world, in mankind, and (among other things) in God, we call faith. But this is not using the word in a strictly Christian sense. Faith is against understanding, faith is on the other side of death. And when thou didst die, or didst die to thyself, to the world, thou didst at the same time die to all immediacy in thyself, and also to thine understanding. That is to say, when all confidence in thyself or in human support, and also in God as an immediate apprehension, when every probability is excluded, when it is dark as in the dark night—it is in fact death that we are describing—then comes the life-giving Spirit and brings faith. This strength is stronger than the whole world, it possesses the powers of eternity, it is the Spirit's gift from God, it is thy victory over the world, in which thou dost more than conquer.

And next the Spirit brings *Hope*, hope in the strictest Christian sense, this hope which is hope against hope. For in every man there is a spontaneous (immediate) hope, in one man it may be more vitally strong than in another, but in death (i.e. when thou dost die from) every such hope dies and transforms itself into hopelessness. Into this night of hopelessness—it is in fact death we are describing—comes then the life-giving Spirit and brings hope, the hope of eternity. It is against hope, for according to that merely natural hope there was no hope left, and so this is hope against hope. The understanding says, 'No, there is no hope'; thou, however, art dead to thine understanding, and in so far as that is the case it holds its peace, but if in any way it gets a chance to put in a word again, it will begin at once where it left off, 'there is no hope'—and it will surely deride this new hope, the Spirit's gift, just as the shrewd and understanding men who were gathered together at Pentecost derided the Apostles and said that they were full of new wine, just so will it deride thee and say to thee, 'Thou must have been drunk when such a thing occurred to thee, at least thou must have been out of thy wits'—there is none closer to knowing tnat than the understanding, and that is very understandingly said by the understanding, for to decease is also to die to the understanding, and the life-giving Spirit's hope is against the hope of the understanding. 'It is enough to drive one to despair', says the understanding, 'however, that one can understand. But that on the other side of this (the fact that there is no hope) there should be a new hope, yea, the hope—that is, as surely as I call myself understanding, that is madness.' But the Spirit which giveth life (which the 'understanding' does not do) declares and bears witness: ' "The hope" is against hope.'

O thou who perhaps to the point of desperation art fighting hopelessly and in vain to find hope, it is this, is it not, which makes thee indignant, that in thine opinion thou canst absolutely victoriously make it evident even to a child or to the stupidest man that for thee there is no hope; and perhaps it is precisely this that embitters thee, that they will contradict this. Well then, entrust thyself to the Spirit, for with it thou canst talk, it acknowledges at once that thou art in the right, it says, 'That is quite right, and to me it is very important that this be insisted upon, for it is precisely from this that I, the Spirit, educe the proof that there is hope: hope against hope.' Canst thou require more? Canst thou think of any treatment better adapted to thy situation in suffering? It is granted that thou art in the right, that there is no hope; thou hast got the justice thou didst demand, and thou didst demand also to be what thou now art, to be spared all this prattle, all these loathsome grounds of consolation, thou art permitted, to thy great content, to be as sick as thou wilt without being disturbed by quacks, thou art permitted to do that which ends pain and quiets unrest, to turn away thy face and die, liberated from the baleful medical treatment of those who cannot bring new life but strive painfully to keep thee alive or hinder thee from dying—and in addition to all this thou dost get the 'hope' which is against hope, the Spirit's gift.

Finally, the Spirit also brings *love*. In other passages I have sought to show (what one cannot often enough lay stress upon, and never can make clear enough) that what we men extol under the name of love is selfishness, and that if we do not pay attention to this, the whole of Christianity becomes confusion to us.

Only when thou art dead to selfishness, and therewith to the world, so that thou dost not love the world, neither the things that are in the world, dost not even love selfishly a single person—

when in love to God thou hast learnt to hate thyself—only then can there be question of the love which is Christian love. According to our merely human conceptions, love coheres 'immediately' with our nature; we regard it as a matter of course therefore that it is strongest in the days of youth, when the heart possesses in immediacy all its warmth and enthusiasm, opens itself to others in devotion, responds to others in devotion. And so too we regard it, if not as a matter of course, yet as the usual course of things, that afterwards, as a man grows older, his nature attaches itself less to others, is closer, does not open itself so receptively, does not so open-heartedly respond—which conviction we also explain as a sorry consequence of sorry experiences. 'Alas,' we say, 'for this glad heart of youth, of our own youth as well, so trusting, so devoted (if in fact this is exactly true!), was disappointed so often, so bitterly, I had to learn to know men from quite a different side, and therefore (so there is a therefore!) a good part of love was quenched also in my heart.'

Oh, my friend, how dost thou suppose the Apostles had learned to know man, does it seem to thee that it was from the favourable side? Verily, if ever there was any one (yet among those who are always afoot with much talk about this young, full, loving, friendly heart of youth, such a one is hardly to be found) who was justified in saying, 'I have so learned to know men that I am sure they do not deserve to be loved'—then it was Christ's Apostles! And this is an embittering experience; it is so natural to wish to find in men what one can love, and yet this is not an unreasonable experience when what is sought after is not the other's good, or not that alone. Not to find anything of the sort, to find the very opposite, and to find it on the scale the Apostles found it—ah, that is enough to be the death of one! And in a certain sense it was the death of the Apostles—they died, everything grew dark round about them (it is in fact death we are talking of!), when they had the frightful experience that love is not loved, that it is hated, that it is mocked, that it is spat upon, that it is crucified, in this world, and crucified while the justice which condemns it tranquilly washes its hands, and while the voice of the populace is loud for the robber. So surely they swore eternal enmity to this unloving world? Ah, yes, in a certain sense, but in another aspect, no, no; in their love for God, in order that they might abide in love, they banded themselves, so to speak, together with

God to love this unloving world—the life-giving Spirit brought them love. And so the Apostles resolved, in likeness with the Pattern, to love, to suffer, to be sacrificed, for the sake of saving the unloving world. And this is love.

Such gifts the life-giving Spirit brought to the Apostles at Pentecost—oh, that the Spirit would also bring such gifts to us, there is verily great need of this in our times.

My hearer, I have still a word I would say; but I will clothe it in a form of presentation which perhaps at the first glance will seem to thee less solemn. I do it, however, advisedly and intentionally, because I think that in this way it will make a truer impression upon thee.

Once upon a time there was a rich man who ordered from abroad at a high price a pair of entirely faultless and high-bred horses which he desired to have for his own pleasure and for the pleasure of driving them himself. Then about a year or two elapsed. Anyone who previously had known these horses would not have been able to recognize them again. Their eyes had become dull and drowsy, their gait lacked style and decision, they couldn't endure anything, they couldn't hold out, they hardly could be driven four miles without having to stop on the way, sometimes they came to a standstill as he sat for all he was worth attempting to drive them, besides they had acquired all sorts of vices and bad habits, and in spite of the fact that they of course got fodder in over-abundance, they were falling off in flesh day by day. Then he had the King's coachman called. He drove them for a month—in the whole region there was not a pair of horses that held their heads so proudly, whose glance was so fiery, whose gait was so handsome, no other pair of horses that could hold out so long, though it were to trot for more than a score of miles at a stretch without stopping. How came this about? It is easy to see. The owner, who without being a coachman pretended to be such, drove them in accordance with the horses' understanding of what it is to drive; the royal coachman drove them in accordance with the coachman's understanding of what it is to drive.

So it is with us men. Oh, when I think of myself and of the countless men I have learnt to know, I have often said to myself despondently, 'Here are talents and powers and capacities enough—but the coachman is lacking.' Through a long period of time, we men, from generation to generation, have been, if I may so say, driven (to stick to the figure) in accordance with the horses' understanding of what it is to drive, we are directed, brought up, educated in accordance with man's conception of what it is to be a man. Behold therefore what we lack: exaltation, and what follows in turn from this, that we only can stand so little, impatiently employ at once the means of the instant, and in our impatience desire instantly to see the reward of our labour, which just for this reason is deferred.

Once it was different. Once there was a time when it pleased the Deity (if I may venture to say so) to be Himself the coachman; and He drove the horses in accordance with the coachman's understanding of what it is to drive. Oh, what was a man not capable of at that time!

Think of to-day's text! There sit twelve men, all of them belonging to that class of society which we call the common people. They had seen Him whom they adored as God, their Lord and Master, crucified; as never could it be said of anyone even in the remotest, it can be said of them that they had seen everything lost. It is true, He thereupon went triumphantly to heaven—but in this way also He is lost to them: and now they sit and wait for the Spirit to be imparted to them, so that thus, execrated as they are by the little nation they belong to, they may preach a doctrine which will arouse against them the hate of the whole world, that is the task; these twelve men are to transform the world—and that on the most terrible terms, against its will. Truly, here the understanding is brought to a standstill! In order now, so long after, to form merely a faint conception of it, the understanding is brought to a standstill—supposing that one has any understanding; it is as if one were to lose one's understanding —supposing one has any understanding to lose.

It is Christianity that had to be put through. These twelve men, they put it through. They were in a sense men like us—but they were well driven, yea, they were well driven!

Then came the next generation. They put Christianity through. They were men just like us—but they were well driven! Yea, verily, that they were! It was with them as with that pair of horses when the royal coachman drove them. Never has a man ever lifted his head so proudly in loftiness above the world as the first Christians did in humility before God! And just as that pair of horses could trot, even if it were for a score of miles or more, without being pulled up to give them breath, so these ran, they ran at one stretch for three score years and ten without getting out of harness, without being pulled up anywhere; no, proud as they were in humility before God, they said, 'It is not for us to lie down and dawdle on the way, we come to a stop first . . . at eternity!' It was Christianity that had to be put through; so they put it through, yea, that they did; but they also were well driven, yea, that they were!

O Holy Spirit—we pray for ourselves and for all—oh, Holy Spirit, Thou who dost make alive; here it is not talents we stand in need of, nor culture, nor shrewdness, rather there is here too much of all that; but what we need is that Thou take away the power of mastery and give us life. True it is that a man experiences a shudder like that of death when Thou, to become the power in him, dost take the power from him—oh, but if even animal creatures understand at a subsequent moment how well it is for them that the royal coachman took the reins, which in the first instance prompted them to shudder, and against which their mind rebelled—should not then a man be able promptly to understand what a benefaction it is towards a man that Thou takest away the power and givest life?

JUDGE FOR YOURSELVES!
FOR SELF-EXAMINATION
Recommended to this Present Time

Second Series

by
S. Kierkegaard
[1851–2]

Copenhagen
1876

CONTENTS

[P. Chr. Kierkegaard, Editor]

PREFACE

Well do I know, and I know only too well, how true it is that the world wants to be deceived. In view of this I might perhaps have some hesitation in making public such a piece of advice as the present.

Why is it I have none? Because I have nothing whatever to do with the world. I address myself to the single individual, to every individual, or to everyone as an individual.

So when each individual does as I do when I write, shuts his door, reads for himself, fully convinced, as indeed it is the truth, that I have not in the remotest way thought of wishing to approach him impertinently or to talk about him to others, inasmuch as I have been thinking only about myself; when he reads this as an individual, so that it does not occur to him in the remotest way to think of anyone but himself—then verily I need not fear that he might be angry with me for offering this advice.

For what is it to be or to will to be the single individual? It is to have and to will to have a conscience. But how could a man of conscience be angry at anyone for giving him true advice? He might rather be angry at the contrary. What wouldst thou say: is it insulting to treat a person not merely as a rational being but as a man of conscience to whom one declares the true position of affairs? I should think it would be insulting if one with the conceit of being shrewd were to treat a person like a child who could not endure to learn the truth, or like a fool whom one can induce to believe anything merely by flattering him; I should think that to hide the truth, to deceive, would be an insult to the person who is thus treated, and that the deceived person is most deeply insulted when he is pleased at being deceived.

My dear reader, read aloud if possible. If thou wilt do this, let me thank thee; if thou wilt not only do this thyself but prompt others to do so, let me thank each one severally, and thank thee again and again.

I

1 Peter 4: 7. Be ye therefore Sober

BECOMING SOBER

PRAYER

FATHER in heaven, Thou art a spirit, and they that worship Thee must worship Thee in spirit and in truth—but how in spirit and in truth if we are not sober, even if we are striving to be? Send therefore Thy Spirit into our hearts; ah, it is so often invoked that it may come to bring courage, and life, and power and strength, oh, that it first (this is indeed the condition for all the rest, and that the rest may be to our profit), oh, that first it might make us sober!

M Y hearer. When the Apostles came forward on Pentecost, filled for the first time with the Holy Spirit, 'then the people were amazed and were in doubt, saying one to another, What meaneth this? Others, mocking, said, These men are drunk with new wine' (Acts 2: 12 f.). So then no one was able to explain, or ventured to explain, what had occurred here; amazement and doubt seized them all, only the mockers attempted an explanation, that the Apostles were drunk, and at so early an hour, nine o'clock in the morning. Such was the explanation. But it does not suffice; for the striking thing is that they were in this same condition not only that morning, no, if they were drunk, they were drunk also the next morning, and the following, and a month later, and twenty years later, and up to the moment of their death, they were still drunk with that new wine which (according to the explanation of the mockers) they must have drunk that morning—for otherwise the occurrence on Pentecost is not explained by the explanation. Oh, profound mockery of the mockers' explanation!

Here, as in every case, it is evident that the world and Christianity have the most opposite conceptions. The world says of the Apostles, more especially of the Apostle Peter as spokesman, 'He is drunk'—and the Apostle Peter gives the warning, 'Be ye sober.' So the worldly mind regards Christianity as drunkenness, and Christianity regards the worldly mind as drunkenness. 'Only be reasonable, come to thy senses, try to be sober', thus does the worldly mind address the Christian. And the Christian says to the worldly mind, 'Only be reasonable, come to thy senses, try to be sober.' For the difference between the worldly mind and the Christian mind is not that the first holds one opinion and the second another; no, the difference always is that they hold opinions which are diametrically opposite, that what the one calls good the other calls evil, what the one calls love the other calls selfishness, what the one calls godliness the other calls ungodliness, what the one calls drunkenness the other calls sobriety. It is precisely the drunken man, the 'Apostle', who finds it necessary to press upon a sober world (as I can imagine it) the warning, 'Be sober'.

This precisely is the warning which perhaps is most apt to wound the hardened worldly mind, which in general is not very easily wounded or put out of countenance. For the wordly mind can put up with a great deal, one can say pretty nearly anything to it, except to call it drunkenness. 'I', says the worldly mind, 'I stick to what's certain; I don't believe anything, not the least thing, unless I can take hold of it and feel it; and I don't believe anybody, not my own child, not my wife, not my best friend; I believe only what can be proved—for I stick to what's certain. I stick to what's certain, and therefore I have nothing to do in the remotest way with all those high-flown notions about other-worldliness, about eternity, and all that which the parsons (not for nothing) make women and children and simple folks believe; for one knows what one has, but not what one is going to get— this is what I stick to. I stick to what's certain. Therefore I never take part in playing the game people make so much ado about under the name of love, where one is always made a fool of, if one is not the person who makes a fool of the others; no, I don't love a single person—but halt, there is one person I love, I do not say that I love him more than myself (that is so fanatical, and I am not a fanatic), but I love him just as much as myself, for this person is in fact myself; this person I do love, that is certain, and I stick to what's certain. One may call me selfish and heartless and cunning and mean, for the matter of that one may call me a scoundrel and a knave—that would never disconcert me for an instant, I stick to what's certain. The one thing, I believe, which might for an instant disconcert me would be if it should occur to anyone to say that I was drunk, inebriated, to say this of me, the coldest and calmest and clearest intelligence.' Yet the Apostle says, 'Be sober!' and therewith he implies, 'Thou art drunken; unhappy man, if only thou couldst see thyself, perceive that with thee it is as with a drunkard when—disgusting sight!—he hardly resembles a man—to such a degree art thou intoxicated.'

So it is that the worldly and the Christian are related to one another. It was not only of the Apostles it was said, and not only on Pentecost, that they were drunken with new wine; no, it was and continues to be the world's judgement of the Christian life. And Christianity, on the other hand, is of the opinion that precisely the Apostles, and precisely on Pentecost, were in the highest degree sober, sheer spirit. And Christianity is of the opinion that it is precisely the true Christian who is sober, and on the other hand that in the exact degree he is less of a Christian, in that same degree he is more in a state of inebriation. And Christianity is of the opinion that the first effect it has, or the Spirit has, upon a man is to make him sober. In Christianity everything goes by pairs, or every determinant factor of Christianity is in the first instance its own opposite, whereas in the merely human or worldly sphere each is simply and directly what it is. Thus, in a merely human sense, a spirit which makes alive is a life-giving spirit, and nothing more; in Christian experience it is in the first instance the Spirit which killeth, which teaches how to 'die from'. Exaltation, in the merely human sense, is exaltation, nothing more; in the Christian sense it is in the first instance humiliation. So likewise inspiration, in the merely human sense, is inspiration; in the Christian sense inspiration is in the first instance to become sober.

And it is about this we would speak, about

BECOMING SOBER

When in a merely human way distinction is made between being sober (spiritually understood) and being drunken, one is apt to associate sobriety with common sense, discretion, shrewdness, and all that goes with this; and with drunkenness (spiritually understood) to associate enthusiasm, being venturesome, and such venturesomeness as leaves probability out of account. The common-sense, prudent, and shrewd man, who calls himself sober, therefore regards the enthusiasts with all their ventures as drunken persons, says this scornfully of them, and warns others not to be led astray by them.

And perhaps in one sense they are right, even according to Christianity's opinion. For Christianity is very far from extolling every enthusiasm, every venturesome risk, and Christ

Himself, who required that the 'disciple' should leave all to follow Him, give all to the poor, and even forbear to bury his father, even He says also (implying thereby that He does not require of every man absolutely that he should be a 'disciple'), 'that one who intends to build a tower, will sit down first and consider the cost, whether he have sufficient to finish it'.

So Christianity also is of the opinion that there is a venturesome risk which is foolhardy, not praiseworthy.

But then in fact Christianity is in agreement with these common-sense, prudent, shrewd ones who, humanly speaking, are the so-called sober people? No, far from it; no, not with a single one of them. For between these so-called sober people there is a difference to be observed. Some employ their common sense, prudence, and shrewdness to coddle themselves in every way, so that they remain pitiful half-men, forgetting (what surely needs to be remembered in every sermon in Christendom) that not only thieves and murderers and whoremongers but also flabby and effeminate persons cannot enter into the kingdom of heaven—ah, when some day the reckoning shall be made of the countless multitude of the human race, there will be found a greater number under the rubric 'The flabby', than under all these rubrics taken together: 'Thieves', 'Robbers', 'Murderers'. Thus it is with some of the so-called sober people. Others, however, possess a stronger will-power, have more violent passions, a deeper urge for decision and action; and they employ their prudence and shrewdness somewhat differently. They venture farther out, tax their strength more, do not flee from every danger; but one thing stands fast for them: probability. Within the bounds of probability they have at their disposal more possibilities than the others, they extort from probability declarations which it (for probability also is prudish and niggardly) refuses to the flabby ones; but one thing stands fast, immovably fast, they will not let go of probability: to let go of that, they say, is to be drunken.

So here is the endless difference from the Christian attitude; for Christianly, indeed merely religiously, considered, the man who never let go of probability never committed himself to God. All religious (not to say Christian) adventure is on the farther side of probability, is by letting go of probability.

But then it is indeed true after all that Christianity is sheer foolhardiness, the common-sense people are right, it is drunken-

ness? No! It is true enough that there are many who thought
they were venturing in a Christian spirit when they ventured to
let go of probability, and it was merely foolhardiness, even in the
opinion of Christianity. For Christianity has its own particular
way of being steadfast. There are, if I may so say, lightly built
men who do not possess any great amount of shrewdness, sense,
and prudence to ensure steadfastness, and for them it is only too
easy to let go of probability and make a venture. Both in a Christian and in a human sense this is drunkenness. But such people
sometimes think that the situation becomes different for the fact
that they refer their venture to God, that their venture is made in
reliance upon God. And undeniably this would indeed alter the
situation entirely—it is just this which must be looked after and
looked into, to make sure that it is really so, that it is reliance upon
God. For to affix God's name to one's wishes, one's desires, one's
plans, that too is easy, only too easy, for the lightly built; but from
this it does not follow that their venture is in reliance upon God.
No, when one lets go of probability in order to venture in reliance
upon God, one has to acknowledge to oneself what is implied in this
letting go of probability, namely, that when one thus ventures, it
is just exactly as possible that one will be victorious as that one will
be defeated. The fact that it is in reliance upon God he makes the
venture affords in fact no immediate assurance of being victorious;
herein precisely we see the precariousness of the venture of these
lightly built men in reliance upon God, in the fact that they
understand it as an assurance of being victorious. But this is not
to venture in reliance upon God, it is to take God in vain. And
what shall deter thee from this is precisely the fact that thou
honestly and candidly hast an understanding with thyself that in
letting go of probability to make a venture in reliance upon God,
thou canst quite as well be said (humanly speaking, for eternally
thy victory is nevertheless sure) to have prepared thereby thy
destruction, as to have paved the way for victory. Lo, this is a
deterrent—not, however, from venturing in reliance upon God,
but from taking God in vain by venturing. Only when thou
hast an understanding with thyself on this point, only then canst
thou venture in reliance upon God. Thou hast let go of probability;
to that extent, humanly speaking, it even may be probable thou
wilt be defeated. But in spite of that thou art determined to go
forth, to go forward, to venture—in God's name. Good fortune

attend thee! But it is true, is it not, thou hast an understanding with thyself that it was not to ensure thy victory thou didst invoke God, but in order that thou (if it should please God not to let thee be victorious—for victory is not impossible, for with God all things are possible; indeed it must not be impossible, for then thy venture would be presumptuous), that thou mightest be in good understanding with God, that He will strengthen thee to bear it if thou must be defeated in a good cause, in a venture made in reliance upon God. But this is deterrent; and just as no living being could sneak past that hundred-headed monster which guarded the entrance to the realm of the dead, and just as no bird flew across the Dead Sea, so does no merely human foolhardiness get past this frightful understanding. However, if thou hast not taken heed that this death-dealing understanding comes between thee and thy venture in reliance upon God, thou hast taken God in vain, thy hardy venture is foolhardiness, the notion that it is made in reliance upon God is a vain imagination.

On the other hand, the Christian principle stands fast, that the true Christian adventure lets go of probability. What cowardliness, worldliness, effeminacy has discovered and had the mendacity to call Christianity is not true—to venture in this way is not tempting God. Oh, abominable mendacity, oh, scurvy slander against all the heroes of the faith, and the martyrs, and the witnesses for the truth, and the patterns! But thus it always is with us! What we wish to be exempted from is danger, and effort, and everything that flesh and blood objects to. Now it is true that Christianity is gentle, it may in the form of an admission[1]—mark well: in the form of an admission!—spare the individual from much, when he humbly confesses how it stands with him, it may also spare him from making the venture proper to Christianity, when he humbly confesses how it stands with him. But the worldliness in us verily will not let itself be satisfied with this; it is never satisfied until it has contrived to get the wrong, the ungodly, made secure as an article of faith, as a duty, as a dogma, as true Christianity—in order that we may renounce true Christianity as ungodliness. So it is with this worldly talk in Christendom about tempting God. It is I that want 'good days', I that want to spare myself; but I will not for a moment confess this; no, I invert Christianity and say, 'To venture out beyond probability is

[1] Cf. 'The Moral' in *Training in Christianity*, p. 71.

tempting God. Fie upon me! Should I—who am a Christian!—should I presume to tempt God?' And should I—who am a cunning rascal!—not desist from that, when by this means I slip out from all effort, and at the same time, at a bargain price, slip into the reputation of being a god-fearing, pious Christian?

No, no, it is not thus! Christianly, it shall stand fast—O my God, support me, that I may be able to make it fast, for this shall stand fast, the fact that this, precisely this, is Christianity, to venture in reliance upon God, to let go of probability, and that one who would be a Christian can be exempted from this only by a humiliating admission! This shall stand fast!—O my God, do Thou make it fast: that as Christianity abominates whoring, murder, thieving, and everything else that can defile a man, it recognizes still another sort of defilement, namely, paltry shrewdness, effeminate common sense, and shabby servitude to probability, and probability, which, Christianly understood, is perhaps the most dangerous defilement. Hence this is emphasized also in Holy Scripture, but these passages one never hears mentioned; it is emphasized, for the Scripture speaks in exactly the same sense of the cowardly and the effeminate as it does of robbers, murderers, and whoremongers; and it says the very same thing about them, that they shall not inherit the kingdom of God. Yes, truly Christianity abominates and regards as defilement what the world extols and regards as the highest thing, to behave always shrewdly; and Christianity abominates this defilement as when it first entered into the world it abominated idolatry—but this deification of shrewdness in our times is precisely the idolatry of our times, Christianity's abomination. Not as though Christianity had any objection to shrewdness regarded as a talent, as a gift. No, far from it! Neither does Christianity ignore how difficult it is when one is shrewd to have to refrain from acting shrewdly. Oh, it is difficult, and seldom is one to be seen who having become addicted to a vice gives it up entirely—and how far more difficult to have shrewdness at hand every instant, to perceive with a shrewd eye what the shrewdest thing is, and the desirableness of being shrewd—and then to have to refrain from acting shrewdly![1] This, however, Christ requires. For, Christianly speaking, this

---

[1] This is a sigh—for S. K. possessed shrewdness, and he often had to complain how hard it was for him to act contrary to the shrewd counsel he was so well able to give himself.

would be the eulogy pronounced, if there was a man of whom it could be said that he was the most sensible man of his times, the shrewdest man in the kingdom; it was known to all that if in a difficult and complicated case one sought the shrewdest counsel, he never went in vain if he went to him, he went in vain only if he went to any other man—but as for acting himself shrewdly, no he never did it! With a purity like that of a virgin woman, like the modesty of a blushing youth, he abhorred acting shrewdly. His life was on the further side of probability, *there* it was he lived, *there* it was he breathed, *there* it was he ventured in reliance upon God—he of all men the most sensible!

This is Christianity! And with this the whole situation is inverted, so far as concerns the distinction between being sober (spiritually understood) and being drunken. We began with the notion that common sense, prudence, shrewdness was what is meant by being sober, and that venturing, venturing to let go of probability, was what is meant by being drunken. But Christianity makes everything new. So it is here: Christianly, this thing of venturing, of venturing to let go of probability, is precisely what it means to be sober—as the Apostles were on the day of Pentecost, were never more sober than when, in defiance of probability, they were merely instruments before God, oh, Christian sobriety! On the other hand, Christianly speaking, common sense, prudence, all this is—how new indeed is the verdict, for that it might be censored is not yet the new, but that it is—drunkenness! Yet what wonder? For it is not eternity, nor God, nor becoming transparent to oneself before God—it is not this which inebriates. How indeed could it? Intoxicating drinks are always composite, fermented, as is that to which common sense and prudence and shrewdness are related, namely, probability.

We will now go further in this Christian discourse about becoming sober and will see more particularly what it means.

To become sober is *to come to oneself in self-knowledge, and before God, as nothing before Him, yet infinitely, absolutely, under obligation.*

To come to oneself. So then: to live on in complete ignorance of oneself, or entirely to misunderstand oneself, or to venture with blind reliance upon one's own powers and such-like, that is (therein we are in agreement with the merely human view), that is not to come to oneself, it is to be drunken. But then, to live on, having accurate knowledge of and shrewd calculation upon one's own powers, talents, qualifications, possibilities, and in the same measure familiar with what human and worldly shrewdness teaches the initiated—is that to come to oneself? Yes, according to the opinion of the merely human view. But not according to the Christian opinion; for this is not to come to oneself, it is to come to the probable; on that road one never gets any farther. And to come to the probable is the way to become more and more drunken, more confused in one's head, and more and more heavy and uncertain in one's gait—all this with the delusion that one is completely sober. For one never drinks oneself sober in the probability. The intoxicating effect of the probability as construed by a merely superficial knowledge of men and of the world is not so dangerous; on the other hand, the more profound the knowledge of men and of the world which is employed to distil as it were the probable, so much the more dangerous is its intoxicating effect. The probable blends within itself the knowledge of good and evil *indifferently*; and even if the probable seems clear, it has *in truth* never become clarified. The man who inquires about the probable, and about that alone, in order that he may attach himself to that, does not inquire which is the right and which is the wrong, which is the good and which is the evil, which is the true and which is the false—no, he inquires indifferently, 'Which is the probable, that I may believe it—for whether it be true is a matter of indifference, or at least of minor importance—which is the probable, that I may attach myself to it and keep to it—whether it be evil, whether it be wrong, is a matter of indifference, or at least of minor importance, if only it is the probable or that which offers probability of attaining power.' Knowledge of the probable, the deeper it is, does not in a deeper sense lead a man to himself, but farther and farther away from his deeper self; it is only in the sense of selfishness that it brings him nearer and nearer to himself —this is what the merely human view calls sobriety: Christianity calls it drunkenness.

To come to oneself *in self-knowledge*. In self-knowledge. For in all other knowledge thou art away from thyself, forgetful of thyself, absent from thyself. This, however, is what the merely human view calls sobriety. To forget oneself, to come not to but away from oneself by losing oneself in knowing, in understanding, in thinking, in artistic production, &c., precisely this is called sobriety. In the Christian view it is drunkenness. And is it indeed not so? Do we not say of a man who is a victim to strong drink that he forgets himself, drowns himself or his self? And when he has completely succeeded in this, when he has quite got rid of himself, we do not say, 'He is sober'; no, we say just the contrary. So it is with knowledge: there is only one sort of knowledge which brings a man to himself entirely, and that is self-knowledge; this is what it is to be sober, the true transparency. On the other hand, the merely human view thinks that self-knowledge is drunkenness, that it produces what drunkenness produces: dizziness. This, however, is not so. No, it is precisely then a man grows dizzy, physically, when he has forgotten himself in strong drink; and then it is that he is dizzy, spiritually understood, when he has lost himself in the knowledge of something else, or, as he puts it, in objective knowledge—call him, and thou shalt see, he awakes as it were from a dream, he has to rub his eyes as it were, to find himself, to remember what his name is, like a drunkard.

To come to oneself in self-knowledge, *and before God*. For if self-knowledge does not lead to knowing oneself before God, then indeed there is something in what the merely human view says, that it leads to a certain emptiness which produces dizziness. Only by being before God can a man entirely come to himself in the transparency of sobriety. The merely human view thinks, on the contrary, that this thing of engaging oneself with God, with the infinite—that nothing is more certain than that this is drunkenness, that this is just as certain as that one who from a ship gazes at the waves, or that he who from a lofty place peers down into the depths, or from a lesser height looks out over endless space where nothing arrests his gaze—that it is not so certain this man will become dizzy as it is that he will become so who engages himself with God. It may seem, too, as if this might be so, and yet in Christianity's opinion it is just the opposite, precisely this is the way to become entirely sober—so it is that a stronger drink is employed to make a man sober who has become drunk with a weaker beverage, although of course this stronger drink, by a frightful misuse of it, may be used for drunkenness.

To come to oneself in self-knowledge, and before God, *as nothing*. The merely human view thinks that to become something is to become sober; Christianity thinks that precisely to becoming nothing—before God—is the way, and that if it could occur to anyone to wish to be something before God, this is drunkenness, or is wishing to abuse the stronger means which can be used to make a man sober.

To become nothing before God, *and yet infinitely*, *absolutely*, *under obligation*. The merely human view holds the contrary opinion, that being sober is recognizable precisely in the fact that one is moderate in all things, that one observes the sober maxim, 'to a certain degree'. So it is also in the case of duties: 'That indeed would be the sure way to becoming deranged in mind, the sure way to drunkenness or madness, if one were to abandon oneself to the absolute and, as this implies, abandons oneself absolutely to it.' Christianity thinks that it is precisely the absolute, and this alone, or that the impression, the pressure, of the absolute is capable of making a man entirely sober, when he (for otherwise he has not received the impression of the absolute) absolutely surrenders himself to its sway; and that, on the other hand, this maxim, 'to a certain degree', is precisely what intoxicates, anaesthetizes, makes one heavy and lethargic and torpid and dull, pretty much like an habitual drunkard, of whom it is said that he falls into a state of drowsiness.

And so it is in fact, the absolute precisely is the only thing that can make a man entirely sober. Let me represent this in figurative language, and let it not disturb thee if the language does not seem solemn enough; I intentionally put it thus in order that thou mayest get an impression all the more true of what is represented. If thou wert to ask a peasant, a cabman, a postilion, a liveryman, 'What does the coachman use the whip for?' thou shalt get the same reply from them all: 'Of course it is to make the horse go.' Ask the King's coachman, 'What does a coachman use the whip for?' and thou shalt hear him reply, 'Principally, it is used to make the horses stand still.' This is the distinction between being a simple driver and a good driver. Now further. Hast thou ever observed how the King's coachman comports himself? Or if thou hast not observed that, then let me describe it to thee. He sits high on his box, and just because he sits so high he has the horses all the more under his control. In certain circumstances, however, he does not consider this enough. He raises himself in his seat, concentrating all his physical force in the muscular arm which wields the whip—then one lash falls; it was frightful. Generally one lash is enough, but sometimes the horse makes a desperate plunge—one lash more. That suffices. He sits down. But the horse? First a tremor passes through its whole body, actually it seems as if this fiery, powerful creature were hardly able to support itself upon its legs; that is the first effect, it is not so much the pain that makes it tremble as the fact that the coachman—as only the King's coachman can—has wholly concentrated himself in giving emphasis to the lash, so that the horse is aware (not so much by reason of the pain as by something else) who it is that delivers the lash. Then this tremor decreases, there is left now only a slight shudder, but it is as if every muscle, every fibre quivered. Now this is over—now the horse stands still, absolutely still. What was this? It got the impression of the absolute, hence it is absolutely still. When a horse which the royal coachman drives stands still, it is not at all the same thing as when a cab-horse stands still, for in the latter case this means merely that it is not going, and there is no art required for that; whereas in the first case, to stand still is an act, an effort, the most strenuous effort, and also the horse's highest art, and it stands absolutely still. How shall I describe this? Let me use another figure which comes to the same thing. In daily speech we talk in a way about its being still weather, though it perfectly well may be blowing a little, or there may be at least a slight breeze, it is only what in a way we call still weather. But hast thou never noticed another sort of stillness? Just before a thunder-storm comes up there sometimes is such a stillness; it is of a different sort entirely; not a leaf stirs, not a breath of air, it is as though all nature stood still, although in fact a slight, almost imperceptible shudder passes through everything. What does the absolute stillness of this imperceptible shudder signify? It signifies that the absolute is expected, the thunder-storm—and the horse's absolute stillness, that was after having got the impression of the absolute.

But it is about this we were talking, about the fact that the impression of the absolute makes one sober, and at the same time alert ('watchful' is the word which the Apostle adjoins in our text) —is not that horse a symbol of this as it were? It got the impression of the absolute, and it became absolutely still, sober, as it were, and watchful. Perhaps it was quite a young horse, which thus needed the impression of the absolute, perhaps it was an older horse, but one which in its old age had become shrewd, sober, in its opinions, and hence thought that everything should be 'to a certain degree', including this thing of standing still, so that one does not stand quite absolutely still, or one makes oneself a bit comfortable, because it is such an effort to stand still in this absolute sense. At all events, the royal coachman was of a different opinion, he conveyed the impression of the absolute. And that the King's coachman constantly does. When one is only a simple driver, there is no cracking of the whip; a cab-driver or a peasant has no snap to his whip—what need of such a luxury when he prefers to belabour the beast with the butt? But the gentleman's coachman cracks the whip, especially when he is driving the gentry; and when he draws up he sits and encourages the horses by cracking the whip. He expresses the fact that he is a good driver, but he does not give expression to the absolute. The King's coachman, on the other hand, does not crack the whip, he gives expression to the absolute, His Royal Majesty must not notice in any accidental way that the coachman is driving. He keeps—absolutely still. Then he arrives home; he throws down the reins—that very instant the horses understand that 'he' is no longer driving. Thereupon out come several grooms—and, lo! the absolute is over with for the time being, then one can cool off or make oneself comfortable according to the circumstances, one is no longer in a solemn sense altogether oneself, altogether sober, the absolute is over with for the time being.

For only the absolute makes one entirely sober.

But that we all of us are surely, we have surely received the impression of the absolute, the absolute impression of it? For what is Christianity? Christianity is the absolute—and we indeed are all of us Christians! And what is the preaching of Christianity? It is the preaching of the absolute—and we have in fact a thousand parsons!

Yet I have never seen any one of whom I could venture to say, what I would not at all venture to say of myself, that his life expressed the absolute impression of the absolute, or that he was entirely sober. Alas, we have all of us to a certain degree become addicted to this intoxicating, 'to a certain degree', with the difference which is observable also in drunkards, that some drink openly, making no concealment, and others, the worst of them, drink on the sly—so likewise there are some who expressly admit that since their lives express only this thing of 'to a certain degree', their Christianity is after all not really Christianity; others whose lives express only this thing of 'to a certain degree' seek to maintain the appearance that they are true Christians, that their Christianity is all right, that it is the true Christianity.

Wouldst thou have a picture of life in Christendom, showing how it compares with the Christian life? then I will present to thee such a picture, to show how it is we live Christianly, and how our life compares with Christianity, the absolute. And be not disturbed by the notion that the form of presentation is perhaps not serious and solemn enough, for, believe me, the solemnity of solemn Sunday discourses is so far, in a Christian sense, from being real seriousness that it rather diverts attention from the one really serious question, what reality looks like, what our life is, where we are. And do not by any means suppose that I speak as I do because I feel myself to be better than others; no, no, already I have made the admission about myself, and I here repeat it, that I am coddled like all the others; and, on the other hand, my life has always expressed sincere sympathy with the experience of being tried by the bothers and cares which are capable of tormenting so greatly a poor human being. But nevertheless Christianity requires us to be spirit, to strive thereafter, and the serious question is, what life we lead. So then, I hope, thou also wilt willingly, honestly, and candidly, with seriousness and with due attention (not mocking me, which would divert attention), apply thyself to this investigation. Imagine a candidate in theology. Let it be me, I also indeed am a candidate in theology. He has already been a candidate for some few years, and now he enters upon that period of life when it is said of him that 'he is seeking'.[1] 'A candidate in theology'—'seeks': when the riddle is proposed in these terms, one does not need a particularly lively imagination to guess at once what it is he 'seeks'—of course it is the kingdom of God (Matt. 6: 33). However, thy guess is wrong; no, he seeks something else, a parish, a living—he seeks this almost absolutely; in other respects the affair has nothing to do with the absolute, nor does it betray any impression of the absolute. He seeks. In his search he runs from Herod to Pilate, recommends

---

[1] This tale of the candidate who 'seeks' was retold, more briefly and far better, in one of the numbers of the *Instant*; and it is said that in Denmark every candidate in theology knows it well.

himself before ministers and secretaries, he writes and writes, one sheet of stamped paper after another—for the supplication must be written on paper which bears the stamp of the government, perhaps one might call this the impression of the absolute, otherwise there is nothing of the sort here. A year passes; he had almost worn himself out with his running and seeking, which can hardly be said to be in the service of the absolute, except (as has been remarked) that he seeks 'absolutely everything'. Finally he gets what he sought; he finds the Scriptural text confirmed, 'Seek and ye shall find'; but the absolute he did not find, it was only a small living—but after all it was not the absolute he was seeking. Still, he is at peace; and indeed he is now in need of repose, so that he can rest himself and his legs after the much seeking. However, when he makes himself more precisely acquainted with the income of the living, he discovers to his dismay that it is a few hundred dollars less than he had supposed. This is exceedingly calamitous for him, as, humanly speaking, one can well understand and can agree with him about it. It is doubly unpleasant for him because at the same time he has found something else which he sought concurrently, namely, a wife, which quite obviously is related to a living, and maybe each year more so. He loses heart. He buys again a sheet of stamped paper, is already afoot to put in a supplication to be allowed to withdraw. However, some of his friends get him to give this up. So the thing is decided. He becomes a parson. Now he is to be installed by the Dean and is himself to deliver the inaugural address. The Dean is a man of intelligence and learning, not without an eye for world-history, much to his own profit and that of the congregation. He presents the new parson to the congregation, makes an address, and chooses for his text the words of the Apostle, 'Lo, we have left all and followed Thee.' Upon this text he speaks pithily and forcefully; he shows that, especially in view of the movements of these times, the minister of the Word must now be prepared to sacrifice everything, though it were life and blood—and the very reverend speaker knows that the young man he installs (yes, as I have said, we can very well understand the young man, for that is human; but we cannot so well understand the Dean) happened to be desirous of withdrawing because the living was a few hundred dollars too little. Thereupon the new parson mounts the pulpit. And the Gospel for the day, upon which he is to preach, is—very opportunely!—'Seek ye first the kingdom of God.' Truly, when one recalls what this young man had to go through with during the laborious year of seeking, this 'seek first' is the last thing one would be likely to think of! So he preaches. And it was in every respect a good sermon; even the Bishop, who was present, said: 'It was a capital sermon, and excellently delivered, he is really an orator.'—'Yes, but then, if it were to be judged Christianly.'—'Good gracious, it was an entirely Christian sermon, it was the sound, unalloyed doctrine, and the stress he laid upon *first* to seek God's kingdom was not without thrilling effect.' —'Yes, but now, Christianly judged, I mean, how far was there here a correspondence between the preacher's life and his discourse? I could hardly free myself entirely from the thought that the speaker—who for me is a true picture of us all—cannot precisely be said with truth to have sought first God's kingdom.' —'That's not at all required.'—'Oh, excuse me, but that is what he preached about, that we first should seek God's kingdom.' 'Quite so, that is exactly the way he should preach, that is what is required of him. It is the doctrine that has to be attended to, the doctrine has to be preached pure and unalloyed.'

This represents about the way Christendom stands related to Christianity, the absolute. After running round about on a score of errands (alas, humanly speaking, after having had to put up with a great deal) one gets one's finite existence made secure, and then we get a sermon about seeking first the kingdom of God.

Is this sobriety or is it drunkenness? The merely human view thinks that precisely this is to be sober, this assuring oneself first of the finite, and then *next* preaching about *first* seeking God's kingdom. We hold the Holy Scripture in high honour. When e.g. an oath is to be particularly solemn, we swear by laying the hand upon the Holy Scripture—which forbids swearing. When one has first, after long seeking, made oneself secure of the finite, one then swears by laying his hand upon this book which bids him to seek first the kingdom of God. And this we men regard as sobriety, this thing of first making the temporal secure—I do no better myself.

Yes, in truth, by putting myself seriously to the test I have been obliged to admit that in case I were *contemporaneous* with one whose life expressed the fact that he first sought the kingdom of God, and so expressed the absolute, and that he absolutely related himself to the absolute, or that he was 'spirit', lost to, a stranger to, dead to all temporal, finite, earthly motives—I could not keep up with him, every instant I should lose my patience and be tempted to call him a drunkard, him who is the only sober one.

For the true situation is this. We men are all of us more or less drunken. But with us it is as with a man who is full, but not entirely full, so that he has not lost consciousness, no, he has just the consciousness that he is slightly full, and just for this reason he is careful to hide this from others, if possible from himself. What does he do then? He seeks something to hold on to, thus he walks close to the houses, and so walks straight without turning dizzy—a sober man. But across an open square he will not venture to walk, for thus it would be revealed, what he himself knows, that he is full. So it is, spiritually understood, with us men. We have a suspicion of ourselves, we know fairly well within ourselves that we are not thoroughly sober. But then shrewdness and common sense and discretion come to our aid, so that by this help we can get something to hold on to—the finite. And then we walk straight and with confidence, without turning dizzy— we are entirely sober. But in case the absolute were absolutely to cast a glance at us (yet from this glance we withdraw, it is for this reason we hide among finite things, as Adam hid among the trees), or in case we were to cast a glance infinitely at the infinite (yet we keep ourselves from doing this, it is for this reason we busily employ our eyes upon errands in the service of finitude)—in case the absolute were to cast a glance at us or we at it, then it would be revealed that we are drunk. Such is the true situation. But in our thieves' Latin we men express it differently, we maintain that we are shrewd, sensible, and discreet persons, that we are sober, and that it is precisely the absolute which would intoxicate us. This is as if that drunken man were to say, 'I am sober; but if I were to walk across a large square, that large square would make me drunk.'—'But, my good man, a large square surely is not something to drink. How can it make one drunk? And a sober man can perfectly well walk across a large square without getting drunk.' This means that the large square, or wanting to walk across it, reveals that the man is drunk; but the man says it is the square that does this, that he is sober. For in fact he rubs along the side of the houses, or at the most walks in the middle of the way when it is through narrow alleys where the houses still are a support—then it is not noticed that the man is full.

This is Christianity's opinion. It is not the absolute which intoxicates, but it is the absolute which reveals that we are drunk, which we know well enough ourselves, and therefore shrewdly keep a hold on finite things, rub along the walls of the houses, remain in narrow alleys, never venture out into the infinite. And it is Christianity's opinion that it is precisely the absolute which makes sober, after it has first revealed that we are drunk. Oh, how cunning we men are, and how cunningly we know how to employ language! We chatter as nearly in imitation of the truth as possible; heard cursorily it is as though we were saying the same thing. We leave out the little subordinate clause, 'it reveals', and so we say, 'The absolute makes one drunk.' This is thieves' Latin. Christianity says: 'The absolute reveals that thou art drunk, and there is only one thing that can make a man entirely sober: the absolute.'

When the Apostles spoke on the first Pentecost they were never more sober than precisely on that day, their lives completely expressed the absolute, they had completely come to themselves in self-knowledge before God as nothing, that is, as mere instruments in His hand, lost to and delivered from every personal aim, burnt out to sheer spirit, completely sober—but derision said, 'They are full of new wine'; and the shrewd, sensible, discreet, merely human view might say, 'They are drunk.'

TO BECOME SOBER IS: TO COME SO CLOSE TO ONESELF IN ONE'S UNDERSTANDING, ONE'S KNOWING, THAT ALL ONE'S UNDER-STANDING BECOMES ACTION

Here again of course the merely human view holds exactly the contrary opinion, that this is just drunkenness, whereas that is sobriety which the shrewd, the common-sense, the discreet people exemplify, taking care to keep their understanding, their know-ing, at a due distance from their lives, or their lives at a due distance from it, not letting it acquire power over them—'such a thing could occur only to a lunatic or a drunkard'. For to 'know', that is pleasure; and no sensible man, no cultured person, wants to be ignorant of what the right thing is, he would be insulted if anyone were to charge him with not knowing it—but to do accordingly, that is an exertion. To 'understand' is a pleasure; also this thing of understanding, of knowing, precisely how cunning and crafty we men are, that we all know how to talk about the Good, no cultivated person would endure to be in ignorance of this and not to be able himself to describe it profoundly and tellingly; for this thing of understanding, though it be an understanding of the mystery of craftiness, is a pleasure. But then to want to strive to be oneself the honest, the sincere, the disinterested man—no, that would be an exertion. On the other hand, even the greatest exertion (if one will) in relation to knowing, to understanding, is only a pleasure, as the huntsman's exertion, his sweat and toil, to capture a beast, or as the fisherman's perseverance, is a pleasure; but to do in accordance with what one knows, what one understands, that is an exertion.

Therefore we men, cunning as we always are in relation to God and godly truth, have concentrated our whole attention upon understanding and knowing; we pretend that it is here the difficulty lies, and that then the consequence naturally follows that if only we understood what is right, it then follows as a matter of course that we would do it. Oh, tragic misunderstanding, or cunning invention! No, infinitely farther than from the profoundest ignorance to the clearest understanding, infinitely farther is the distance from the clearest understanding to doing accordingly; indeed, in the first instance there is only a difference of degree, in the other there is an essential difference of kind. All my labour with respect to knowing has no effect upon my life, upon its lusts, its passions, its selfishness; it leaves me entirely unchanged —it is my action which changes my life. However much therefore an earlier age in Christendom may have erred, compared with our age it was generally in the right when it translated at once Christian thought into action, which is the real Christian simplicity. For indeed in our age also they talk about the importance of presenting Christianity simply, not elaborately, and grandiloquently—and about this subject they contend in the barter of thought, they write books about it, it becomes a science all for itself, perhaps one may even make a living out of it and become a professor in this faculty, but they forget or ignore the fact that the truly simple way of presenting Christianity is . . . to do it.

To do it, however, is an exertion, an exertion like the death-throe, it is in fact to 'die from' (*afdøe*); but to depict Christian

truth, that is a pleasure. And by 'doing the Christian doctrine'
thou wilt at the same time lose men's friendship, perhaps even
stir them up to persecute thee—and what wonder, indeed, for
how could living men, who with their whole soul cling to this life
and all that belongs to it, how could they tranquilly put up with
having a deceased (*Afdød*) person among them? On the other
hand, by merely depicting Christianity (especially when at the
same time thou dost assure thyself of profiting by it, so as to
become very popular and perfectly well understood by means of
. . . the profit thou hast) thou wilt even be able to have great
success among men. For—oh that I had a voice which could
make itself heard, that I could impart to it the significance a
dying man's word has, and that what is said might continue to
reverberate, it is so decisively important! In the possibility
Christianity is easy; and merely as depicted or entertained as a
possibility it pleases: in reality it is so hard, and expressed in
reality, or as action, it incites people against thee. How often
I have come back to this point! When thou seest an orator who
merely with some talent depicts Christianity, but no more than
that, depicts Christianity and so presents it as a possibility—he
is honoured, highly esteemed, almost deified by people. How
natural it is to argue thus: If then in addition to this his life gave
expression to it, how greatly he then would have been loved! O
my dear man, let him guard himself well against that!

And this, this precisely, the shrewd, discreet man understands,
and hence (for he is sober) he is so prudent in establishing a
yawning gulf between his understanding, his knowing, and his
life; for he is sober.

But Christianity says, 'He is drunk, he maintains himself in a
state of drunkenness, for he shudders at the consequence of being
sober even for a single day.' And as a drunken man does not know
what he does, so neither does the shrewd, sensible man know
what he does, that it is to his own destruction he thus develops
his knowing, his understanding; for as a sober man has said, 'A
man is proud of his understanding and does not reflect that it is
according to that he shall be judged.' For the more one has
understood, and the better he has understood it, the severer the
judgement when one day eternity will compel him to be sober.
But sober he certainly is not, any more than a man is sober
because with great shrewdness he knows how to calculate exactly

what he needs in order to assure himself of being in such a condition that consciousness does not awaken disturbingly. He extends his knowing, his understanding; there is nothing in that, he thinks, which resembles drunkenness. He defends himself against his knowledge; with prodigious shrewdness he knows how to defend himself against his knowledge—there is surely nothing in that, he thinks, to indicate drunkenness. But why does he defend himself against his right knowledge? Why? Because at bottom he knows it would reveal to him that he is drunk—as it will do when one day eternity shall prevent him from defending himself against it.

The true situation is this. In every man there is a talent, understanding. And every man, the most knowing and the most limited, is in his knowing far ahead of what he is in his life, or of what his life expresses. This disproportion, however, we men are less concerned about. Upon knowing, on the other hand, we lay great store, and all strive, each one for himself, to develop his understanding more and more.

'But', says the sensible man, 'the thing one must be careful about is the direction one's knowing takes. In case my knowing turns inward towards myself, in case I am not careful to prevent this, then my knowing becomes highly intoxicating, it is the way to become completely drunk; for then there comes about a drunken confusion between knowing and the knower, so that the knower himself will come to resemble, will actually be, the thing known. And this is drunkenness. That this is the case thou wilt promptly discover. For if thy knowing takes such a turn, and if thou dost give in to it, the end will soon be that thou wilt come toppling into reality like a drunkard, pitching thyself heedlessly into heedless action, without giving understanding and shrewdness time to take due heed of what is advantageous, what is profitable. That's why we, the sober people, give warning—not against knowing and extending one's knowledge, but against letting one's knowledge take the inward direction, for then it is intoxicating.' This is thieves' Latin. It makes out that it is one's knowing which intoxicates by thus taking the inward direction, instead of saying that just in this way it will reveal that one is drunk, drunk through clinging to this earthly life, the temporal, the worldly, the selfish. And this is what one is afraid of when one throws upon knowing the blame for being an intoxicant. One is afraid that his knowing, turned against himself inwardly, will illuminate the drunken condition inside, will illuminate the fact that he prefers to remain in this condition, will drag him with it out of this condition, and by the consequences of this step will make it impossible for him to slip back into the beloved condition, into drunkenness.

Christianity, on the contrary, says that just the fact that one's knowing turns against oneself inwardly, that just this is what makes one sober, that only that man is quite sober whose understanding, whose knowing, is action, that therefore it is not at all necessary to expend so much effort upon developing one's understanding, if only care be taken to ensure that it gets an inward direction, that it is craftiness to direct all one's attention and concentrate all one's powers upon developing one's understanding, that a man with only a slender understanding, but with this turned inward and so translated into action, is sober, and that a man with the greatest understanding, but turned in the opposite direction, is completely drunk.

A competent judge of such matters has said that it was rare to see anyone write humbly about humility, doubtfully about doubt, &c. This means that it is rare to find a presentation of which it can be said that the presentation is the thing presented, so that (to cite one of his examples) doubt is imparted in a doubting form, as the Greeks did it, whereas in our age one must first become (how reassuring!) a professor, decorated, married, to impart as an article of faith to believing hearers 'doubt about everything'. But still rarer than such a presentation which is the thing presented, still rarer is it than a man's understanding of a thing is his action, that the fact of his understanding what ought to be done is expressed by—oh, noble simplicity!—his doing it!

No, there is nothing more deceitful than the human heart, and never perhaps does it display itself more clearly than by this disproportion between our understanding and our action. If this were to be severely judged, the verdict might be that we are all hypocrites. The Apostle is milder, he says only that we are drunk—but we shrewd, sensible, discreet people say, 'On the contrary, it is we who are sober, it is the Apostle who is drunk. Or is it not drunkenness to let one's knowing get such a power over one that it hurls itself upon one and therewith ("reminds him that he is drunk") drags him out into the extremest decisions, so that instead of having soberness and joy in his knowing, one might rather curse his knowing which makes him unhappy, just as one may become unhappy by owning up to something in a state of intoxication which he never would have acknowledged in a sober state.' This is quite true when it is understood in a contrary sense: the sensible man, sure enough, is so sober that he will not acknowledge that he is drunk, although he is. But then the first requisite for being truly sober is to acknowledge that one is drunk.

For entirely sober, according to Christianity's opinion, is only he whose knowing is acting. So it ought to be. Thy understanding must at once become action. At once! Alas, it is not thus with us men! When we have understood something, there is a long time to wait before an action follows, or before the translation of it into action. But in the right relationship the action follows at once, and just because of this the translation is so accurate, it is thy understanding whole and complete. If the action does not follow at once, this translation into action of the thing understood becomes distorted. Alas, so it is with our actions! How much do they resemble our understanding? Perhaps like the musical notes thou dost reproduce with the violin-bow? Perhaps like the faithful reprint of a picture? No, like blotting-paper compared with the script on which it has lain.

Thus, for example, there is one who has understood what will be, as he thinks, of profit to the whole human race, and perhaps he is in the right. There is a severity which is needful; he understands so clearly that only severity can save, so clearly that he has the courage also to be severe against everyone—with one exception: himself. Is this what it means to be sober? Yes, the merely human view is surely of this opinion; if he succeeds in his undertaking and doesn't get himself into trouble by it, people see his discretion and sobriety in the fact that he knew how to direct this fearful thought in such a way that all were wounded by it . . . except himself. Christianity, on the contrary, is of the opinion that he is drunk, that he would have been sober if *at once*, upon discovering the saving power of severity, he had *at once* turned it against himself.

Then there is one who has understood something true, he has understood it, oh, it stood out before him so vividly, so convincingly, with such power of eloquence, that he thought he must be able to convince the whole world of it—and that he essayed to do, and he succeeds, he convinces his whole generation of the triumphant joy of self-sacrifice. Yet there was one man he did not convince: himself. He swung off in a wrong direction from what he understood, or away from understanding it aright, not in the direction of action, but into poetical and oratorical production. At the instant when it stood out so convincingly before him, so irresistibly, that self-denial is the triumphant joy, precisely at that instant a little self-denial was required of him. If he had acted then—perhaps the whole masterpiece about the triumphant joy of self-denial might never have come into existence . . . but self-denial, yes! Now, on the contrary, the masterpiece came into existence—that surely was not self-denial. Is this what it means to be sober? The merely human view is certainly of this opinion; 'For,' it will be said, 'although a person doesn't himself do it, when he can win thousands—that surely is the main thing!' Christianity is of the opinion that this alone is the main thing, this little act of self-denial which was lacking, that if this had come about, and at once, and as a complete rendering of his understanding, that would have been to be sober.

Let me take still another example. There was a time when art essayed to present a picture, the Saviour of the world, Jesus Christ. This no doubt was misunderstanding, for in this way it is not possible to present Him, inasmuch as His glory is the glory invisible, the inward glory, and He is 'the sign of contradiction' (what a contradiction to want to depict this!), *hidden under a contrary* exterior. So art will essay in vain to do this. But what if the art of words should essay to do it? Imagine now a man seized by this notion, and he will then employ all the potentialities of speech to depict the Saviour of the world. But to this end he must have repose, says he, an environment favourable to this work; and there must be nothing to disturb him, says he, and furthermore he must be assisted by everything that can serve to keep him in the humour.[1] So in a delightful region he chooses the most lovely environment, and he beautifies everything with art and good taste, and never has there been such allurement for any poet as

---

[1] Here we can perceive that this 'example' is not imagined; it is S. K. himself, the poet, in whom the aesthetical, as he said, was not abolished by the religious—and not at once dethroned. The Journals show that not long before this time he still talked like the 'example'—'I am a poet, I must have repose', said he.

for him—but we must remember also that this is indeed the most important task. From the outset he is already famous, people look up to him with admiration, they look forward with admiration to the production of his masterpiece, and the newspapers have already announced it, giving him part-payment in advance of the praise he is to receive—but we must remember also that this is the most serious subject. Is this what it means to be sober? The merely human view is surely of this opinion, thou canst hear it indeed from the newspapers, thou canst see it in everybody's sympathy for this undertaking, which presumably will completely compensate us for not being contemporary with Christ—which on other grounds is no little advantage to us, however much the parsons may protest that (inexplicable!) their most fervent longing is to have been contemporary with Him. But Christianity is of the opinion that this is drunkenness, that in comparison with this even the slightest self-denial is sobriety. For Christianity is of the opinion that being sober means that thy understanding is thy action, that as the Temple-tribute was paid in its own proper coinage, so is thy understanding constantly to be expressed as action, warm, full, and whole, issuing instantly the instant thou hast understood something.

'But to become sober in this way is frightful, there is nothing indeed in this to arouse enthusiasm!' 'What!' Christianity will reply, 'were then the Apostles not enthusiastic? were not the martyrs?—old men who then for the first time felt enthusiastic and became like youths again, young maidens who precisely then learned enthusiasm!' However, every man to his taste. For the man who is accustomed to get enthusiasm from wine there seems to be little enthusiasm in water-drinking—but what if after all there might be enthusiasm in water-drinking! For the man who finds enthusiasm in sensual enjoyment there seems to be nothing to prompt enthusiasm in the notion that self-denial is to be the occasion of enthusiasm—but in case after all there is enthusiasm in self-denial! For the man to whom, according to his opinion, the relationship to God ought to signify that he is to get everything from God, there is no enthusiasm in the thought that the relationship to God means to renounce everything—and yet what is the most blessed thing (and so also the most apt to prompt enthusiasm): to be able with God's aid to get everything; or to be obliged, but also with God's aid, to do without everything?

What truly arouses enthusiasm is not the gifts but God; but in the first case thou canst readily look mistakenly at what thou gettest (and that is indeed the lesser motive to enthusiasm); in the second case thou art compelled to look upon God alone—and that is the greatest motive to enthusiasm.

My hearer. To become sober was the task proposed; and 'seriousness' is this: what does reality look like? where are we?

Where are we? What is the situation in Christendom? To say what it is is not difficult; it is more difficult to alter it.

We have so mixed up together the finite and the infinite, the eternal and the temporal, the highest and the lowest, that they all coalesce and it is impossible to tell which is which, in other words, the situation is one of impenetrable ambiguity—it is not so difficult to cut a view through the thickest growth of a primeval forest as it is to get the ideals to throw light into this ambiguity, where everything is murky, where we live well secured against the ideals, more especially because a sensible point of view has shoved itself between us and them, so that we are in understanding with one another about every striving after something higher . . . when it is advantageous, but would find that a really higher striving which waives all claim to advantages is of all ludicrous things the most ludicrous 'exaggeration'.

In newspapers, in books, from pulpits, from university chairs, in conventions, there is a tone of solemnity, of importance, of such grave importance, as though everything turned upon spirit, upon truth, upon thoughts. And perhaps too it does . . . perhaps. And yet perhaps it all turns upon livings, upon careers . . . perhaps. Is it the living, the career, which arouses the enthusiasm of the candidate in theology, or is it Christianity? One does not know. He takes the living, he *protests* that it is Christianity. Is it the living, the career, which arouses the enthusiasm of the candidate, or is it learning? One does not know. He takes the living, becomes professor, he *protests* that it is learning. Is it the number of subscribers which arouses the enthusiasm of the newspaper writer, or is it the cause? One does not know. He gloats over the subscribers, he protests that it is the cause.[1] Is it love for the many which moves a man to put himself at the head of the crowd?

---

[1] Here S. K. has in mind especially Goldschmidt and the *Corsair*—the experience which first revealed to him the baseness of the press.

One does not know. He takes advantage of standing at the head
of this mighty power, that one can plainly see; he *protests* that it
is out of love.

And with all this it is maintained with might and main that
Christianity exists, even that we are all Christians, so that Christianity surely never has flourished so luxuriantly. By what then
does one prove that Christianity exists? Maybe by the fact that
there are 1,000 parsons? Capital!—so thus it is proved also that
'the Idle Hustler'[1] is not ridiculous, as has hitherto been supposed;
no, he is in the right when he proves that he has a great deal of
business, proves it by the fact that he employs four clerks! And
yet the situation here is a different one. For at least the four clerks
are not in any way a refutation of his claim that he has a great deal
of business; but the existence of the 1,000 parsons is rather a
refutation of the existence of Christianity than a proof of it. For
what does it prove? It proves that there are 1,000 livings, neither
more nor less. Is this Christianity? Or will this help Christianity
to make its way in the world? Or will it not rather have the
contrary effect? For the congregation is shrewd, too. The parson
may declaim, weep, pound the pulpit, 'protest'—all right, if it
can be supposed that by *this* the congregation will get the impression of Christianity. No, the congregation says dryly, without
tears, 'It is his living.' One single act performed with true self-
denial, in renunciation of the world, is infinitely more of a revival
and more of Christianity than 1,000 or 10,000 or 100,000 or a
million parsons, so long as they keep it ambiguous which is
which, whether it is the living, the career, the advantages, which
arouse their enthusiasm, or Christianity; so long as they keep it
ambiguous, for in case they say outright that it is the former, they
do no harm.

'But is it thy notion then that a man can live on air, or is Christianity perhaps of the opinion that it is inadmissible to work for
one's livelihood?' Not by any means, not in the remotest way.
On the other hand, it is Christianity's opinion that a man can and
must keep these things separate from one another, make it clearly
evident where it is he labours for his own advantage, and where
for a cause, for ideas, for the spirit, for the higher interest, and
that he should not be tempted at any price to let this coalesce
with the other, this which is the most diverse, the infinitely diverse,

[1] A character in Holberg's comedy of this name.

the heaven-wide diverse. Christianity's opinion is that to seek at the same time one's own advantage . . . in the service of truth, to seek at the same time one's own advantage . . . in labouring for ideas—that this is bosh and the way to hypocrisy, since the latter is infinitely higher than the former, and since it is neither the truth nor the idea which is served by my getting a living and making a career, but it is I alone. Christianity's opinion is that 'protests' are the meanest invention of the father of lies, that in relation to striving for the higher aim, there is only one sort of protest, the fact that my life expresses it—and then I have no need to protest; and that in the opposite case my protests are bosh and the way to hypocrisy.

'But in speaking thus thou art forgetful of reverence for the parson.' His Reverence! Most certainly I shall not treat insolently his Very or his Right Reverend Reverence, I wish that what reverence is fairly and honestly due to him may be meted out to him, but not a bit more. But here again we encounter that ambiguity. There are two sorts of worth, which are to be regarded with different sorts of reverence. When a person lives blamelessly among us he is entitled to be treated with respect. Perhaps at the same time he is especially talented and employs this talent of his with diligence and efficiency, thereby earning his livelihood, so that he can be said to be especially worthy.[1] So, for example, an actor. On the other hand, there is an entirely different concept of worthiness and reverence which may properly be said to have come in with Christianity. That was upon a time when Christianity was preached by Apostles. However, that we will leave out of account. But there was a time when Christianity was preached by witnesses for the truth—there were no livings in those days, inasmuch as Christianity (incredible as it is!) had come in without any help from livings. Such a teacher of Christianity had claim to a special sort of reverence, it was his life which justified it. But, lo, it is this concept of reverence the parsons are still squinting at, although their lives have become precisely the opposite to the lives of these glorious ones, and the preaching of Christianity, being entirely secularized, has become just like every other business. And this concept of reverence is

---

[1] The translation of this paragraph cannot but be awkward for the reason that the Danish honorific address to the clergy is, like the sermon, not 'reverend' but 'worthy' —*Værdig*.

not due to them. A parson in our days cannot lay claim to any other reverence than that which pertains to every man in his own profession, in proportion to his efficiency. If he is a distinguished preacher—very well then, there is due to him the same reverence as to a distinguished physician, for example, or artist, or actor, &c.; the mediocre men rank with the mediocre; ordination cannot decide anything personally, for when the ordained man's life is completely secularized he cannot personally plead that he is ordained, rather might the actor, the artist, the physician, &c., demand that they also be ordained. Such is the situation in the midst of Christendom, where people still sometimes doubt whether an actor may be buried in consecrated ground, whereas no doubt whatever is entertained as to how far the parsons have a right to be buried in consecrated ground.

'But this then will bring everything to confusion.' Not at all, the matter seems quite simple to me. My notion is this. Humble before God, and for the rest childishly joyful and delighted, I am fully convinced that it is the most honourable thing in the world for a man to work for his livelihood. So I will do that. I will, frank-heartedly before God and with a good conscience, earn my bread, for example, by preaching Christianity. But, but, but my congregation shall not have occasion to let me understand slyly that this is my livelihood, for I intend to say to them myself directly, with such cheerfulness and confidence that it will be a delight: 'It is my livelihood; it is not for Christianity's sake I have got a living, it is for my own sake.' Truly it is not at all dangerous for the congregation to get to know, what it does know anyhow, that I also am a man, requiring something to live on. Neither is it dangerous for the congregation to get to know, what is the truth, that I am not so strong in faith, so alive in spirit, that I could bear (as Christianity undeniably would prefer) to preach Christianity in poverty. It is not at all dangerous for the congregation to get to know which is which. No, no, not only is it not dangerous, it is the only way to truth and salvation and Christianity. The dangerous thing is if I were to pooh-pooh the living while hiddenly I look sharply after it; for if I am so superior, so strong, I ought to express this by doing without it. The dangerous thing is that I assume a dress of solemnity and reverend dignity, pretending that it is for Christianity's sake—as if it were that which stood in need of my getting a living and making a career, as though it were not I rather that stand in need of Christianity's indulgence for thus making my preaching a means of livelihood; the dangerous thing is that I assume this dress of solemnity and reverend dignity while the congregation laughs at me in its sleeve and understands the situation very well, or it understands which is which. The long and short of it is, if the fact is that this is my livelihood, if this, Christianity, signifies that I am a beggarly wretch (which, however, is a monstrous falsehood)—well then, dangerous it never can be that the congregation gets to know that I am a beggarly wretch. If I were a beggarly wretch, the dangerous thing is that the congregation did not get to know it officially and directly. And however one may turn and twist the thing, never was he a beggarly wretch who had the courage and intrepidity to acknowledge, 'I am that.' No, the man one might quite properly call a beggarly wretch, him thou wilt in all probability find hidden under the rags of solemnity and reverend dignity.

O ye revered figures whom Christianity so touched and moved that it and ye conquered your hearts, and ye resolved, and kept the resolve, to preach Christianity in poverty and lowliness, the genuine preaching—I do not press insolently into your ranks; no, I stand afar off, bowing humbly, but for the rest, childishly joyful and delighted, frank-hearted, with a good conscience. But one thing I shall never do (I would make myself a good conscience thus, and if I were to do it, I should also be making myself a conscience, a bad conscience to have to bear), I shall never defraud you of what is justly your due, I shall rather by God's help succeed in illuminating your glory, ye revered figures, in illuminating it . . . at my expense! I shall never let everything coalesce into one, as people do nowadays, and say: 'The doctrine, the objective teaching, is the main thing, it makes no difference if it is my livelihood, my career, whether one does it gratis, another for money and station, one in voluntary poverty, another in the way of a flourishing business, one for the sake of the sacrifice and its perquisites, the other as himself sacrificed, all this is neither here nor there, the doctrine, in fact, is and remains the same.' What an abomination! What a lie! An abomination! They have distracted men's attention precisely from that which is really the decisive thing. Or is there anyone who does not know in his heart, know for himself and know along with all the others, that this, precisely this, endlessly differentiates a man, namely, the question whether he is to obtain advantage from his striving, or exactly the opposite? A lie! For it is not true that it is and remains the same doctrine, since in the one case the act of preaching is the doctrine, which is truth and remains truth in the preaching; in the other case the preaching makes the same doctrine falsehood—so the doctrine does not really remain the same.

But to return again to the beginning of this last exposition: the situation of our age is determined precisely by the fact that we have got the infinite and the finite, the highest and the lowest, so confounded that the situation is an impenetrable ambiguity. So it surely is necessary to become sober in order to get out of this condition of drunkenness.

My intention here is remote from the profane proposal when they talk about the congregation desiring perhaps to save something on the parsons, scrape something off their salaries—oh, wretched meanness! If I were in control, the result would be that people would make it a point of honour to reward them more liberally. On the other hand, this requirement of 'Christian reverence' must go, if there is to be any truth in the situation. Either one thing or the other: either a life of strenuous exertion, exertion in self-denial and renunciation, exertion in witnessing for the truth and against lies—in 'reality', not in declamations delivered during 'quiet hours' under the sway of seventeen illusions —and then the requirement of Christian reverence; or else the milder forms, where the parson's life is not more severely taxed than all other people's—and then abandonment of the claim to Christian reverence. To combine both of them is falsehood. So this will be the conclusion of the matter. Every one of the more capable parsons will also surely be able to see this for himself, every one of the younger men will surely find it reasonable and be willing to accede to it. If there should be one or another who has got only too much accustomed to this false reverence and solemnity, so that he cannot readily resolve to make admissions, but would rather hold on to a thing which, in a moment so critical for Christianity as this, might have the most dangerous consequences—that is his own affair.

But this will be the conclusion of the matter, that we sober men must come to the point of admitting where we are, and where Christianity is. People say that Christianity is a 'doctrine', and they go on to recount that 'this doctrine has transformed the face of the earth'. Oh, what fools we are . . . or how cunning! No, never has any doctrine (served by what weighs it down and drags it into finiteness, by men of titular rank, namely, who are salaried officials of the government) transformed the face of the world, that is just as impossible as to make a kite rise by means of that which pulls it down, the weight attached to it; never has any doctrine, thus served, ever been able to stir up a little persecution, which surely is absolutely necessary if there is to be any question of transforming the world. But that is a thing the person concerned takes good care to avoid. No, but Christianity was served by witnesses for the truth who, instead of having profit from the doctrine, and every sort of profit (and here is the decisive point which made this doctrine something else than a doctrine), made sacrifices for the doctrine and sacrificed everything: it was served by *witnesses for the truth*, who did not live on the doctrine, along with a family, but lived and died for the doctrine. Thereby Christianity became a power, the power which mastered and transformed the world. Thus it was served for wellnigh three hundred years; thereby Christianity became 'the power' in the world. There was now, if I may say so, an immense capital investment accumulated; the only question was how it should be employed. Alas, by this time there had already begun the retrogression, the illusion: instead of transforming the world, they began to transform Christianity. Worldly shrewdness hit upon the idea of turning the life of these witnesses, their sufferings, their blood, of turning it into money, or into honour and prestige; people shrewdly spared themselves suffering, but the fact that the 'departed' had suffered, the preachers turned to their own advantage. And in this they succeeded only too well; many centuries passed, and the good-natured, simple-hearted people did not notice what had occurred, that those whom one honoured and glorified and rewarded in every way were not the 'departed' who had made the sacrifice and got no thanks for it, but a cunning tribe who took the thanks. And so it went on. And shrewdness became more and more cunning in finding out new and newer, cleverer and cleverer forms of the deceit, which spares me suffering and permits me to acquire dexterously pecuniary advantages, besides honour and prestige . . . from the fact that others have been scourged, crucified, burnt, &c. The deceits became shrewder and shrewder. But unfortunately the shrewdness in seeing through the deceits also became greater—by which, however, it is not affirmed that the shrewdness in seeing through the deceits is any better than the deceits.

No, but shrewdness in deceiving has encountered an equally great shrewdness in seeing through it. Period. This is a standstill. The capital investment acquired in these three hundred years has been consumed, ladies and gentlemen; it is impossible by new deceit to squeeze more out of it, for shrewdness in seeing through the deceits has become precisely as great. The capital investment has been consumed, this is status; the standstill is a *fact*, this is the situation; Christianity has reached the point where it has to be said: 'Now then I have to begin all over again.' Is there no one I can move to prevail over his heart and be willing to understand what Christianity is, and that to preach Christianity means to make sacrifices, to be ready to suffer? If such a man is to be found, if there are to be found several of them, then Christianity begins again to be a power, as for many ages 'this doctrine' has not been, and as it could not become so long as merely being a Christian (not to say parson or professor) was a livelihood, a career.

It is a standstill. And that this may become a standstill of soberness and truth, pains should be taken to make clear that it is a standstill, lest it become something else, something external, a worldly revolution. Hence (since this is a matter which verily interests Christianity only in the slightest degree, and only in the slightest degree would serve its cause) the parson should not be deprived of any least part of his lawful revenues, not fourpence even, nor of his titles and dignities. Not this by any means. No, but one thing should be made evident and notorious: that it is not for Christianity's sake he has secured this, but for his own sake; and that he has not obtained it by means of Christianity, inasmuch as it would be Christianity to relinquish it, and there is need of an indulgence from the part of Christianity for striving after it and possessing it. But above all there is need of watchful care lest there might come about the most frightful of all confusions, that one might hit upon the notion of wanting to be a reformer—in such a way, be it observed, that the reforming becomes pleasure, profit, &c., whereas instead the will to reform implies sacrifices, suffering.

People have wanted to perform the astonishing trick of saying: 'Christianity is an objective doctrine, it makes no difference how it is served, the "doctrine" is the whole thing.' This is what has abolished Christianity. It is easy to understand. There is an existential determinant of Christianity which is the unconditional condition, without which Christianity cannot be applied. This is what it is: to die unto the world (*afdøe*). Try it out now. There comes one who preaches Christianity—and whose livelihood and career it is to do this—he says to a man, 'Thou shalt die unto the world—the price is ten dollars.'—'How is that? Ten dollars? Paid to whom?'—'To me, for it is my livelihood, my career, to preach that one must die unto the world.'[1] Between God (who requires, 'Thou shalt die unto the world') and me, the single individual, the poor man who is to take a bite of the sour apple and die unto the world, there is introduced as the intermediate term (in the way of preaching) a living, a fat and good living for a man with a family, and a rank equivalent to that of councillor, and the prospect of advancement—this is an impossibility, the preaching contradicts itself. And even if the whole human race were to put up with this, it's no use, it's an impossibility, it can't be done; one, two, three! It is impossible, so let the hammer fall, let it for ever be determined that it is impossible. And since, as is well known and readily understood, what a man's life proclaims is a hundred thousand times more effective than what his mouth proclaims, so is that sort of preaching as remote as possible from being able to bring Christianity in effectually, or to bring anybody to die unto the world, inasmuch as the hundred thousand times greater effectiveness of that preaching is substantially expressed thus: 'No, so far remote is it from inducing anyone to die from the world that even the preaching that one should die unto the world has become one among the many and various roads leading to a rule of life—"Enjoy life's warmth ere comes the winter's snow; and cull the flowers ere the roses go." ' That simply doesn't go.

This they noticed themselves. So Christianity became mild—or rather, they whose career it was to preach Christianity found it necessary (out of love for men—not to say self-love) to make Christianity a saleable article. So it became merely 'consolation'. A family is living in the enjoyment of all possible pleasures, then a man announces himself as a preacher of Christianity and says, 'Have you no use for the gentle consolation of eternity, which,

---

[1] Substantially the same story was more tellingly told in the Journal. I have translated it in my *Kierkegaard*, p. 533.

without praising my own wares too highly, I venture to call one of life's greatest comforts and pleasures, which serves to mitigate sorrows and to give joys their proper zest?—It costs 50 dollars.'—'Why, that's a fair price.'

But to sell Christianity thus, without laying any obligations upon life, is peddling indulgences, it is trafficking with Christianity.

'And yet,' says the preacher, 'we preach also that one must live accordingly.'—'O dear, Sir, what of it that thy mouth preaches thus, when thy life preaches that this is thy livelihood, a path to a plentiful competence for thee and thy family, a path to worldly honours and prestige, so that really it is humbug your wanting to put others under the obligation of "dying from the world"— for the obligation to die from the world cannot be preached with emphasis by one whose livelihood, whose career it is to do this.'

And here again we are at a standstill. Dying from the world is the first and the last word of Christianity strictly understood. This was expressed also by those who in the first age of Christianity preached Christianity: they were departed souls. Now the turning-point has been reached: the preaching of Christianity, or the preaching that Christianity requires thee to die from the world, is exactly the opposite of dying from the world. This simply doesn't go.

To make it go (if one will agree with me that to make something go there must be, *either* in one way *or* in another, some sense in it) —to make it go there must first be an admission that this preaching of Christianity which in a worldly way (with worldly arrangements, worldly norms, worldly securities) is the preacher's livelihood and career, the admission that this is not really Christianity, however truly one may preach the doctrine, 'the sound doctrine'. And the trouble is, in my judgement ('in my judgement' because I am only an unauthoritative poet, who at the most contends for the admission of our weakness; the authoritative teacher might pass a much more decisive judgement upon us), the trouble is that no one for a long while past has made the admission that this whole thing of the 1,000 parsons is not really Christianity, but a softened form, made a whole quality softer as compared with genuine Christianity. It is far from my meaning to say that for this cause such preaching is entirely without profit;

but it is quite another thing to say that Christianity, in order to maintain its majesty and be able to assume command, must require the admission that this is not properly Christianity.

There have been times when this preaching of Christianity, though it was not, as it never is, deserving of unstinted praise, was less offensive—in times, that is to say, when the congregation was less knowing, could not so clearly discern between a striving after the infinite and a striving after the finite, or discern what the protestations really mean. As the situation now is, the preachers of Christianity cannot attain frank-heartedness and a good conscience in the face of an all-too-knowing congregation without having publicly attested which is which, whether it is the finite they want, or the infinite. This 'also'—to want also the infinite, or to want also the finite—to want to have one's mouth full of flour and also to want to blow, is not merely 'also', but purely and simply, or solely and only, bosh. The protestation that it is the infinite one desires, while one takes the finite, doesn't do any good, it does not conceal the fact that there is a knowingness in the preacher and in the congregation, and if it is there, it is indecent not to attest it publicly by an essential change: *either* by letting go of the finite and finite advantages; *or* by making the admission that this preaching is after all not really Christianity. It is like bashfulness. In the case of a very small child bashfulness is one thing; as soon as it is assumed that the child is old enough to be knowing, bashfulness is another thing. After a knowledge has come about, and so after it can be assumed that there is knowledge in both parties, and a mutual knowledge that there is this know-ledge—after this has come to pass, to wish to conserve the first bashfulness would not only not be bashfulness but an ex-tremely depraved and depraving immorality. The preaching of Christianity, or its preachers, have long enough—both pecuni-arily and with respect to honours, titles, and dignities—*lived off of the fact . . . that there have been* those who sacrificed everything for Christianity. This is no longer convincing to a knowing congregation. Speaking frankly, one cannot blame them for it. How could a contradiction be capable of convincing?—the contradiction of *hearing* a man prove the truth of Christianity by the fact that there have been those who sacrificed everything for Christianity—and of *seeing* that the preacher lives off of this, by the aid of it is in possession of earthly goods of various sorts, which in fact is a contradiction of the proof. The dangerous situation is when there is knowledge in the preacher, and knowledge in the congregation, and mutual knowledge of this knowledge—then not to be willing to come out with it in speech, to wish to preserve a loftier, a more solemn tone, the untruthfulness of which one is secretly conscious of; this is the dangerous, the demoralizing thing. The congregation has need of getting a sight of that true proof—not the consideration that I am living off of the fact that there have been people who sacrificed everything—in any case (for I, an unauthoritative poet, must stick to the easier thing, only too much entangled with this life, and therefore a coward, as poets commonly are, yet with the courage to acknowledge it, which poets do not always have), the congregation has need (of that which both I and everyone else must be capable of furnishing) of the truth, the admission, instead of being fed with protestations, which signify nothing to shrewd and knowing men. And surely the preacher also has need of getting the truth clearly uttered, if only for the sake of doing people a little good. And verily, according to my notion, he can do them much good, if he is true in this fashion, admitting that this really is not Christianity if the preaching is to provide everything earthly for himself and family, and that rather abundantly, if preaching is to be his worldly career. So it is one of two: *either* there is real renunciation of the earthly, in order with sacrifice and suffering to preach Christianity; *or* one assures himself of the earthly, the temporal, but makes then the admission that this preaching is not properly Christianity. The first form one man has no right to require of another, he has a right to require it *of himself*. The other form we men have a right to require of one another; for, after all, there must be truthfulness in the situation, and an end must be put to this game of duplicity played by protestations between knowing parties, which are therefore protestations made by one who knows only too well how little protestations mean, and made to those who know only too well how little protestations mean, and made with a suppression of the true state of affairs.

Oh, these 'protestations'! From generation to generation the thing has gone on, while people continued in tranquil acquisition and possession of the earthly and kept on with the protestation: 'In case it were required of me, I should be willing to leave all, sacrifice everything, for the sake of Christianity.'[1] And the individual, continuing in the tranquil acquisition and possession of the earthly, kept up, twenty, thirty, forty years—in short, a whole lifetime—this protestation: 'In case it were required of me, I should be willing to leave all, to sacrifice everything, for the sake of Christianity.' In the meanwhile the world has beheld an almost complete moral dissolution—but none of the protesters discovered that this was required of him, he merely continued to protest that, 'In case . . .' So he continued to acquire, to strive after, to possess the earthly; but at the same time he was a hero; it was no fault of his that this was not made evident: *in case* it should be required, he was willing enough—he protested that 'in case . . .' In my youth there was a young man who never succeeded in passing his first examination in the university, but said regularly, 'Next time I make it', for which cause we never called him by his proper name but by 'Next time I make it'. So it is with the protestations, but they succeed in keeping it up longer than that young man, who after only a few years was found out.

However, now the time for protestations is past! Three hundred years of immortal achievement[2]—what wonder that they saved up, if I may say so, an immense reserve, upon which (though it is always a confusion and absurdity to suppose that one man draws upon another's deeds of heroism) one might draw by means of protestations, might keep on drawing for a long time before it became clear how confused a thing this is. But the reserve for protestations, the specie which a bank in order to be a bank always must possess, and which in this case Christianity's bank did possess,—it has been consumed, ladies and gentlemen! Instead of being able to draw on the bank, a new bank must first be founded, by means of what in this case is the specie, namely, actions, actions in the role of a Christian.

If I cannot do this—well then, one thing I can do, one thing I must do, and that one thing I will do, I will at least refrain from mendaciously ascribing something to myself by means of protestations, or from defrauding you, ye glorious ones, of your rightful due, the reward of admiration and gratitude for your life, your deed, which ye bequeathed to the race, not that some shrewd

---

[1] S. K. heard Bishop Mynster utter these words in a sermon, and he religiously noted them in his Journal.

[2] A play on words, for *Bedrifter* means also business ventures.

people might turn it into money and such-like, but that it might prompt us men of a later time to imitation. I shall not 'protest'. If I am not capable of being a hero (which in every sense of the word I doubtless am not)—well then, at all events I shall not protest that 'in case . . .'; in other words, I shall not pretend that it is the fault of circumstances (because they didn't require it of me) that I do not show what a hero I am, I shall not pretend that at bottom I am a hero, waiting merely for the occasion, while my life expresses the fact that I am (as I only too readily find occasion to be) just as greedy of money and just as greedy of honours as every other man. No, if (as has been said) I am not capable of being a hero, then it shall be made evident that I am not capable, and that there is a lot of fudge in this *in case* it is required', especially when the condition of the world is a moral dissolution such as not even ancient times have seen, such as did not exist even when Christianity came into the world, so that if no other man will, I will vow, in the name of Christianity and of God, to say to everyone who protests that 'in case . . .', to say to him, 'If there be nothing else to prevent thee from stepping forth in the role of the hero which thou art, except the notion that it is not required of thee—oh, my dear, my honoured friend, it is not only required, it is the last moment, if it is not too late; therefore haste, haste!'

So then, the time is past for protestations—protestations, the most dangerous of all hypocritical inventions, more dangerous than the Pharisees' righteousness of works, for after all to live so strictly is a real something, but the protestations are nothing, and yet mendaciously assert the highest claim. And if their time is past, then let there be no more twaddling, no vacillation, whereby a man is entangled with them again, let there be resolute decision: away with them, away with protestations, the most dangerous of all drunkenness! Let us be sober! If my life constantly expresses, year after year, that I am just like the common run of men, at least I shall hold my tongue from protestations that 'in case . . .'

Yet perhaps the learners, the audience, the congregation, or, more accurately, the Christian public, will have divers objections to make if the protestations are abolished, perhaps they would even make a little effort to recall the 'protestations'. For though it is the preachers who employ protestations, it is perhaps the hearers, the world, that get the most use out of forcing the preachers to resort to this falsehood so that Christianity may not become too serious.

In earlier times (when people really related themselves to the patterns in such a way that they either, as in the truest examples, understood that they must imitate them; or, although careful to spare themselves suffering, nevertheless held the patterns in high honour, almost too high, inasmuch as they were not far from worshipping them, which was a rather sly device for exempting themselves from imitation), in earlier times they required that the preacher's life should express the doctrine: this was, as we now say, the 'security' which the preacher had to put up. In our times (when a completely worldly sapience has inserted itself between us and the patterns, has got rid of them, that is to say, or put them at an almost ludicrous distance from us, so that if we were *contemporary* with such a life, with such a striving, we should find it of all ludicrous things the most ludicrous), in our times the preaching of Christianity in that way might readily become too serious a thing for the Christian public. The requirement now is therefore a different one. If thou wouldst have success in the world with thy Christian preaching, it is now required of thee that thy life express pretty much the opposite of what is preached, or it is required that thy life, by expressing pretty much the opposite of what is preached, shall provide 'security' that the preaching is an artistic entertainment, a dramatic presentation, with tears, movements of the arms, and such-like.

Take a few examples. Is it this thou wouldst preach, this Christian thought, that the Christians despise the world's honours and distinctions, rank and titles, stars and ribbons—and thou thyself art literally nobody, and in addition to this it is notorious that thou wast not willing to attain such honours, although it was in thy power: my dear fellow, this is not a subject for thee to talk about; it might seem indeed like seriousness; and the Christian public would become furious, as if Christianity were something which had a right to put one's life under obligation, instead of being as it is a consolation, a consolation, for example, for those especially who have not been fortunate enough to attain rank and title, &c., in spite of their zealous effort to get it. As I have said, this is not a subject for thee to talk about. No, try first to get a high rank, procure then a few (or rather, not a few, the more the better) of the stars and ribbons—and then preach mightily about the Christians despising rank and titles, stars and ribbons: thou hast the applause of the Christian public, both before and behind, both before and after, thou hast it expressed, if thou wilt, in tears, for thy life furnishes security that thy preaching is an artistic production, and surely in the theatre more tears are shed than in church.—Is it this thought thou wouldst present, that after all Christianity has a predilection for the unmarried state—and thou thyself art unmarried? ah, my dear fellow, this is not a subject for thee to talk about; the Christian public would be ready to believe that this might be seriousness—and then God have mercy upon thee. No, take time, look out first to procure a wife—and then preachify about Christianity having a predilection for the unmarried state, and weep a little at the same time; the Christian public will be moved to weep with thee in the quiet hours; for thy life furnishes the security that the preaching is an artistic production.—Is it this thought thou wouldst present, that in the matter of marriage Christianity is of the opinion that a person ought to marry only once—and thou thyself art married for the first time? ah, my dear fellow, this again is not a subject for thee to talk about, perhaps there is a long look ahead before thou canst preach about such a thing, perhaps thou wilt never be in a position to do it; in any case, wait; if it be that thy first wife dies and thou art married a second time—then the moment has come, now preachify about Christianity's opinion that a person should marry only once! Thou hast the applause of the Christian public; for thy life furnishes security that thy preaching is objective.

Yes indeed one is so ready (and this doubtless is the way to become the darling of the Christian public), so ready to lay the blame on the preachers of Christianity, to seek the defect in them; and yet perhaps it is rather the Christian public which would compel the preachers by the fear of men (to which certainly the preachers dare not yield) to deceive this Christian public. The world, which in every field requires 'security', has also taken pains to secure itself against Christianity becoming through its preaching a power, a power which has the right to put a man's life under obligation; and hence this world requires the reliable security that the preacher's life makes preaching a punching of the air. For the world *wants* to be deceived; it not only is deceived (ah, then the thing would not be so dangerous), but it *wants* to be deceived; vehemently, more vehemently perhaps than any 'witness' has struggled for the truth, the world struggles to be deceived, and gratefully it rewards, with money, with prestige, everyone who wants to do what it wants, wants to deceive it. And never perhaps has the world needed so much as in our time . . . to become sober.

For, to say it short and sharp: this is the very definite utterance of the New Testament, that Christianity, and the fact that one is truly a Christian, must be in the highest degree an 'offence' to the natural man, that he must regard Christianity as the highest treason and the true Christian as the most scurvy traitor against humanity, a treason and a traitor which never can be punished severely enough. It is also easy to see that Christianity, being the thing which defines man as spirit, must so appear to everyone who has not by 'dying from' been reborn as 'spirit'.

Now I have never seen a single man about whom it could in the remotest way occur to me to think that his life (for the 'protestations' must be stricken out) expressed the fact that he was dead and had become spirit, just as little as I count myself to be such a one. How in the world has it come about that entire states and countries are Christian, that we are Christians by the millions, that there is a rush and crush to become teachers in Christianity?

This is only to be explained by the fact that we have transformed Christianity into something quite different, which the authoritative teacher might with right and reason call treason against Christianity.

So soon then as one might try to display Christianity in its true form, that same instant there would be this outcry against him: 'He is a traitor to us!' Aha! Even so weak, so mild, so humble an effort as I have made to display Christianity somewhat more truly—I am convinced that there are some who secretly judge thus about me: 'He is a traitor to us, he betrays us.' They do not say it aloud; perhaps they think this would not be shrewd, lest attention might be directed to this matter, and perhaps lest I, or at least the matter itself, might be brought to a heat by further elucidations. Yet if I were to display Christianity more strongly—yet no, I am not spirit, and therefore cannot do that—but if I could display Christianity more strongly, and if I did it, that same instant the judgement would be loudly expressed: 'It is treachery against us!' Aha! We have got Christianity turned into something quite different from what it truly is, and so the judgement passed upon it has become a different one. So soon as Christianity is again presented in its true form, then the true judgement will come out (cf. the New Testament prophecy): 'It is treason against humanity.' Not even the astronomer's calculation of the movements of the heavenly bodies is more certain. We extol our age for the fact that Christianity is no longer persecuted. That I can well believe: Christianity doesn't exist. If it existed in its true form, persecution would instantly persecute this treason against humanity.

I understand this capitally just because I am not spirit. I understand also that for this reason I can tranquilly invite the reader to follow me, to confide himself to me; for I shall not carry the thing to a greater extreme than a little admission—and that hardly can be called treachery, except to those who are entirely lost in untruth, and presumably stricken also with blindness, so that they do not see what otherwise surely would help them, like a corporal chastisement, to open their eyes to the fact that if the profane world were to raise objections against Christendom as it actually is, before it has guarded itself by making admissions, the situation would be another and a good deal worse. The average men—the class to which I belong—will have enough sense of truth to be disposed to be willing to have it made clear, if it can be, that what we call Christianity is not properly Christianity, and then also to be willing to be convinced of it, and (if nothing more is exacted of them) to admit it. For if what is exacted of me and of others was simply that we should really become spirit—then doubtless we should all of us become in the highest degree embittered.

But I do not carry the thing so far as that. Strange as it may seem for one to justify oneself in this way (since in a higher sense it is an accusation against myself), I can truly say that I am guilty of no treachery against us men, and that I am not spirit.

Yet if now the situation is thus with a Christian world, Christian states, &c., is it not then true that we have the very greatest need to become sober? And is it not then the mildest possible thing (yet what wonder it is so mild, since it is I that propose it, I who am the weak, unauthoritative poet!)—is it not the mildest possible thing when there is no question of anything but the admission of it? And what will it profit us finally in eternity that we have put this off, intoxicated by sheer illusion? In truth I myself feel only too deeply how wretched and mediocre is the thing I seek to attain, but for all that there is some sense in it. In eternity (if in the meantime I have not got farther on than I am now) I will say: 'That which we called Christianity was not Christianity, it was a very much softened interpretation of Christianity, a something remotely related to Christianity; but this I have conceded, I have made the admission aloud and very audibly, that it is not properly Christianity—do with me, O God, as Thou wilt, according to Thy grace! I know well that in every age, and so too in this age of mine, there have lived men who required that we be Christians in a stricter sense—with them I have never been able to take part. No, to me this seemed a truer way: to take a milder form, an accommodation—but then to concede that this is not properly Christianity. So I come! Sober—no, I feel that I am not that, for only "spirit" is sober. But at all events I do not come with a head completely muddled, drunk with the illusion that this softened form was the true Christianity, nor drunk with the self-conceit that, in contrast with this modified Christianity in which the majority live under the name of Christians, I am the true Christian—no, I come with this admission, and indeed it is to Thy grace I come, O God! This is not to be sober (for in that case my life must have been far more strict, expressive of "spirit", and yet for all this taking refuge unconditionally in grace— whereas I apply grace also in a second place,[1] that is, to spare myself in human sympathy for myself), this is not to be sober, but it stands in relation to becoming sober.'

No honest man (and what advantage is there after all in any dishonesty in relation to the pretence of being a Christian? In eternity, where the question first becomes important and decisive, dishonesty is impossible) can truthfully say that this is too severe, too hard. Oh no! It is quite another question whether God in heaven will not say that it is too mild. But in any case it stands in relation to becoming sober. And certainly there is an infinite difference between this: to act as if Christianity were in existence, and were in existence in all of these millions, and in these thou-

---

[1] S. K. says 'also' because he was accustomed to insist especially upon the necessity of using 'grace in the first instance', i.e. prevenient grace, which saves from sinning, since he perceived that people were inclined rather to rely upon 'grace in the second instance', the grace which forgives sin already committed, and were taking it in vain as a dispensation to sin.

sands of parsons—there is an infinite difference between that and this: to admit that this whole thing is not really Christianity but a human accommodation, which precisely by the help of the admission (for without this the accommodation is a breach with Christianity) stands in relation to true Christianity, stands in relation to becoming sober.

II

CHRIST AS THE PATTERN

OR NO MAN CAN SERVE TWO MASTERS

Matt. 6: 24 to the end

CHRIST AS THE PATTERN

PRAYER

O LORD JESUS CHRIST, it was not to plague us men but to save us that Thou didst say, 'No man can serve two masters'—oh, that we might be willing to accept it, by doing it, that is, by following Thee! Help us all and everyone, Thou who art both willing and able to help, Thou who art both the Pattern and the Redeemer, and again both the Redeemer and the Pattern, so that when the striver sinks under the Pattern, then the Redeemer raises him up again, but at the same instant Thou art the Pattern, to keep him continually striving. Thou, our Redeemer, by Thy blessed suffering and death, hast made satisfaction for all and for everything; no eternal blessedness can be or shall be earned by desert—it has been deserved. Yet Thou didst leave behind Thee the trace of Thy footsteps, Thou the holy pattern of the human race and of each individual in it, so that, saved by Thy redemption, they might every instant have confidence and boldness to will to strive to follow Thee.

THE HOLY GOSPEL IS WRITTEN BY THE EVANGELIST MATTHEW IN THE SIXTH CHAPTER, BEGINNING AT THE TWENTY-FOURTH VERSE

No man can serve two masters: for either he will hate the one and love the other; or else he will hold to the one and despise the other. Ye cannot serve God and Mammon. Therefore I say unto you, Take no thought for your life, what ye shall eat, or what ye shall drink; nor yet for your body, what ye shall put on. Is not the life more than meat, and the body than raiment? Behold the fowls of the air: for they sow not, neither do they reap, nor gather into barns; yet your heavenly Father feedeth them. Are ye not much more than they? Which of you by taking thought can add one cubit unto his stature? And why take ye thought for raiment? Consider the lilies of the field, how they grow; they toil not, neither do they spin: and yet I say unto you, That even Solomon in all his glory was not arrayed like one of these. Wherefore, if God so clothe the grass of the field, which to-day is, and to-morrow is cast into the oven, shall he not

much more clothe you, O ye of little faith? Therefore
take no thought, saying, What shall we eat? or, What
shall we drink? or, Wherewithal shall we be clothed?
(for after all these things do the Gentiles seek): for your
heavenly Father knoweth that ye have need of all these
things. But seek ye first the kingdom of God and his
righteousness; and all these things shall be added unto
you. Take therefore no thought for the morrow: for
the morrow shall take thought for the things of itself.
Sufficient unto the day is the evil thereof.

'No man can serve two masters', it is the Gospel's own word.
So take this word, go out into the world, observe if possible what
the lives of all these millions of men express; imagine one who
has been contemporary with all the generations of the departed
and has observed what their lives express. What do they express?
They express as with one mouth what even the mouth says too:
'Never has there lived a man who has not, more or less, served
two masters. And as for the assertion of the Gospel that it is not
possible to do it ("No man *can* serve two masters"), there must be
a misunderstanding, for it is only too possible to do it, as the whole
experience of the world attests. It would have been more com-
prehensible if the Gospel had said that no man *should* serve two
masters—but that no man can do it is not true; the thing no man
can do, on the contrary, is what the Gospel requires. The other
thing is easy to do; and if thou wouldst become something in this
world, thou must be alert to take the line of serving two or more
masters; for he who would take seriously the notion that he can
serve only one master had better look out, it is back-breaking
work.' Yet perhaps the world and the Gospel are talking about
entirely different things. The world, naturally, talks about this
world, simply and solely about this world; it knows nothing and
wants to know nothing about the existence of another world.
That indeed would be for 'this world' a discovery involving deadly
peril. Another world! The Gospel talks in terms of the eternal,
and about this other world, about eternity. No man can serve
two masters—no, not in all eternity; and if no one can do it in
terms of the eternal, then no one can do it; for the fact that it

seems as if one could, yes, even if it were so that one could in these few seconds of temporal existence, that is neither here nor there so far as concerns the truth, whether one can or whether one cannot. How a man is to fare in this world is something which the Gospel (in contrast with novels, romances, lies, and other amusements) does not amuse itself by considering. No, for the Gospel these seventy years are like an instant, and its talk hastens on to the decision of eternity; nor does it deludingly hold out to men bright prospects for this life and for this world when (eternally unchanged) it proclaims the eternal truth, 'No man can serve two masters.'

'No man can serve two masters', it is the Gospel's own word. So take this word, observe the men who are willing at least to understand it as it would be understood, who also have tried perhaps to comply with it, observe these men, and thou shalt behold that their lives, if not their mouths, express unanimously: 'But this is too high for us men, it is not possible to serve one master, nobody can do it'—but the Gospel says (eternally unchanged), 'No man can serve two masters.' And if thou wilt observe these men more closely in the moment of despondency—even though they put constraint upon their mouth, yet their life expresses: 'It is too high for us men, yea, it is a cruelty to require of us such a thing, and never with less right has anything called itself glad tidings than precisely this Gospel! So let us rather remain under the Law with its inflexible severity, anything rather than this smiling cruelty: that the requirement is if possible still greater than that of the Law—and that this is what is called glad tidings!' This is 'the offence'—even if the mouth is silent. When discouragement weighs heavily upon a man's soul, the offence is not far off, and it is such thoughts as these that find a dwelling in the offended man. And let us get these thoughts into the open, in order if possible to get them out—not out into the world, but out of the world, or at least out of the heart; for to constrain one's mouth to be silent, or even maybe to say the opposite, is of scant avail when one cannot constrain one's mind to let go of these thoughts.—Is then the requirement actually so cruel, or is the Gospel really not glad tidings? For if it is so that this is eternal truth (and we have the Gospel's word for it, and in any case the honest man would recognize that it is so, whether the Gospel said it or not), if it is so that this is eternal truth, that no man can serve two masters, how should the Gospel be able to say anything different, and how should the Gospel, the very truth, be able to wish to suppress it, or how could it be cruel to tell the truth? Consider well whether it would not be cruelty to conceal it from thee! Moreover, dost thou not believe that the Gospel knows what it is to be a man, recognizes our weakness, knows how far every man is from being able truly to serve one master? 'But', says the Gospel, 'it is just for this reason I preach a redemption—is not this glad tidings?' 'However,' continues the Gospel, 'if my first was not true and did not stand eternally firm, namely, that "no man can serve two masters", then there would in a deeper sense be no need felt for a redemption, and this glad tidings would never be heard. Is not this really glad tidings, this, that "no man can serve two masters"? When I, the Gospel, say this, by saying that "no man can serve two masters" I condemn all, absolutely all; and yet in the same breath I call all, absolutely all, unto me, proclaiming that God wills that all should be saved, and that this is the Gospel. But how could all be saved if all do not feel the need of being saved, and how could all feel the need of being saved if the requirement were not such that no man can perfectly fulfil it?'

'No man can serve two masters', it is the Gospel's own word. So take this word, observe the lives of those of whom it can be said that in striving to fulfil this word they were, humanly speaking, very far ahead, so that if they were to compare themselves with us, they readily might be tempted to ignore us and to be not far from thinking that they had attained perfection—observe their lives, and thou shalt see that in times of temptation (*Anfægtelsen*), even if the mouth is constrained to silence, they give expression to this: 'The requirement, however, is too high for men; as it is said of a spendthrift that no amount of money suffices him, but that to give him money is like casting it into a bottomless pit, so this requirement is not exhausted by any striving, not in the remotest degree; before God, at this instant when, humanly speaking, I have got farthest along, I have not come one inch, not a millionth fraction of an inch, nearer to God than the man who never strove, no, nor even than the man who strove with might and main for the opposite. Oh, weariness! oh, impotence! to have to do with the infinite, the absolute! As the forces of nature mock human undertakings and transform them into childish foolery, so does the absolute mock absolutely every human striving. The absolute is not for man, it is too high for him.' But can then that which is expressly designed to humble, can that be too high? Or when a man feels as if it were too high for him, is it not because he has put himself in relation to it incorrectly, so that by putting himself in the wrong place he gets the stress in the wrong place, so that the requirement falls upon him crushingly? Instead of this, the requirement, by humbling a man, should exert a stress which results in exaltation, in rejoicing at 'grace', and in boldness through grace. O thou who in this way art tempted—I have need to hear thy speech, thou hast not in the same degree a need to hear mine; yet this being granted, permit me to speak. I would say: 'What then is exaltation? Is not all exaltation proportionate to the stress of humiliation? But if the stress may be too strong in the direction of humiliation—complaint against it might be interpreted to mean that the exaltation was too high. It is a fact that in the world of sense one can lift by means of a weight—in case then one misunderstood and supposed that he had to lift the weight instead of being lifted by the weight—then indeed he is crushed. But the misunderstanding lay not in the weight but in him. So it is with the unconditional requirement; if I must lift it, I am crushed. But this is not the intention of the Gospel, its intention is that I, through humiliation, shall be lifted up in faith and worship—and then I am as light as a bird. Or what is most exalting: the thought of my own good deeds, or the thought of God's grace? And again, when does it reach a climax, so that one's head swims in ecstasy, is it not then when my best deed is before God transformed to vileness and grace becomes all the more great? An admirable man has said admirably that a great benefaction is only properly rewarded by unthankfulness. Capital! For when the great benefaction is rewarded with thanks, not to say with much thanks, maybe with a thankfulness equal to it, the benefaction is diminished. But the great unthankfulness as a reward keeps the benefaction unchangeably great. And so there is to be found neither in heaven nor upon earth, nor in any relationship between man and man, an exaltation like this, when I turn away humbled and ashamed from my best deed as from a vileness and find repose in 'grace'. Let the pagan with his proud neck strike the heavens, or try to—from this humiliation comes the exaltation which blissfully reaches heaven. Thou canst not worship God by good works, still less by crimes, and just as little by sinking into a soft slumber and doing nothing. No, in order to worship aright and rightly to have joy in worshipping, a man must so comport himself: he strives with might and main, spares himself neither day nor night, he tries to produce as many as possible of what upright men, humanly speaking, might call 'good works'. And then when he takes them and, deeply humbled before God, beholds them transformed to wretchedness and vileness, that is to worship God—and that is exaltation.

'No man can serve two masters', this is the Gospel's own word; eternally it is repeated unchanged: 'No man can serve two masters.' 'But if it is true that no man ever has done this—is it not then a reasonable demand on the part of mankind that the requirement be changed, that it be abated? And because less enlightened ages have put up with this state of affairs, being unable to perceive the absurdity of it, and because the human race in its cowed condition did not dare to breathe a murmur, being all too strongly stamped with the marks of intimidation by the law, does it follow that an enlightened, broad-minded, cultured age, or at any rate (since it must be admitted that there is still a great mass which is both uncultured and inti-midated), does it follow from this that an enlightened, broad-minded public is bound to put up with the same thing? To require men to perform the absolute is at bottom sheer madness, a ludicrous exaggeration, which (as any sensible man can readily see) revenges itself, like all exaggeration, by producing an effect exactly the opposite to that which was intended. All human reason is comprised in this glorious and golden rule, "up to a certain point, everything within reason"—or in "both—and" or "also". This precisely is the mark of ripe seriousness, that it requires the requirement to be such that a man can with pleasure and satisfaction fulfil its obligations fully by steady and not too strenuous effort. What none of us has done, none of us of course can do; and if none of us can do it, the requirement must be changed to correspond with what we have shown we can do by the fact that we have actually done it—more cannot be required. And therefore we require a Christianity which can be brought into harmony with all the rest of our existence, in view of the change which, with the increase of enlightenment and culture, has taken place in the human race, or at any rate in the cultured public, which is like the heart-pulse of the race.'

This voice (even if it were not heard in the world, as indeed it is, and very loudly at that) finds a sympathetic echo in many a heart. It is well then that it should be heard. That this world has become changed, who will deny? But is it for the better? Yes, that is a question. That the world has become sheer common sense, who will deny? But is it a gain? Yes, this too is a question. But it is eternally certain that nothing is so great an offence to common sense as the absolute, and (to stick to the immediate context of our discourse) this may also be recognized in the fact that common sense is never willing to acknowledge any requirement absolutely, but always requires that it shall be the one to require what the requirement shall be. To require that Christianity be done away with, or to give up Christianity, is therefore in perfect accord with this common sense. But to require that Christianity be changed is a misunderstanding. For Christianity cannot undergo change— herein again we can recognize that it is diametrically opposed to 'common sense', whose secret is that it can change in every way at the stroke of the clock, depending upon what the age, the public, the main chance, demand, or upon how the wind, the leaves, or the leaves of the newspapers (*Blad og Bladene*) happen to turn. No, Christianity cannot undergo change; to require this reduction of its requirements is an attempt to change it, which remains, however, totally without effect; indeed, as a mountain might look at a child which went up to it and said, 'Get out of my way', so must Christianity listen to this talk which requires of it the eternally impossible, that it be changed.

Christianity cannot undergo change, nor is it so situated that where everything and everybody changes it also is changed; nor is it put to embarrassment like human authority by the fact that all men change—but that it should be forced upon anybody is not Christianity's will and never has been. On the other hand, it has been its will from the very beginning, and it is its will that it be presented unchanged, in all its absoluteness, so that every man can weigh in his own mind whether he will have anything to do with it or not. Though not even one single person will accept it, Christianity remains unchanged, not one tittle does it yield; though all accept it, not one tittle must be changed. It is God's love to men Christianity proclaims, for every single man, the poorest, the most wretched, the most forsaken; for his sake God has as it were set heaven and earth in commotion; but though all men who now live or have lived were united in requiring only one tittle of change—no, never! Every single man, the poorest, the most wretched, the most forsaken, if only for his own best interest he wills as God wills, is, according to Christianity, of infinite importance—incomprehensible love! But, on the other hand, the countless millions of the race are before God no more than a gnat, or not even so much, if they do not will as He wills.

How then should common sense and Christianity be able to come to an understanding with one another when they mutually repel each other like opposite poles? For in these sensible times it is not this which constitutes an obstacle between Christianity and men, that we men fail to live up to the requirement. Christianity can put up with that, as it did in other ages when people had an infinite conception of the requirement and were willing to admit their own imperfection, to admit that the fault lay in them, not in the fact that the requirement was absolute. No, what in these sensible times constitutes the obstacle between Christianity and men is that people have lost the conception of the absolute requirement, that they cannot get it through their heads what use there is in having an absolute requirement, what good it can do, seeing that no one fulfils it, that the absolute has become the unpractical, the foolish, the ludicrous, that they (in rebellion or in self-conceit) invert the situation, seek the fault in the requirement, and become themselves the requirers, requiring that the requirement be changed. 'To will the impossible', say they, 'is madness; the sensible thing is to will what we are capable of doing. But to require the absolute is to require that one shall will the impossible, shall squander on this his strength, his time, his life, without getting an inch farther—and this is madness, a ludicrous exaggeration.' *Common sense* is a rebellion against the absolute, though not a loud-voiced rebellion, at least in the first instance— common sense would regard that as injudicious, and a more refined common sense always wishes (for certain reasons) that attention be not drawn to this, that it remain a secret between us that we have made this revolt, whereas the appearance is maintained that nothing at all has happened. Sneaking slowly onward, this common sense eats away the absolute bit by bit, undermining faith in and reverence for it—and then finally perhaps an impatient common sense bursts forth boastfully into speech, loudly proclaiming its wisdom, that the absolute is madness. Along with the growth of common sense there gains ground a certain sort of human lore, the lore concerning what we men actually *are*, or *are* in these times, the moral situation regarded as the product of natural causes, explained by geographical situation, climate, prevailing winds, rainfall, distribution of water, &c. Whether we men are deteriorating from generation to generation is of no concern to this human lore, which merely reports with precision what we *are*, according to the current quotation of the bourse and the market price—in order that by shrewd acquaintance with this it may be possible to guard oneself against men and to make use of them, to succeed, to win advantages in this world, or to be able to justify and gloss over one's own wretchedness and mediocrity, or get leave to express with a good conscience of a sort (a scientific conscience) one's suspicion of anything better which might occasionally turn up. But how men *ought to be*, about God's requirements, about the ideals—about this less and less inquiry is made in proportion as common sense increases. In the end one even finds such talk, if occasionally it is heard, this talk about how a man ought to be, one finds it a flat and insipid sort of thing, something rather countrified. 'No sensible man wants to listen to that sort of thing, indeed he ought not, if he would not waste his time and his life. If it be a parson who talks about such things, one can tolerate it, with the proviso that it is a parson who properly preserves a sense of decorum, limits himself to declaiming this in quiet hours in the church—but otherwise does not presume to press it. In such a case it may be tolerated, after all it is the parson's business, and common sense is too reasonable to interfere with this, though it is certain that, in rather a different way than poetry and art, a parson (who generally is neither poetry nor art) is a superfluity.' For if it is true that people have sometimes misused Christianity to intimidate the world—certain it is that now the situation is inverted, and the world with its common sense would intimidate Christianity, would intimidate the parsons, who for the sake of being tolerated become actors and declaimers, neither more nor less—alas, many of them do not need to be intimidated to this effect by the world, they are perhaps only too willing to be seduced.

If only this might be said and heard, this truth: that 'common sense', which thinks the requirement must be altered to suit men; Christianity, which maintains that man must be altered to suit the requirement, or that at all events the absolute requirement must at least be absolutely asserted—that these two, common sense and Christianity, cannot come to an understanding with one another. For my part I shall always feel grateful to common sense and some respect for it, if it is honest enough to come out openly in speech and say that the absolute is ridiculous.

This is not the dangerous thing, at least not for Christianity; for it is never dangerous for men to get to know how things really stand, least of all for that power which has truth so thoroughly on its side as has Christianity. On the other hand, it might be dangerous for Christianity if one holds down the truth, if not in unrighteousness, at least in ambiguity. As if, e.g., one were to get the notion that the text was doubtful, or that this saying, 'No man can serve two masters', was difficult to understand, so that in the one case profound research is needed, and in the other case long investigation, and that as a matter of course (seeing that research and investigation are not everybody's affair) there must be a few professors on hand, whose livelihood it then becomes to make research and investigation, for which cause they surely (either for the sake of science, or at least for the sake of their living) would take good care to make the research or investigation last just as long as they lived. This, however, does not succeed so well in our times. But there is also another way of holding down the truth in ambiguity: one may let the absolute requirement continue to resound, but in such wise that something else is surreptitiously understood, namely, that in actual life one has nothing to do with such a thing, so that the absolute requirement becomes a Sunday solemnity, a *divertissement* enacted by parsons —and in other respects a man's life remains entirely secure, untouched by the painful disturbance of the absolute requirement.

No, Christianity takes the absolute requirement seriously, and though it may be that not a single person has been able to fulfil the requirement—yet One has fulfilled it, fulfilled it absolutely, He who uttered the saying, 'No man can serve two masters', He who here, as in every situation, not only uttered the truth but was the truth, He who was the Word also in this sense, that what He said, He was.

It is about Him we will speak, about the Pattern. He has said, 'No man can serve two masters'—and His life gave expression to the fact that He served only one master. By paying attention to His life we shall see the absolute requirement, and we shall see it fulfilled. Meanwhile we constantly recall to mind that Jesus Christ was not only a pattern but also the Redeemer, in order that the Pattern may not alarm us to desperation; and we recall it to mind also at this moment, when, as the Gospel we have read prompts us to do, we speak about

CHRIST AS THE PATTERN

or

NO MAN CAN SERVE TWO MASTERS

We shall see how His life from the very beginning had to be arranged, and how it must be to the very end, if He would give expression to the requirement of serving only one master. Moreover, we shall see how (especially since He could not wish to live apart in concealment, but, as the Pattern, must wish to make evident before men what it is to serve only one master), we shall see how it fared with Him, and must have fared with Him in this world, among us men, who all more or less serve two masters, and to such a point that we cannot calmly endure that there is One among us who will serve but one master, more especially if He will not retire into obscurity, but draws to Himself the attention of all, and that with the claim that He is the truth.

He let himself be born in poverty and lowliness, and not this only, but in despicable condition, of a betrothed virgin to whom the upright man who was betrothed to her showed a kindness in not putting her away secretly, which at first he proposed to do, and which itself would have been an act of forbearance. So it was He came into the world, in such wise that He remained outside the world, cast out of the world by His very entrance into it, 'without father, without mother, without descent', by His birth not connected with any man whatsoever. But thus it behoved Him to be early attentive to what His life was designed to express: only to serve one master. Just as he who is to contest in a race is dressed accordingly, just as he who is to strive in battle is armed accordingly, so is His life from the very beginning adapted to make it possible only to serve one master. For birth (and it need not be the birth of a scion to an ancient noble house, or of an heir to the throne), birth itself, when through it a child becomes a member of a family, birth itself is a bond which at once unites this human individual with other persons in a close connexion; and it is connexion with the world, and all that is of the world, and so too connexion with other men, which makes it so difficult only to serve one master, and makes this impossible if the connexion is not broken, albeit love remains. On the other hand, the illegitimate child, knowing nothing of race and belonging to none, excluded from society, brought to birth at midnight behind a bush by one whose pregnancy was concealed—so it was He let Himself be born (because there was no room, as also He was crucified because the world had no room for Him!) in a stable (for in the case of the despised maiden there was no family connexion with a layette in readiness), laid in a manger. If there is any question of connexion, it must be with the horses.

True enough, this birth may be regarded from another side, from God's side: a heavenly glory irradiates this birth. It is not as at other times that the stars of the night shine unchangingly upon the earth; no, His birth—which certainly did not seem like an important event on earth—was an event in heaven, the most important event, one star particularly shines upon the place of His birth, diffusing—blessed is the eye that sees it!—heavenly splendour over the stable and the despised maiden and the dishonoured husband and over the babe in the manger. This glory is superhuman, but just as Christianity always puts contradictions together, so that glory is not directly recognizable as glory, but is to be recognized inversely by lowliness and humiliation (the cross which is associated with everything Christian)—so it is also in this instance. For the Christian cross is not superficiality, outward show, 'both—and', without depth, a mere decoration, a cross in a star; no, seen from the one side it is quite literally, with frightful literalness, a cross, and no eye can behold the cross and the star combined in a higher unity, so that perhaps the lustre of the star would become somewhat less glorious, but also the suffering of the cross somewhat less painful. From the other side, conversely, it is the star that is seen; but the star is not worn (that is a later invention!), alas! it is the cross that is worn (cf. the Gospel), as a decoration, a badge. This, however, has always been and always will be an offence to common sense. For common sense says, 'too little and too much spoils all, everything in moderation, the middle of the road, middle size, this is the true way'. Common sense would therefore be well content to dispense with the star at the nativity—this is too much, or so much is not needed—but also it would insist upon birth in lawful wedlock, and in an honest, well-to-do, middle-class family, at the very least. But the Christian mind is different; it has at its disposition the heavenly—but of the earthly not a thread. When, for example, Christ sends out His disciples—well, surely He might have provided them with the necessaries; but no, they must possess nothing, and on the other hand, 'Whosoever shall give to drink unto one of these little ones a cup of cold water only in the name of a disciple, verily I say unto you, he shall in no wise lose his reward' (Matt. 10: 42). This is very superior. The mightiest monarch of all earth's mightiest monarchs cannot pay in this fashion for a drink of cold water—but of course he takes good care that his emissaries or ministers are not at a loss for a glass of water. The disciple, on the other hand, is in absolute poverty, he is literally in want of the prime necessity of life, a cup of water—and he has no money, he has nothing (God can be as niggardly as that, and then the next instant single out this same man by miracles), nothing to give for it; oh, yes, he has, it is true, he has a cheque payable in heaven, and, rightly considered, that is (but unfortunately not in this world) of greater worth than all the glories of the world, but money he has not, and nothing earthly—which is unfortunate in this world, where money (rightly considered!) is still of more worth than all the glories of heaven. It is related of a traveller that far back in the country he found himself in pecuniary embarrassment, in spite of the fact that he was in possession of a bank-note of a very high denomination . . . which nobody was able to change. So it is with the Christian disciple. To common sense this, like everything Christian, is an offence. 'Too little or too much', says common sense, 'spoils all; let us dispense with this heavenly cheque, so much is not needed; but then let this thing of preaching Christianity be at least an assured good living, with a few fasts in the course of the year and some prestige in the community; the other thing, either way you take it, is an exaggeration. Why must the opposites be held apart from one another in such frightful tension? Why may there not be a little reduction made with respect to the miraculous, and then a little addition made with respect to the less divine perhaps but more directly human wish to be a bit comfortable in the world? Moreover, why this superiority, which makes so much ado, and such a strange ado, disdaining to possess a shilling, and then resorting to miraculous expedients? It is not genuine superiority, but a far-fetched and affected exaggeration; the simple and natural thing would have been to give the disciples some money to take with them. If there is to be a miracle in addition, very well, then let it be performed thus: by one miracle once for all a fund is raised once for all, so that the disciples are provided for, and there is no need for more miracles. The other way is a double exaggeration, both with respect to too little and with respect to too much.' And this is what common sense is very apprehensive of, the thing it would on no account allow itself to be guilty of, it is the thing which common sense, the instant it sets eyes upon it, judges to be madness, it is exaggeration. But without exaggeration it is impossible only to serve one master; and on the other hand, for common sense, closely connected with one person and another and with the whole world and all that is of the world, it is an easy matter to serve two or more masters.

So then His life is as if calculated to make it possible only to serve one master; He is without family and family connexions.

But the star in heaven has betrayed something—only inquire of common sense, and thou shalt hear how well it knows that heavenly glory is not one of the good things a person might wish to have in this world, that it is generally a mortal danger. The star, as has been said, betrayed something: the king of the country took notice, and the despised family must flee with the child out of the country. The despised family; true enough, a generation later (that is, too late) it was called the holy family—but only inquire of common sense, and thou shalt hear it say, 'To belong to a noble or a rich family may be all very well; I, however, do not ask for so much, I am content to belong to a middle-class family; but in this world to have to belong to the holy family, no, I thank you, that would be the last thing, it is certain torment and wretchedness. But hypocrisy has long let it be forgotten that this family was despised as long as it lived upon earth, hypocrisy makes parade of "the holy family", it would make us and others believe that this condition of humiliation is glory, that heavenly glory and earthly glory come to the same thing. And hypocrisy is offended when the humiliation is depicted—it is annoying, and in self-defence it calls this the blasphemy of us freethinkers.'

The family (if one will call it such, for it is no family) flees then with the child. And now this child has no country. But this is as it should be, in order to make it possible for Him to express what it is only to serve one master. Just as he who is to contest in a race is dressed accordingly, and just as he who is to fight in battle is armed accordingly, so is His life from the beginning adapted to make it possible only to serve one master. For second only to the connexion which binds together the family comes the connexion which unites a people.

In a certain sense, it is true, glory shines here also: the insignificant child which was born in a stable suddenly becomes so important that the ruler has all the infants under two years put to death, in the hope of putting this infant to death among the others. 'Again, too little and too much,' says common sense, 'again an exaggeration. Let its birth be an event, and so be a link in the chain of cause and effect; but the child is born as less than an insignificance—and then suddenly the birth is such a frightful event. If it is so important that this babe be born, it is nearly incomprehensible that it is born in a stable, where something might have befallen it. And on the other hand, what a frightful exaggeration, that the importance of this babe should be determined by the murder of infants of the same age, not to speak of the fact that it is this babe of whom it is said that he is to be the salvation of the world, and who begins by causing the death of a host of infants!'

So then the child is now without a country. However, the family returns again, but must live in hiding. During a visit to Jerusalem at the festival the child is missing. And here is an incident which corresponds to and symbolically describes what was or became this child's work in life, to express what it is only to serve one master. The child stands alone, it was without family, without country; but now it is also without the two who were its support, who were anxiously seeking the child, and find it (very significantly) in the Temple, and the child says (is not this significant?), 'Wist ye not that I must be about my Father's business?' The mother does not understand these words (that is not strange), she treasures them in her heart (that was pretty).

Nothing further is known about His childhood and youth. He doubtless played with the poor parents, was subject unto them and helpful to them—which is no obstacle to serving one master; on the contrary, this one master is served precisely by obeying them whom He wills that one should obey. So He grew up, became a man; but He was and remained, as we say, nobody. Nor did He possess anything or acquire anything to possess. Just as he who is to contend in a race is dressed accordingly, and just as he who is to fight in battle is armed accordingly, so was His life calculated to the end of being able to express what it is only to serve one master. Ah, but to become something in this world (not to say to will to become something in the world), to possess something (not to say to acquire something to possess)—for this a connexion with the world and with other men is unavoidable, and, on the other hand, it is only too easy to avoid serving but one master. It is true that I have both read and heard sermons by men who themselves had become something in the world, sermons which, among other things, dealt with the subject of seeking first the kingdom of God; but I take the liberty of holding the opinion that this something which these men had become in the world they must have become in some other way than by seeking first the kingdom of God. I do not doubt that these men and every honest man will substantially agree with me that in case a person makes a serious business of seeking first the kingdom of God, nothing is more certain than that he will become nothing in this world, which, more jealous than heaven, insists that only he who seeks shall find, and where (as is not the case in relation to heaven—for though it is true that the way to heaven is narrow, this is not because it is too much thronged) the throng of seekers is so great that not even all who seek can become something, though they perhaps always become a little more than one who seeks first the kingdom of God, for it is quite certain that he becomes nothing in this world. There is nothing that can be more easily substantiated; God forbid that anyone should be so dishonest or so impudent as to require me to substantiate it. I do not make myself out better than others. Indeed, in a certain sense, I surely have not become anything—it is just this which offends several people, because they think that I might have been able to become something. So then, according to the judgement of such people, I have not become anything. However, I dare not count upon that when it is the Gospel which is to pass judgement. When it is the Gospel which is to pass judgement I must admit with shame that I have become something, though it is very little. Yet I must bear witness that this something which I have become I did not become by seeking first the kingdom of God, and I tranquilly await the attempt of the reverend parsons to substantiate the proposition that one can become something in this world by . . . seeking first the kingdom of God, a thing which, inasmuch as it is to be done first, takes precedence of every other seeking, and, inasmuch as it is the kingdom of God, is heterogeneous with the world and with all that is in the world, including this thing of becoming something in the world.

Therefore, to changing the requirement or abating it, as common sense would have it, I am heartily opposed, as Christianity is opposed. Nor is it my desire that people should give the impression that we men comply with the requirement even in the remotest degree. No, this is the way I think about it. If I am to have anything to do with God—and, oh, that surely ought to be a man's joy, his bliss, so that he is not inclined to bother about the whole of Europe, nor about the public, nor about comparisons with people here at home, &c., if only he may be permitted to have to do with God, every day plucked in his examination, it is true, yet having to do with God, which, according to Christianity, is a favour granted to all men—if I am to have to do with God, I must put up with it that the requirement is the absolute; if the requirement is not the absolute, then I have nothing to do with God, but only with this stifling thing, 'the others', myself, the public, &c. No, no, O God in heaven, above all never recall the absolute requirement! For really it is Thee men would do away with when they would do away with the absolute requirement; and it is for this reason I cling so tight to the absolute requirement and execrate the common sense which by doing away with the absolute requirement would do away with Thee. No, above all let it remain the *absolute* requirement! If I, while recognizing what the true situation is, might wish to become something, if I for the sake of finite necessities must try to become something in the world— that is quite different from wishing to do away with the requirement, and hence I can continue to be in relationship with Thee

nevertheless, for I do not make a right-about-face, do not turn
my back upon Thee, do not treat what I become in the world as
life's seriousness; no, I let the absolute requirement continually
transform me and what I become into beggarliness and wretchedness. On these terms I can still—is it not so?—have to do with
Thee, O God, remain in relationship with Thee.

Let then the annihilation, the inward annihilation before God,
possess its frightfulness, its pain—a man's enthusiasm ought to be
the more blissful. Frightful it would be indeed if, in view of
the fact that before Thee the most honest effort is as nothing, a
man were to take occasion to abandon himself to inactivity, or if
he were to give up entirely having to do with Thee, in order
now to become a serious person who seriously strives to become
something in this world.

So His life, the life of Him who was the Pattern, was from the
very beginning calculated with a view to being able to express
what it is only to serve one master. He belonged to nothing and
to nobody, stood in no connexion with anything or anybody,
foreign to the world, in poverty and lowliness, without a nest,
without a hole (as foxes have), without having whereon to lay
His head. Like the straight line which is tangent to the circle
at only one point—so was He, in the world and yet outside the
world, only serving one master.

He might then have lived on in quiet obscurity, His life might
have been worship in secret, belonging only and belonging
entirely to one master, until death finally came.

But this was not His thought. Even apart from the fact that
He suffered Himself to be born to save the human race, to be the
atonement by His suffering and death—even apart from this,
even if He had only wished to have been the Pattern, He would
not in any case have lived in obscurity. No, this was His work,
this His meat and drink, only to serve one master, but He would
make this evident in the world, and hence He must step out, so
to speak, upon the world-stage so as to fix upon himself the attention of all. He Himself knew only too well what the consequence
would be, that the attention of all directed to Him would mean
His suffering, that to be heterogeneous with the others closest to
Him, not to say absolutely heterogeneous with all, and yet to will
to remain among them, is more dangerous even than when the
soldier in battle falls out of step with the others, which so easily

may end with his being trampled under foot. And He remained in the world, He did not retire from the world, but He remained there to suffer. This is not quite the same thing as when in our age preachers inveigh against a certain sort of piety—which by the way is not exactly what is practised in our age (and hence it is strange to inveigh against it now)—but it was practised in an age gone by, a piety which seeks a remote hiding-place, far from the world's noise and its distractions and its dangers, in order if possible in profound quiet to serve God alone. They inveigh against this piety, they say that it is cowardice, &c. Wherefore nowadays we do differently and better, we pious people, we remain in the world—and make a career in the world, shine in society, make ostentation of worldliness . . . just like the Pattern, who did not retire cravenly from the world! Oh, depth of craftiness! To remain in the world, in the sense that one says good-bye to God and godliness, defining oneself and one's life in conformity with the world—this sort (of piety!) is certainly not higher than the piety of the cloister. It mendaciously promises a double profit: first one plucks for oneself all possible pleasure (which the quiet dwellers in the cloister at all events renounced), and then one is impudent enough to require that this worldliness (what a delicate refinement!) be regarded as a higher sort, a higher sort (who ever could dream of such a thing!), a higher sort of piety, higher than the cloister's quiet retirement. Oh, disgusting! No, it certainly is not the highest thing to seek a remote hiding-place where it might be possible to serve God alone; it is not the highest thing, as we can perceive in the Pattern; but even though it is not the highest (and really what business is it of ours that this other thing is not the highest?), it is nevertheless possible that not a single one of us in this coddled and secularized generation is capable of doing it. However, the highest thing it is not. The highest thing is: while being absolutely heterogeneous with the world by serving God alone, to remain in the world and in the midst of reality, before the eyes of all, directing upon oneself the whole attention of all—for then persecution is unavoidable. And this is Christian piety: to renounce everything in order to serve God alone, to deny oneself everything in order to serve God alone—and then to have to suffer for it, to do good and have to suffer for it. This is what the Pattern expresses; and this also (to mention a mere man who was a distinguished teacher of our Church) is what Luther again and again insists upon, that it belongs to true Christianity to suffer for the teaching, to do good and to suffer for it, and that to suffer in this world is inseparable from being a Christian in this world. We shall now see how it fared with Him who only would serve one master, how it fared with Him, that is to say, how it must fare with Him in this world; for as it fared with Him, so must it fare with Him, so would it fare with Him in the world in any age.

He would express what it is only to serve one master, where all more or less serve two masters or many; and He would not live in obscurity, no, He would make this evident, He would direct the attention of all to Himself—what then will the consequence be? The consequence will be that He will come into hostile collision with the whole world, with all men, and that they will seek in the most various ways to move, to persuade, to entice, to tempt, to threaten, to compel Him to become like them and unfaithful to Himself and to His task. And the world will stake everything upon carrying this warfare through, it will not let go of Him until the most shameful death has brought His life to an end. And what the world wills is the same thing that an evil power also wills, the prince of this world, who (like God!) requires that he alone be worshipped, which is impossible nevertheless, seeing that he is not 'the Lord',[1] the one master, so that everyone whose only master he is does not serve one master. This collision with the world, with the human race, which is instigated by the evil power, is from now on the history of the Pattern.

He serves only one master; and just as he who is to contend in a race is clothed accordingly, and he who is to fight in battle is armed accordingly, so also is His mode of existence calculated with a view to being able to serve only one master.

He is absolutely an alien in the world, without the least connexion with anything or with any single person in the world, where everything else is in connexion. It is harder for a rich man to enter the kingdom of heaven than for a camel to go through the eye of a needle; but it is impossible for that man to serve only one master who has even the least connecting bond.

He is not bound as a husband to a wife; no, He has not even any father, no mother, no brothers or sisters, He is connected with no family, He says (pointing to the disciples), 'These are My father and mother and brothers and sisters.'

[1] In Danish, *Herre* means lord as well as master, and *Herren* is the Lord.

'But then after all He has disciples?' Disciples, yes; but if they are true disciples, there is no bond in the connexion, for in relating Himself to His disciples, He relates Himself at every instant first to God, serving Him alone; and if the disciples wish to form any bond of connexion, they are not disciples. No, it is not as difficult to grasp and hold tight with the hand what by reason of its smoothness slips through the fingers, as it is impossible for connexion to capture him who only serves one master.

He makes His appearance as a teacher, and almost at the same instant He has the whole attention of that little land.

He teaches: 'No man can serve two masters.' 'Well, what He teaches would be all the same to us, if only He didn't go ahead and do accordingly; for then it becomes impossible to stay with Him. On the other hand, it is perfectly feasible that this thing about no one being able to serve two masters, that this thing might become (here is true seriousness!) an objective doctrine—and then a kingdom of this world, where He, the teacher, becomes king and prince, and we who have stood closest to Him, now find ourselves closest to the throne.'

He made His appearance as teacher in the little nation, which as usual is divided into two parts: the mighty, and what one calls the masses. Both sides are observant of Him—which of them will He join, which will have the good fortune to win Him to a connexion with it? Neither by birth nor by outward condition does He belong to the mighty; but they perceive well enough that He *is* a might. By birth and condition He seems to belong most closely to the masses, and they joyfully perceive in Him a might. But He serves only one master, solitary and alone—ah, certain path to suffering, to destruction! If thou dost behold in a winter's storm one who is clad in the lightest summer garments, not even he is so painfully exposed as he who wills to be a solitary man in a world where all persons are in connexion, and consequently require, with the selfishness characteristic of connexion, that one must hold together with them, until the individual secures himself against several connexions by entering into one connexion, whereas the solitary individual, as soon as it becomes evident that he will hold with none, has against him (grandiose connexion!) all connexions united in one connexion.

He would only serve one master; but He is (as everyone can see), He is a prodigious might. His contemporaries behold Him with wonder. At this moment there is no question of opposition, not even envy has asserted itself. No, all is wonder—wonder at this man who, almightily almost, as it might seem, holds all possibilities in His hand, is capable of becoming whatsoever He will. It is like a fairy-tale, and wonder curiously attempts to guess the riddle: 'What will He be now? But something He must want to be; and whatever it is He wills to be He must be able to attain it, and if it is what He wills it is sure to be something great'—and then the united recognition of His contemporaries, or at least the united recognition of many of the contemporaries, will attach itself to Him enthusiastically. For human recognition is like natural love, friendship, &c., it is selfishness. Where there is direct ground for recognition, where the fact that someone is an eminent man is recognizable by worldly power, prestige, by 'gold and goods'—there also human recognition is prompt. In fact (even if the individual is not always conscious of it as the sly reaction of natural selfishness) it is the result of a very simple computation: by recognition in this instance I get the advantage of being on the side of the mighty, of being in the game by taking the part of the mighty, and at the same time I appear to be an amiable person whose soul is not shrivelled by petty interests but is expanded by disinterested enthusiasm. On the other hand, where direct reasons for recognition are lacking or are withheld, recognition is without profit, it is a severe effort, it means sacrifices—hence it is not shown, just as natural love and friendship fail to show themselves in cases where Christian love would be manifested. If God in heaven were to take the form of a lowly man, if He, divinely prodigal, if I dare say so, were to scatter on all sides cheques upon heaven—human recognition will not go in for such grand behaviour. Human mediocrity which has attained popularity—there is the thing the speculative mind loves to recognize. In case there is a child in the family who has eminent qualities, and this fact is directly recognizable by worldly honour and prestige, a European fame, stars and ribbons—ah, then of course the family is sheer (disinterested!) enthusiasm. If he had been thus eminent, but without the direct signs of recognition, the family would soon feel him to be a burden, an infliction, and would wish rather that he was an entirely insignificant person. So it is with human recognition—and He who only serves one master wills to be absolutely . . . nothing.

With the resources of omnipotence—for that He has, although the use He makes of it hides this from the eyes of many, it is indeed like lunacy to employ, to have need of, the resources of omnipotence to become nothing—with the resources of omnipotence He assures Himself of becoming nothing. And then He must come to the point of breaking with all men. Humanly speaking, He must make unhappy, immeasurably unhappy, the few who were so very dear to Him, the mother must feel it like a sword piercing her heart, the disciples must feel it like the bitterness of death—and it was He who held and holds all possibilities in His hand! Oh, soul-felt anguish of misunderstanding! And He must—even in the case of the dearest, the best, the most upright—He must come to the point of making it manifest that everyone, the dearest (alas, the dearest!), the most upright (alas, the most upright!), is nevertheless, when it comes to the pinch, a cowardly wretch, a traitor, a hypocrite. Fearful! What after all is so comforting in life and in death as to have or to have had a favourable and good impression of a person? What so comfortless as to get the opposite impression of a person one has loved and trusted? Oh, my friend, reflect upon this! There is a young man, he learns to know a girl, and this dear girl becomes his wife—they reach seventy years of age, their day of life was a lovely summer's day, then in the evening she dies, and with deep emotion he says, 'Whatever other men have experienced, I have had the experience that there is such a thing as faithful love.' Happy man! Appreciate then, not only what thou hast had, but what thou hast, thy happiness, the happiness of thy sorrow; oh, happy sorrow, that death did not take faithfulness from her, but only her with her faithfulness from thee! For if this man had been obliged to lead this girl out into great and decisive tests, he would have got to know something else, that nevertheless she also was (to use the mildest term) a shabby lot, that he himself was the same, as I would of myself have the experience in great and decisive tests.—There live two youths, they unite themselves closely to one another in the days of youth, and old age finds everything unchanged, as it remained throughout all of their obscure life; then the friend dies, friend is separated from friend, and the friend who stands by the grave says, 'Whatever others have experienced, I have had the experience that there is such a thing as faithful friendship.' Happy man! Enviable happiness, from experience, from so long an experience, to learn to know something so joyful! [S. K. may have meant to have depicted a different possibility, as in the other instances, but he did not do so.]—There is a man, perhaps older than thou, yet of such an age that thou couldst speak of him as thy contemporary; in him thou beholdest greatness, loftiness, and it chances to be in a season of calm weather ye live together—then he dies, and at his grave thou dost say joyfully, 'Whatever others have experienced, I have had the experience that there is such a thing as noble character.' Happy man! For be assured that what thou didst really learn to know was that it was calm weather; if a storm had arisen, thou wouldst have seen that he is shabby, like thee and me. Oh, most bitter of all sufferings (far more bitter than to discover how paltry one is oneself), to have to make it manifest that this (ah, one would give everything if only it might be truth as one thought it was!), that this to which one looked up as to something great and lofty (oh, take this away from me, let me be exempted, if this must be made manifest, so let it be, but let it not be I that must make it manifest!) is shabbiness, paltriness! And this He had to do who only served one master; if He were to continue to the end only to serve one master, He must make this manifest of all, also of them —yet here there can be no question of looking up to anyone, but we can say, also of them He loved, whom He loved as only He could love who alone was love. O Thou who wast love and leniency—they were indeed willing to suffer everything for Thee and with Thee; couldst Thou not have abated a little bit, a tiny scrap, and therewith have spared them from getting this annihilating impression of themselves: Paltry wretch that I am! Oh, soul-piercing torment, not to be able to spare them! Oh, agony, not to be able in love to abate the least bit, the least scrap . . . because in love one would save them!

He serves only one master; He employs the resources of omnipotence in order to ensure Himself continually of being nothing! He employs just as much power in order not to budge an inch from the spot He has resolved to occupy and where He is determined to stay: in the midst of reality, before the eyes of all, where He will express, 'My kingdom is not of this world.' And finally He employs just as much power in order to direct the attention of all upon Himself. This (as His contemporaries also felt) is like an attempt at wanting to compel the human race to lose its senses, for in fact He would press upon them, or impress in them, the qualification of 'spirit', which the human race has always considered a superfluity, and considered it necessary to protect itself by warfare unto death against this exaggeration of lunacy and 'possession', which must come from one who 'has a devil'. This is like wanting to compel a person to lose his senses. For the law of relationship between being nothing and attention is this: what corresponds very reasonably to being nothing is obscurity, no attention drawn to one; what corresponds to being something is attention drawn to one—then he comes up and looks around and says, 'Sure enough, here is something, it was reasonable that I was heralded, that attention was drawn.' To being something in a high degree corresponds a high degree of attention; and being something quite extraordinary may, without disturbing this law, draw to one the attention of the whole contemporary age. But here comes the crazy thing: to be nothing—and with that to have the whole attention directed to one. This is just as crazy as to wish to erect in the midst of this world a kingdom which is not of this world. For if one would not have it be of this world, it is pure chicanery and caprice (in fact madness) to select a place for it right in the midst of this world; one might take his kingdom along and try to find another world, or at least seek a remote place in this world to set up a kingdom which is not of this world. But to select a place right in the midst of this world, that is playing for high stakes—either he is mad, or the rest of us are; and this is a fight unto death: either he conquers, or we do, but we do not unite, any more than fire and water do.

He, however, serves only one master; He does not yield a tittle by way of becoming uniform with this world or letting Himself be forced into any sort of uniformity by becoming something in this world, nor does He yield a tittle by way of letting Himself be forced outside this world, into remote seclusion. No! Hence in the end the whole world, everybody united, turns against this man. How shall one get rid of him?

How shall one get rid of him? To liberate oneself from him by declaring him insane, and then tranquilly assuming again the attitude of being that something which every single individual is—no, that's not practicable, he is too powerful for that, both with each individual and with the generation as a whole, he has wounded them too deeply; this would be—so everyone must feel—just as foolish as for the ants to liberate themselves from the funnel of the ant-lion by declaring that it is lunacy. So there is nothing else for it: one must protect oneself against him by resorting to the qualification 'guilt', by declaring that his life is the most terrible egoism, the most revolting pride. This, however, does not suffice, he is too strong for the human race. There is only one resource left: we men, the whole race, are to retire cautiously behind the quality 'God', and from that vantage ground aim at Him and direct the attack against Him, with God on our side; the accusation is found: He blasphemes God.

So that will be the accusation! His last hour draws near. He has had disciples; at the decisive moment, when He is struggling in anguish unto death, He finds them without anguish, He finds them sleeping—they could not watch with Him one hour. One of them, however, did not sleep—he employed the decisive moment to betray and sell Him. So He is seized—and the disciples awake from sleep and open their eyes. They flee. The most faithful of them denies Him.

He stands before His judges, accused, or rather condemned, scourged, arrayed with every possible insult, derided, spat upon —then it occurred to Him: yet some time Thou must say what Thou art, now is the moment for it, now it is almightily ensured against being taken in vain—so He says, 'Nevertheless I am a king.'—'It is enough to cause a person to lose his mind, to become furious with the man, that He says this now. It is this we were all waiting for, that He should have said it at once, and he would have become that, nothing is more certain—He seems only to have been waiting for this moment when it is absolutely too late, since He Himself has made it absolutely impossible, in order then to say, "Nevertheless I am a king."'

He still might have got off with His life; the governor of the land is so kind as to refer the case of the accused to the so much lauded human compassion, which—who knows?—might perhaps have interested itself in Him, had He not with so proud a mien up to the last made Himself unworthy of sympathy, proved incorrigible up to the last, without indicating in the remotest way by the least sign that He, won back to life and to the world, might yet have a desire to live in order to become something in the world. The people have the right to vote, to vote either for the acquittal of a robber, or for that of the accused. They vote for

the robber. And that is natural—the other also was a far more
terrible robber. For what is it after all to have assaulted travellers
on the highway perhaps a dozen times, what is that compared to
His assault upon the whole human race and upon the very notion
of what it is to be a man! For just think, a thief can steal my
money; so far as that goes we disagree; but in another sense we are
entirely in agreement, for truly the thief is of the same opinion
as I, that money is a great blessing. And the slanderer can steal
my honour and reputation; but truly the slanderer is of the same
opinion as I, that honour and reputation are a great blessing, it is
for this reason he deprives me of them. But in a much craftier
way one can as it were steal from us all our money, honour,
reputation, &c., steal out of the life of us men that in which we
live. And that indeed is what He did, the indicted man. He did
not steal the money of the rich—no, but He took away the estimation attached to having money. 'Oh, paltry, contemptible
mammon', this is what His life expressed, 'paltry mammon, with
which a man defiles himself by hoarding it, which he heaps up to
his own destruction, which he possesses to his perdition, so that
finally in hell he will eternally execrate himself. Oh, if thou didst
understand me, the thief who stole everything from thee thou
wouldst regard as thy greatest benefactor, who helped thee as
thou hadst need to be helped—for it is easier for a camel to go
through a needle's eye.' Neither was He a slanderer who diminished anybody's honour and reputation—no, but He took away
the estimation from human honour and reputation. 'Oh, paltry
costume of buffoons, all the more paltry the higher it goes, the
more it shines and sparkles. Thou knowest it not, it fares with
thee as with that king who by mistake put on a shroud instead of
the royal apparel—it is not this mistake thou hast made, it is truly
enough the royal apparel thou dost wear, but look out, precisely
this is the shroud, the shroud in which thou shalt travel to hell,
without needing to fear that anyone will deprive thee of it, for
there it will be a torture to thee, as a punishment thou must
continue to wear it—cast out because thou hast not on a wedding
garment.' 'But what is the good of it then that I am allowed to
keep the money, that I am allowed to keep the purple, the stars
and ribbons, what is the good of it that everywhere they present
arms, that all fall upon their knees, when I make my appearance,
what good does this do me when He puts through His point of

view? For indeed He has taken away the estimation attached to all this, and if He prevails, it is rather I who am a fool every time they present arms, every time they kneel before me. If perhaps it is too severe to impose capital punishment for thievery and highway robbery—for this sort of robbery which He has exercised against us all there is only one punishment, the death penalty.'

So then as a blasphemer He was condemned to death. His crime was—a warning to imitators!—that He would only serve one master. In human legislation this stands inalterably firm, since public security requires it.

So He is crucified. The death-struggle is a time for converse with Himself and with God. He does not say much. Once every half-hour He utters a word. The suffering overwhelms Him, and He bows His head; He cries, 'My God, my God, why hast Thou forsaken Me?' But thus with bowed head He is not to die. 'It is finished!' 'What is He talking about? Sure enough, it is finished, at least it can't be long before it is finished, for death cannot be very much delayed.' 'It is finished!' So then, it is finished. Now as He is dying He lifts His head towards heaven: 'Father, into Thy hands I commit My spirit!'

'No man can serve two masters', this is His word, and *He was* the Word: He served only one master. So He was not only right in saying this, but right also in saying what He said in the Gospel: 'No man can serve two masters.'

Yet lest the thing might become too serious for us men, a deadly anguish to us, He diverts our attention from Himself and directs it to something else, almost as a diversion and recreation: 'Consider the lilies of the field, behold the birds of the air.' So He does not say, 'No man can serve two masters . . . look at Me', no, He says, 'No man can serve two masters . . . consider the lilies of the field, behold the birds of the air.' He might have said with truth, with infinitely great truth, if thou wilt, 'Look at Me.' For lilies and birds do not literally express anything, and only He is the truth of that which the lilies and the birds symbolically denote. But thus the seriousness would have been mortal. Hence He employs the lilies and the birds, and yet the seriousness remains; for the serious thing is that He says it. In relation to the communication of truth, if it is really to be true, the first question to be asked is whether it is true, and then, who the speaker is, what his life expresses. If a frivolous person, a spendthrift, or a miser, in a moment of poetic feeling utters this true saying, 'Consider the lilies of the field, behold the birds of the air', this is not then seriousness, but fudge and nonsense. When 'the Pattern' says it, on the other hand, it is seriousness, for His life is the truth of it. But seriousness is softened almost to jest by introducing the lilies and the birds. However, it is not something to laugh at—strange as it is that the sparrow also has now become a professor, and professor of the most serious science or art, notwithstanding that (differing in this respect at least from other professors) to-morrow it is sold for a farthing and eaten—no, it is not something to laugh at, for the Teacher's presence in the classroom ensures that no one will dare to laugh. And He never laughed—as it is said in an old hymn: 'Why does He weep who never laughed?' One might be tempted, however, to suppose that He said with a smile, 'Consider the lilies of the field, behold the birds of the air.' Ah, this is so gentle, so divinely gentle— when the speaker is Himself the only one who ever has expressed what it is only to serve one master, when He knows that it will cost a life, then to be able as it were to forget all this and say, 'Let us talk about the lilies and the birds—not about me!' Ah, when it costs Him His life, and heart-felt suffering every blessed day, every hour—then to be able to impart instruction so delightfully! With a man it is different. When he has merely a little more than usual to think about, not to say when he is involved in strenuous and self-sacrificing effort, he will hardly be inclined to pay attention to a sparrow or a lily; with man's stolid and surly vanity he thinks this something far too insignificant, something for children, womenfolk, and idlers. But the Saviour of the world says, just as if it were a Sunday afternoon or a holiday when one has nothing else to do: 'Consider the lilies of the field, behold the birds of the air.' How childlike, how wholesome! For quite different is the sickly thing one sometimes beholds: that a man who has become tired of dealing with men and tired almost of being himself a man, in a sort of uplifted mood now gets the notion of living with sparrows, a notion which, melancholy though it is, and perhaps sometimes wittily expressed, is very far from being seriousness.

Consider the lilies and the birds! Take time, take plenty of time, and yet, in another sense, embrace the instant—remember that now it is autumn. Lovely is the autumn; but notwithstanding it is itself one of the seasons of the year, ah, the most beautiful, it is at the same time as if it were a remembrance of the season now vanished, or a reminder that it is now about to vanish—embrace the instant. Then comes winter, the long winter; then thou wilt hear or see nothing of the lilies and the birds, then they have long ago decamped, these itinerant schoolmasters, who in this respect are different from the itinerant schoolmasters in the country, that the latter make use especially of the winter season and do not commonly hold school in summer, presumably lest they might conflict disturbingly with the lilies and the birds. Embrace the instant, be swift to learn—but as for the lilies and the birds, have no concern, there is nothing about them to suggest that so soon it will all be over; always with the same assurance as in summer-time they deliver the lecture they have to give; the instruction they impart, being what they have learned by themselves (and it is so profitable to a man), is always even, uniform, constant, with no sudden alterations of mood, but 'always the same and about the same thing and in the same way',[1] eternally unchanged in an incomprehensible way, yet always abreast of time and fitting into the instant. Oh, the beneficent peace out there, yet it is just what man is so greatly in need of, needing more especially to have it within him, the peace which is out there with thee and in thee, thou lily of the field, thou bird of the air, the peace which would banish so many real or imaginary sorrows and cares and worries, the peace which means repose or to repose in God.

So give heed to the bird! It sings and twitters, and twitters this refrain—oh, listen!—along with what—oh, heed it well!—it is saying to Sorrow, the refrain of an ancient hymn: 'Yes, yes, to-morrow.'[2] And so the bird rejoices in 'to-day'. Then thinks Sorrow, 'Only wait, I will yet be on the watch for thee; to-morrow ere the day has dawned, and ere thou art risen from the nest, and ere the devil has his shoes on (for I am ever earlier afoot than he; I am one of his servants and forerunners who come first to prepare an entrance for him), then I shall come.' And to-morrow . . . the bird is there no more. 'How is that? it is there no more?'—'No, it has gone on a journey, it is away.'—'How

[1] As Socrates said of his teaching.
[2] The Danish phrase (*Ja, ja imor(g)en*), having fewer consonants, and one of them elided, might be more easily recognized in the song of a bird.

gone on a journey? Its passport was sequestrated, and I swear by Satan, I know it has not journeyed without a pass.'—'Well then, they may not have exercised sufficient vigilance, for it has gone on a journey; it left a greeting for you, the last thing it said was, "Say to Sorrow, Yes, yes, to-morrow."' Thou art shrewd indeed, thou winged traveller, an incomparable professor in the art of living! Oh, to be able thus to say to Sorrow, 'Yes, yes, to-morrow'; and then, after saying it, to enjoy to-day, to enjoy it almost doubly for the joy of having said this! And thus to hoax Sorrow—not for a few days (for what does that avail? Sorrow may as well come first as last), but to keep on saying this until, when Sorrow finally comes in earnest, it is a visit made in vain; to let it come running up every blessed day only to hear the reply, 'To-morrow'; and when finally it might at last become a serious business, that then it comes in all seriousness, only to depart in vain. And the lily! It is pensive, it inclines its head a little, it shakes its head, as a sign to Sorrow: 'Yes, yes, to-morrow.' And to-morrow the lily has a legitimate excuse for absence,[1] it is not at home, it is away, the Emperor has lost his rights over it, if ever he had any, and Sorrow may just as well tear its claim to pieces, it has no validity; and that's the end of it, even if Sorrow becomes furious and says, 'The excuse is invalid.' Oh, to be able thus to say to Sorrow, 'Yes, yes, to-morrow'; and then to be able to remain quite tranquilly on the spot, charming in carefree joy, more joyful if possible for having had its jest with Sorrow: 'To-morrow.' Not to hoax it for a few days, for a week; no, to keep on saying to Sorrow every time it presented itself, 'It is too early, thou dost come too soon', to keep on saying this until when it comes in earnest it is . . . too late! Oh, what a master of the art of living! One almost shudders, while admiring the master one almost shudders, for this is a matter of life and death. One almost shudders—and yet, no, the master's art is so great (a thankless thing to be a great artist!) that one does not observe even the least shudder, and one surrenders oneself to this as the most charming and pleasant jest.

Give heed then to the lilies and the birds! To be sure, there is 'spirit in nature'[2]—especially when the Gospel inspirits it; for

[1] A grim play upon words: *Forfald* also means decay.
[2] An allusion to H. C. Ørsted's famous book *Aanden in Naturen* (The Spirit in Nature).

then is nature nothing but symbols, nothing but instruction for men, it too is 'inbreathed' by God and 'is profitable for doctrine, for reproof, for correction, for instruction in righteousness'. 'Consider the lilies of the field; they sew not, neither do they spin' —and yet the most skilful seamstress who sews for herself, or a princess who with the use of the costliest fabric has her sewing done by the most skilful seamstress, or Solomon in all his glory, was not arrayed like one of these. So then there is one who sews and spins for the lilies? That indeed there is: God in heaven. But as for man, he sews and spins. 'Yes, necessity is enough to teach him that, necessity teaches naked women to spin.' Fie upon thee, that thou canst think so meanly of thy labour, of what it is to be a man, so meanly of God and of existence—as if it were nothing but a house of correction! No, consider the lilies of the field, learn from them, learn to understand what thou knowest: thou knowest that it is man who spins and sews, learn from the lilies to understand that nevertheless really, even when it is man who spins and sews, it is God who spins and sews. Dost thou think that the seamstress, if she understands this, will become less diligent at her work and in it, that she will lay her hands in her lap and think: 'If after all it is really God who spins and sews, the best thing for me is to be free, to be liberated from this unreal spinning and sewing'? If so, then this seamstress is a foolish little maiden, not to say a saucy wench, in whom God can take no pleasure, and who can take no pleasure in the lilies, and who well deserves to have the good Lord show her the door, and then she would see what will become of her. But this seamstress, our own dear lovable seamstress with her childlike piety, understands that only when she herself sews, is it God who will sew for her, and hence she becomes all the more diligent at her work, for the fact that by constantly sewing she constantly must understand—oh, blissful pleasantry!—that it is God who sews every stitch, for the fact that by sewing constantly she must constantly understand —oh, the seriousness of it!—that it is God who sews every stitch. And if she has understood this, through the instruction of the lilies and the birds, then she has comprehended the significance of life, and her life has become in the highest sense significant; and when at last she is dead, it may truly be said of her at the grave, with the greatest possible emphasis: 'She has lived'. Whether or not she was married is of no decisive importance.

'Behold the birds of the air!' How does it come about? Thou art troubled, thy mind is dejected, thine eyes are fixed upon the ground! What is the meaning of this? It was not thus God created man, as can be learnt from every child's primer. What distinguishes man from the beast is the upright posture. So then, if you please, up with the head! 'Oh, won't you leave me in peace?' —No, let us advance by easy steps. It would perhaps be too brusque a movement for thy sick mind, too abrupt a change, if suddenly thou wert to look up from earth to heaven. So let the bird come to our aid. It is sitting upon the ground where thy glance is fixed. Now it rises—so much thou canst surely endure as to lift thy head so that thy glance may follow it. It mounts, so lift thy head a little more, and a little more. Now that is right: now the bird is high up under the sky—and thou art in the correct attitude. Behold the bird in the sky—oh, and acknowledge to thyself that as little as the vault of heaven can be said to press down, just so little is it God who depresses thee; no, the depression comes from the earth, or from the earthly in thee; but as the vault of heaven is uplifting, so it is God who would uplift thee. 'Behold the birds of the air, they sow not, neither do they reap, nor gather into barns.' Yet the birds certainly do not live on air any more than men do. So there must be one who sows and reaps and gathers into barns for them? That there is indeed, namely God, the great caretaker and provider, or, as we call Him, Providence. He sows and reaps and gathers into barns, and the whole world is, as it were, His immense store-room. Tiresome people have had the tiresome notion of wanting to turn the whole world into an immense barn, so as to get along without God. That is foolish mimicry. No, when it is God who does this, it is delightful— oh, the delight of the birds of the air, which sow not, neither reap, nor gather into barns! But this is what man does, he sows and reaps and gathers into barns. So learn then from the birds of the air to understand what thou *knowest*. Thou knowest that it is man who sows and reaps—learn to understand that when man does this, it is really God who does it. 'What bosh! When I with the sweat of my brow go out into the field and reap, so that the sweat pours down me, I have good reason to know with certainty that it is I who reap, at least it is I who sweat. Or is it perhaps really God who sweats? Or, if it is God who reaps, why do I sweat so? Thy talk is grandiloquent, unpractical nonsense.'—Oh, man,

man, obdurate human mind, wilt thou never learn from the birds
to be out of thy mind in order to become man? Wilt thou never
learn in godly exaltation, like the birds, to understand what work
means? Thou wilt certainly come far closer to the truth than thou
art, even if thou wilt merely regard the matter inversely, understanding that to work is not a sheer trouble and burden from
which one would preferably be exempted, that far rather God has
granted man the power to work, in order to bestow upon him . . .
a delight, a sense of independence, which is not bought at too
high a price by the sweat of the brow—for the fact that one sweats
or does not sweat is not decisive; indeed, a dancer also sweats,
but one does not for this reason call dancing a labour, a trouble,
and a burden. This is the only godly understanding of what
work means—and with this one is very far from bemoaning the
sweat of the brow. Take, for instance, a child and the parents'
relation to it. Little Ludwig[1] is taken daily for a ride in his baby-
carriage, a delight which usually lasted an hour, and that it is a
delight little Ludwig understands very well. And yet the mother
has hit upon something new which will delight little Ludwig
even more. Couldn't he pull the carriage himself? And he can!
What? He can? Yes, look Aunty, little Ludwig can pull the
carriage himself! Now let us be men,[2] and not put the child out;
for we know well enough that little Ludwig cannot, that it really
is the mother who pulls the wagon, and it is only to give him
delight she plays the game that little Ludwig can do it himself.
And little Ludwig puffs and groans. Does he not perhaps sweat?
Yes, by my troth, he sweats, the sweat stands out on his forehead,
in the sweat of his brow he pulls the carriage—but his countenance
beams with joy, he is intoxicated with joy, we might say, and he

---

[1] It perhaps adds nothing to the instruction of this passage that it can probably
be regarded as S. K.'s reminiscence of his own early childhood; yet there is some
interest in the fact that Ludwig was a name he somehow associated peculiarly with
himself. He constantly thought of himself as Ludwig. Psychologists at least may be
interested in this curious mental trait. If in this passage, as in several others, Ludwig
is S. K., then we have here a reference to his mother—an affectionate reference and
(psychologists may observe with interest) the only reference he made to her in any
of his works, the Journal included.

[2] 'Let us be men!' Perhaps this is another reminiscence. For in his university
years S. K. seems to have been so much addicted to this exclamation that when
Hans Christian Andersen held him up to ridicule in one of his stories, he represented
him as a parrot which knew how to utter no other phrase.

becomes even more so every time the aunt says, 'Why, look, little Ludwig can do it himself.' It was a peerless delight. The sweating? No, being able to do it himself. So it is with being able to work. Rightly understood, understood in a godly way, it is sheer delight, something God himself has hit upon to give delight to man, concerning which God said to Himself, 'Decidedly it will delight him more than to be carried constantly in a baby-carriage.' Here, as in every other case, the way one regards it makes all the difference. When it is to thy liking, for the sake of pleasure, thou dost not bemoan the sweat. Well then, let thy work be thy delight, understand it a something God has hit upon to delight thee; ah, grieve not His love, He believed it would delight thee well!—But there is a still higher godly understanding which we·learn from the birds: that after all it is God who works, God who sows and reaps, when man sows and reaps. Think of little Ludwig! He has now become a man, and so he understands very well the true situation, that it was the mother who pulled the carriage; he has now therefore a second gladness in the reminiscence of childhood, thinking of the love of the mother who could thus invent something to delight the child. But now he is a man, now he really can do things by himself; he now is led perhaps even into temptation by this really being able to do things by himself—until that reminiscence of childhood reminds him how much he still is in the same situation as the child, that when a man works, it yet is another, it is . . . God who works. Dost thou think that therefore he will be inactive or slothful and say, 'If after all it is God who works, it is best that I be exempted'? If so, then that man is a fool, not to say a shameless scoundrel, in whom God can take no pleasure, and who can take no pleasure in the birds, and who well deserves to have the good Lord show him the door, and then he can see what becomes of him. But the honest, upright, god-fearing labourer becomes all the more industrious for understanding more constantly that—oh, blissful pleasantry!—God is a fellow worker—oh, highest seriousness! Created in God's image as he is, with head erect, he looks up towards heaven at the birds, gay birds[1] from whom he learns that it is God who sows and reaps and gathers into barns. But he does not sink into inactivity, he is alert, attentive to his work—otherwise he is not in a position to perceive that it is God who sows and reaps and gathers into barns.

[1] In Danish *Spøgefugle* means a jester, a wag (literally, jest-bird).

Thou lily of the field, thou bird of the air! How much a man owes to thee! Some of his best and most blissful hours. For since the Gospel installed thee as pattern and teacher, the Law was done away with, and pleasantry was assigned its place in the kingdom of heaven, so that we no longer are under the pedagogue but under the Gospel: 'consider the lilies of the field, behold the birds of the air!'—But then perhaps all that about following Christ, about imitation, becomes a pleasant jest. He Himself helped us by not saying, 'Look at Me', but 'Consider the lilies, behold the birds!' He pointed away from Himself, and we—indeed we men were not to blame for it—we took the hint only too willingly; shrewd as we all are when it is a question of sparing flesh and blood, we shrewdly understood only too well what a concession was made to us in having such patterns, and we became indefatigable in adorning it—thinking only with a certain secret horror of the serious thing, the following of Christ.

No, not quite thus may we be allowed to do, that would be making the Gospel so easy that substantially it would become (what precisely the following of Christ was calculated to hinder) —poetry.

For doubtless the lilies and the birds may be said only to serve one master, but that after all is merely figuratively said, and the obligation of man to 'follow after' them is poetically expressed, as also the lilies and the birds regarded as teachers are without authority. Moreover, if a man, with the lilies and the birds as a pattern, were to live as has been described above, so that he thought thoughts of God in and along with everything, this certainly is piety, and a piety which in a perfectly pure form has certainly never been seen among men. But in the strictest sense it is not yet Christianity, it is properly Jewish piety. What is decisive for Christianity is not at all evinced here, the notion of suffering because one adheres to God, or, as we say, suffering for the doctrine, which properly is the following of Christ.

Alas, yes, it is as if it were entirely forgotten in Christendom what Christianity is. When one would portray it even with only tolerable fidelity, it is likely that people will imagine that it is a cruelty, a torture of mankind, which he has invented—to such a degree does suffering for the Word or for the doctrine accompany Christianity meticulously, that when a person merely depicts it with a tolerable approach to truth, he will draw down upon himself human disfavour. And, as has been said, in spite of the millions of copies of the New Testament which are in circulation and in spite of the fact that everybody possesses the New Testament, is baptized, confirmed, calls himself a Christian, and in spite of the fact that a thousand parsons are preaching every blessed Sunday—for all that it is not unlikely people will say the thing is this man's own invention, when quite simply he draws from the New Testament that which is distinctly enough written there, and in clear words, but which we men, from generation to generation, have jettisoned in the most free-and-easy way, without consistently admitting that what we have retained is anything but the pure, sound, unadulterated doctrine.

'Imitation', 'the following of Christ', this precisely is the point where the human race winces, here it is principally that the difficulty lies, here is where the question really is decided whether one will accept Christianity or not. If pressure is brought to bear at this point, and a strong pressure—in that same degree there are few Christians. If at this point a convenient accommodation is made (so that Christianity becomes, intellectually, a doctrine), many enter into Christianity. If it is done away with entirely (so that Christianity becomes, existentially, as easy as mythology and poetry, while imitation is exaggeration, a ludicrous exaggeration), then Christianity widens out to such a degree that Christendom and the world almost correspond, or all become Christians, then Christianity has triumphed completely—in other words, it is done away with.

Ah, if only attention had been given to this in due time, the situation in Christendom would be very different from what it now is. But since human assertiveness became more and more menacing in refusing to hear anything of this nonsense about imitation; since mercenaries and thralls or at least very weak believers took upon themselves to be preachers of the Word—then the history of Christendom, from generation to generation, became a steady reduction in the price of what it is to be a Christian. Until at last it became such an absurdly low price that soon the opposite effect was produced, that men hardly wanted to have anything to do with Christianity, because as a result of that untrue mildness it had become so mawkish that it disgusted people. To be a Christian—well, if only one does not literally steal, does not literally make thieving one's business;

for to be a thief in one's business can well be combined with being a serious Christian who takes the communion once a year, and a couple of times a year, or definitely on New Year's Day, goes to church. To be a Christian—well, if in committing fornication one does not exaggerate, or deserting the golden mean go to extremes; for cautiously, with decorum, i.e. secretly, with taste and refinement, that still can well enough be combined with being a serious Christian who at least hears one sermon for every fourteen comedies and romances he reads. And that there might be anything to prevent a person who is altogether conformed to this world and by every shrewd device seeks to assure himself of the greatest possible earthly advantages and pleasures, &c.— that there might be anything to prevent him from thinking that this could perfectly well be combined with being a serious Christian—that would be a ludicrous exaggeration, an impertinence if anyone who would enjoin such a thing upon us, and boundless foolishness on the part of him who risked this venture, since there was not a single person who would reflect . . . upon what is written in the New Testament or that it is written there. This is a cheap edition of what it is to be a Christian, yet it is the actual status; for that preachers declaim on Sundays during a quiet hour about the higher virtues, &c., does not alter the actual status on Mondays, since people explain such preaching by the fact that it is the parson's official job and his living, and since the lives of many parsons are not different from that actual status— but properly it is the existence which preaches, the preaching with mouth and arms is of no avail.

However, there also were those who held Christianity at a higher price, but never higher than about up to that quiet piety, which under the lenient régime of grace thinks often about God, expects every good thing from His fatherly hand, seeks comfort from Him in life's need.

'To suffer for the doctrine', following Christ—that is entirely abolished, consigned long, long ago to oblivion. Inasmuch as in the sermon one cannot very well entirely avoid saying something about the following of Christ (although some have known how to manage it in such a way it can be done), one does it by suppressing the really decisive thing and substituting for it something different: that one ought to endure the adversities of life with patience, &c.

But the following of Christ is abolished. Established Christendom, if only for laughter it could listen, would doubtless fall into the profoundest amazement if it were to hear that this is the doctrine of the New Testament (and in accordance with the New Testament, of all true Christians), that it is the part of the true Christian to suffer for the doctrine. To suffer for the doctrine—in such a measure only to serve one master, in such a way to follow the Pattern that one suffers for being a Christian! To suffer for the doctrine—'No, no,' Christendom would doubtless say, 'I believe now that the man has gone clean out of his mind; to require that one must suffer for the doctrine—to become addicted to Christ in such a measure is then far worse than becoming addicted to gambling, drink, or adultery. It is all well enough, as the parsons preach, that Christianity is a gentle consolation, a sort of assurance for eternity, it's all right, that is a thing a man may be willing to give his money for—and perhaps it is paid for pretty dearly with the high tithes now exacted, so that in this respect we might be said to suffer for the doctrine. But to be obliged to pay to have *this* preached, that one must suffer for the doctrine! The man is stark mad.' And yet the blame is not his; the 'stark madness' really is that in preaching Christianity they have left out and suppressed what does not please the worldly and earthly mind, and so have prompted all this worldliness to imagine that it is Christianity.

Oh, if they had held tenaciously to this point, to the following of Christ! If, instructed by the errors of earlier ages, they had truly held to this point! This did not come to pass. So it must come to pass. 'Imitation', which answers to Christ as the Pattern, must (if Christendom is to make sense) be again introduced, but (as I have hinted) in such a way as to show that we have learnt something from the error of earlier ages.

Without introducing 'imitation' it is impossible to get the better of doubters. Hence it is that the situation in Christendom is what it is, that doubt is posited instead of faith. And then they want to arrest doubt . . . by reasons; and in this course they are not yet arrested, they have not yet learnt that it is wasted effort, indeed that it is to nourish doubt to give it a reason for persisting; they have not yet become awake to the fact that 'imitation' is the only force which, like the police force, is able to scatter the disorderly mob of doubt, and to give it a will and a compulsion, if one would not be a 'follower', at least to go home and keep one's mouth shut.

'Imitation', which answers to 'Christ as the Pattern', must be brought to the fore, applied, recalled to remembrance.

Let us take up the matter fundamentally, yet with all brevity. The Saviour of the world, our Lord Jesus Christ, did not come to the world to bring a doctrine; He never lectured. Since He did not bring a doctrine, neither did He seek to prevail upon anyone by reasons to accept the doctrine, nor seek with proofs to substantiate it. His teaching in fact was His life, His presence among men. If anyone desired to be His disciple, His way of going about it, as can be seen from the Gospel, was quite another way than the method of lecturing. He said to such a man something like this: 'Adventure a decisive action, then we can begin.' What does that mean? It means that one does not become a Christian by hearing something about Christ, by reading something, by thinking thereupon, or while Christ still lived upon earth, by seeing Him once in a while, or by going and gaping at Him the whole day. No, what is required is a *predicament* (*situation*):[1] adventure upon a decisive action, so that thou dost become heterogeneous with the life of this world, unable any longer to have thy life in it, dost find thyself in conflict with it—then thou wilt gradually be brought into such a tension that thou wilt be able to be observant of what I am here saying (says Christ). Perhaps also the tension will so affect thee that thou wilt understand that thou canst not support it without having recourse to Me, and so we can begin. Could one expect anything else of 'the Truth'? Must it not give expression to the fact that it is the taught who needs the teacher, 'the sick man who needs the physician'? Not inversely, as Christianity was preached in a later age, that it is the physician who 'needs the patients', the teacher who needs the pupils, and therefore, as a matter of course (like any other salesman, who surely does not require that the highly esteemed public should buy a pig in a poke), must be at your service with reasons,

[1] By the use of a strange word, which I find in no dictionary, and which S. K. parenthetically interpreted by 'situation', he means to indicate such a 'decisive action' as he himself had in mind and was about to perform—it expresses in a new way his constant thought of the necessity of 'venturing far out . . . where God can get hold of one'. 'Decisive action' is a luminous commentary upon many a passage in the Gospels where we have the response of Christ to a man who proposes to be a disciple.

proofs, recommendations from others who have been cured or instructed, &c. But the divine truth! Yet the fact that it behaves differently is not to be attributed to what one might call divine pride of superiority. Oh, no, in this respect the Saviour of the world was doubtless willing, as in all other ways, to humiliate Himself; but it cannot be otherwise.

We will not linger upon the way in which Christianity gradually spread abroad in the world; we hasten on to a definite point which is decisive for the situation in present-day Christendom.

We halt for a moment at the Middle Ages. However great its errors may have been, its conception of Christianity has a decisive superiority over that of our time. The Middle Ages conceived of Christianity with a view to action, life, the transformation of personal existence. This is its valuable side. It is another matter that there were some singular actions they especially emphasized, that they could think that fasting for its own sake was Christianity, and so too going into a monastery, bestowing everything upon the poor, not to speak of what we can hardly refer to without smiling, such as flagellation, crawling on the knees, standing upon one leg, &c., as if this were the true imitation of Christ. This was error. And as is the case when one has turned into the wrong path and pursues it steadily, one gets farther and farther from the true way, deeper and deeper into error, the situation becoming worse and worse—so it was here. What was worse than the first error did not fail to make its appearance, that they got the idea of meritoriousness, thought that they acquired merit before God by their good works. And the situation became worse than this: they even thought that by good works one might acquire merit to such a degree that it accrued not only to his advantage, but that like a capitalist or bondsman one might let it accrue to the advantage of others. And it became worse, it became a regular business: men who had never once thought of producing any of these so-called good works now got a complete assortment to deal with, being active as shopkeepers in selling for money the good works of others at a fixed but moderate price.

Then Luther came forward. 'This situation', said he, is spiritual apathy. It is a dreadful apathy; otherwise you who by good works think to merit the blessedness of heaven must perceive that this is the sure path, either to *presumptuousness* (and with this the forfeiture of blessedness), or to *despair* (and with this the forfeiture of blessedness). For to wish to build upon good works—the more thou dost practise them, and the stricter thou art with thyself, the more dost thou develop in thyself simply anguish of dread, and ever new dread. On that path—if a man is not entirely spiritless, on that path he attains exactly the opposite of quiet and rest for his soul, he attains disquietude and unrest. No, a man is justified only by faith. And therefore, in God's name, to hell with the Pope and all his auxiliary assistants, along with all your fasting, flagellation, and all the monkey-shines which are resorted to under the name of 'following'.

But let us not forget that for all this Luther did not do away with the following of Christ, nor with the voluntary imitation, as the effeminate coterie is so fain to make us believe. He applied imitation in connexion with witnessing for truth, and (without imagining, however, that it was meritorious) in this respect he voluntarily exposed himself to dangers enough. In fact, it was not the Pope who attacked Luther, but Luther who attacked the Pope; and Luther's life, although he was not put to death, was nevertheless a sacrificed life, a life sacrificed to witnessing for truth.

Present-day Christendom (that at least of which I am talking) attaches itself to Luther; it is another question whether Luther could subscribe to it, whether the turn which Luther took may not only too easily lead into a wrong path when Luther is not at hand to make truth of the true turn he took. At all events, if any-one would perceive what may be questionable in the present situation, the best way doubtless is to look back to Luther and the turn he took.

The erroneous path from which Luther turned off was exaggeration with respect to works. And quite rightly, he was not at fault: a man is justified solely and only by faith. So he talked and taught ... and believed. And this was not taking grace in vain, his whole life was testimony to this. So far so good.

But already the next generation slackened; it did not turn in horror from exaggeration in respect to works (of which Luther had had personal experience) into the path of faith. No, they transformed the Lutheran passion into a doctrine, and with this they diminished also the vital power of faith. In this way it was diminished from generation to generation. Works—well, God knows that there was no question any more about them, it would be a crime to accuse this later age of exaggeration with respect to works, and people were not so silly as to presume to claim merit for what they exempted themselves from doing. But then as to faith—is it to be found upon earth?

What Christ required as a condition for reaching the situation where there can be any question of becoming a Christian was a decisive action—there is now no longer any need of that. One's life is essentially homogeneous with worldliness and with this world, and so one hears perhaps a little about Christianity, one reads a little, thinks a little about Christianity, has once in a while a religious mood—and so one is a believer and a Christian. Indeed, one is already a Christian beforehand: one is born as a Christian, drolly enough, and what makes it still more droll, one is born as a Lutheran. That undeniably is a very precarious way of becoming a believer and a Christian; it has very little likeness to the experience of Luther—the experience of horror, when through a course of years he had tortured himself in a monastery without finding rest for his soul or rest from this horror, then in the end to find escape by the blessed path of faith, so that it is no wonder that this much tried man witnessed so strongly against building one's blessedness upon works, not witnessing against works—it was only the sly world which thus misinterpreted him.

But when they had done away with the notion of becoming a Christian by means of a decisive action capable of bringing about the predicament (situation) in which it is decided whether one will be a Christian or not, then (for the sake at least of doing something) they put in its stead the notion of thinking about Christianity, supposing they would become Christians in this way, and intending to advance subsequently beyond faith;[1] for they did not stop at faith—and this is not to be wondered at, for they did not start out like Luther from exaggeration with respect to works and then attain faith, but they began as a matter of course with faith, which 'naturally' every man has. If one would call medieval Christianity the monastic-ascetic type, one might call the Christianity of our age the professor-scientific type. Not all, it is true, could become professors; but nevertheless all acquired a certain professorial and scientific cast of mind. And just as in the first period not all could become martyrs, but all stood in

[1] Hegel and the Hegelian theologians regarded the simple data of faith as inadequate apprehensions of reality which the philosopher and the professor must transcend. Against this going beyond faith S. K. constantly protested.

relationship with the martyrs; and as in the Middle Ages all did not enter the monastery, but all stood in relationship with the monastery and regarded the man who entered the monastery as the genuine Christian—so in our time all stand in relationship with the professor, the professor is the genuine Christian. And with the professor came scientific learning, and with learning came doubters, and with learning and doubters came the scientifically learned public, and then came reasons *pro* and *contra*, and people were swayed *pro* and *contra*, 'for *pro* and *contra* in this case much can well be said'.

The professor! This personage is not once mentioned in the New Testament—from which we can perceive first of all that Christianity came into the world without 'professors'. For the professor changes the whole point of view of Christianity.

And therefore imitation must be introduced. To the professor corresponds Christianity as objective teaching, as mere doctrine.* Thus by means of doubt or by means of reasons this conception of Christianity plays victory into the hands of doubt, and transforms (what Christianity most decisively counts the most decisive thing) decision into postponement from a day to a week, to a month, to a year, to a lifetime. When the 'professor' stands at his apogee and Christendom sees itself in the professor, as once it saw itself in the monastery, the situation in Christendom will be this: Christianity properly does not exist, *adhuc sub judice lis est*,[1] one awaits the result as to what Christianity is or what is Christianity. Faith does not exist, what exists is at the most a mood which fluctuates between remembering Christianity as a thing already vanished, and expecting it as a thing to come. Imitation is an impossibility, for when everything has been put in suspense, it is

---

* It is true that in better times there was in parts some Christian learning; but the individual (the exception) who occupied himself with this scientific learning had the Christian sobriety (expressive of the fact that for him it was decided that he would be a Christian, and that for him the decisive thing was to be a Christian) to live himself as an ascetic, thus expressing far, far more strongly by his life that Christianity is all the same something entirely different from a science, like mathematics, &c., which is indifferent to personality, and that the very, very last way for Christianity to be brought to its apogee is when in homogeneity with this world, by worldly successful docents, it is lectured upon as an objective science, or when with constantly more and more learning, the decision to become a Christian, or to become a Christian otherwise than by 'protestations', is put off, because one is constantly expecting . . . a result from the part of science.

[1] The case is still on trial.

impossible for one to make a beginning with anything decisive, but one's existence drifts as it were with the current, and one employs one's natural self-love to make life as comfortable for oneself as possible. The 'professor' can make nothing fast;[1] the one thing he can do is to put everything in suspense. Sometimes it looks as if what the professor asserts is the most reliable certainty. That, however, is a deception, due rather to his serious mien and protestations, whereas more closely examined even his most secure position is yet within the sphere of scientific doubt and therefore in suspense. Only imitation is capable of making the end fast; but just as the king turned pale when an invisible hand wrote upon the wall, 'Thou art weighed and found too light'; so the professor turns pale before imitation—that also says, 'Thou, with all the weight of thy objective learning, thy folios and systems, art weighed and found too light.' What wonder indeed, for in a Christian sense it is precisely objective learning which weighs least of all in the scales.—When the monastery is the misleading thing, faith must be introduced; when the 'professor' is the misleading thing, imitation must be introduced.

Imitation must be brought to mind, but (as was previously remarked) in such a way that we have evidently learnt something from the errors of past times.

The mildest way to introduce it is . . . in the form of possibility, or (as one might say) dialectically, that is, in such a way that it merely exerts pressure to bring doubt to silence and administer a little justice upon existences. Thus it works quite simply (as I have indicated in a previous book): only he is allowed to advance doubts whose life bears the impress of imitation, or he who at least by a decisive action has got so far out that there could be a question of his becoming a Christian. Everyone else has to hold his tongue, he has no right to take part in speaking about Christianity, least of all *contra*.

This is the mildest way in which imitation can be introduced; it is only the 'professor' that is shaken off, the assumption of scholarly importance that is repulsed; for the rest, everybody is leniently treated who will relate himself beseemingly to Christianity,

---

[1] It appears in the sequel that S. K. has here the analogy in mind which he often makes use of, namely, that in sewing, the end of the thread must first be secured by a knot. In the end he attached to this analogy the tragic thought that the only effective way to make the thread fast is for a man to die as a witness for the truth.

however far behind he may be, however, far from being able to be called a follower of Christ, he is leniently treated, and nobody (this at least ought to be a lesson learnt from a vanished age) is pressed by fear to the point of venturing perhaps beyond his strength—under grace one draws breath freely and frankly. In case anyone would in the strictest sense be an 'imitator'—if that is truth, I will discreetly make place for him and also bow before him. But as the situation now is in Christendom, as I am, who am no better than the others, my notion is that the proposal I have made will already be something won. And I for my part have a dread of this high ideal: in the strictest sense to suffer for the doctrine, to be an imitator, whereas I make no concealment of the fact that this is the requirement of Christianity. But I have a dread—oh, for with this the notion of meritoriousness may so easily come back again; and this is what I am most afraid of. When one arranges one's life as comfortably and enjoyably as possible, and never in the remotest way thinks of sacrificing anything or of renouncing anything which one can get—then it is easy enough to keep clear of the notion of meritoriousness. But truly when a man sacrifices something or much, and then in the daily suffering which was his reward he must drink what humanly speaking is the bitterness of being so rewarded—oh, it may so easily happen to a man in a weak moment of forgetfulness to think that he has merits before God, that he (to speak figuratively, but by a figure which only weakly expresses what I mean), that he as a subject in the presence of the King forgets himself and lays his hand upon his sword. Ah, that is, humanly speaking, only too easy to understand. Frightful danger! I agree entirely with Luther (whether he actually expressed himself in these words or not), that a man who countless times, if that were possible, every blessed day and throughout a whole life, had been guilty of the most dreadful crimes . . . and yet has the comfort left to him of saying to God, 'O God be merciful to me a sinner'; that he may count himself indescribably happy in comparison with him who in the greatest possible self-denial, making every possible sacrifice for the truth throughout a long life . . . a single instant was in error and thought that he had merit before God. Oh, what a terrible curse a man may bring down upon himself, venturing to sacrifice everything, to suffer everything—and then that this should become for him the most frightful torment by reason of presumptuousness before God. This is my belief. There are moments when I do not think that one can acquit Luther of a certain melancholy; but nevertheless I entirely agree with him. And therefore I do not venture to introduce imitation further than as a pressing possibility, which is able to repress doubt into silence and exert pressure in the direction of humility. This is a mild accommodation, I admit; I do not intend to go about modifying Christianity secretively. No, I announce with all possible solemnity that I do it. Some have, even according to my mild conception, illicitly modified Christianity. It is not against this I protest; but they have done it as secretly as possible, they have said to themselves, 'Tut, nobody will observe it.' This, to my mind, is revolting. Of whom might I be afraid? Of men? Them I fear not and ought not to fear. Of God? But what is the use? However secretly I do it, He sees it nevertheless; and what perhaps He does not forgive me is just this, that I keep it secret.

Imitation must be introduced, to exert pressure in the direction of humility. It is to be done quite simply in this way: everyone must be measured by the Pattern, the ideal. We must get rid of all the bosh about this being said only to the Apostles, and this only to the disciples, and this only to the first Christians, &c. Christ no more desires now than He did then to have admirers (not to say twaddlers), He wants only disciples. The 'disciple' is the standard: imitation and Christ as the Pattern must be introduced. That as a consequence I am plucked or barely pass is a thing I can humbly put up with. But I and every man shall be measured by the ideal, in accordance with the ideal it shall be determined where I am. It shall not—oh, God be praised that it shall not—(for it is but a sorry and pitiful short-sightedness to sell one's lofty dignity, i.e. to take to the ideal the attitude of the pass-man, in order to gain the imaginary satisfaction of mediocrity by comparison with others, a short-sightedness like that of Essau when he sold his birthright for a dish of lentils), it shall not be so that we men are permitted to abrogate the ideal requirement, saying that the thing is not for us, and then to hunt up a certain mediocrity, and then begin there and make that the standard, and then perhaps become distinguished . . . merely because the standard has been altered to suit us.

Let me illustrate what I mean by a picture. Take a school, suppose that there is, as we can imagine, a class of 100 pupils of equal age who have to learn the same thing and are graded by the same standard. To be from No. 70 down is to stand very low in the class. What then if the thirty pupils from No. 70 down got the notion that they might be allowed to form a class to themselves? If so, then No. 70 would accordingly become No. 1 in the class. That would be to get up higher. Yes, if one likes to put it so; but according to my conceptions it would be to go still lower down, to sink down in pitiable, mendacious contentment; for to be truly willing to put up with being No. 70 according to a real standard is to be nevertheless much higher up. So it is in real life. What is it to be *bourgeois*? What is spiritual apathy? It means to have the standard changed by leaving out the ideals, it means to have the standard changed to correspond with what we men who now live in this place actually are. The whole of Europe may be *bourgeois*, and a little out of the way provincial town may not be. All depends upon whether the true standard is used. But sensual well-being is no friend of the ideal standard.

Here we see why things have gone backward in Christendom. It is because they have abolished imitation, and not even employed it to exert pressure—this being the exact reverse of the Babylonian revolt against heaven at the Tower of Bebel, the exact reverse, for that (very far preferable in spite of denial) was a rebellious attempt to take heaven by storm, the other is an attempt to get rid of heaven and the ideals by a disclaimer made in self-conceit and self-contentment. Let us imagine a Christian city. Christianly understood, the standard is the disciple, the follower. On the other hand, there is, e.g., Pastor Jensen. He is a talented, shrewd man, and there is much to be said in his favour. So let us make him No. 1 and regulate ourselves by his example; that is a sensible thing, for thus one may become something in the world. 'Yes, but according to the ideal standard Mr. Jensen (to recall that picture) is only No. 70 in the class.'—'Pshaw! A fig for the ideals! If we have to have them with us, nobody can want to live.'—And what is Mr. Jensen's view? His view is (and thereby we recognize that he is not even No. 70), his view is that he can aptly serve as the standard and model, that these exorbitant requirements are fantastical. And thus they play in the city the game of Christianity: Pastor Jensen, a society man, as if created expressly for this social sport, becomes the genuine Christian in the game, even an

Apostle, is acclaimed in the newspapers as an Apostle, in the capacity of an Apostle (capital!) is overwhelmed with all the comforts of life, which also (in the capacity of an Apostle?) he well knows how to appreciate.

Here we see how *bourgeois* a thing it is to accommodate oneself in self-styled Christianity in such a way as to abolish Christianity. What the requirement of Christianity is is not a fixed thing, it depends upon what sort of people one lives amongst. Instead of imitation, what one really gets is the notion of being what people for the most part are, and to be a little better is to be great. But when the price of becoming a Christian is so cheap, then comes idleness, and then comes doubt, and then the real truth comes to evidence, that one cannot conceive why Christianity need be. And that is perfectly true; for if the requirement is no greater, then a saviour, a redeemer, grace, &c., become fantastic luxuries, and in so far as one does not let go of Christianity but continues to make movements in terms of it, one becomes as ridiculous as a child who wears his father's clothes. What Christianity pre-supposes, namely, the tortures of a contrite conscience, the need of grace, the deeply felt need, all these frightful inward conflicts and sufferings—what Christianity presupposes in order to intro-duce and apply grace, salvation, the hope of eternal blessedness—all this is not to be found, or is to be found only in burlesque abridgement—at bottom it is sheer superfluity which at the most one imagines the need of. And so in the end one becomes tired of Christianity; for the pressure of imitation was lacking, the ideal, Christ as Pattern.

To suffer for the doctrine, to *will* to suffer for the doctrine, not incidentally to suffer for it by chance—well, that kind of Christianity has gone out of use. The next kind of Christianity (where in any case there is no question of the decisive criterion of suffering for the doctrine) is perhaps hardly any more to be found: a Christianity where the psychic states which Christianity pre-supposes are, as one says of a disease, recognized by their symp-toms, the characteristic symptoms of an anguishing conflict of conscience, fear and trembling, and in addition to this the shock received from Christianity, profound and perilous, the apprehen-sion that Christianity is to the Jews a stumbling-block and to the Greeks foolishness—also this kind of Christianity is hardly any more to be found or at least very seldom in our time, and in any case there is no question here of suffering for the doctrine. It is hardly to be found, and how could it be in our time when the whole mode of life is calculated to prevent the mind from acquiring the contemplative inwardness which makes it possible for such psychic states to assume character? In our time (this is truth, and it is significant for the Christianity of our time), in our time it is the physician who exercises the cure of souls. People have perhaps an unfounded dread of calling in the parson, who, however, in our time would talk possibly pretty much like the physician. So they call in the physician. And he knows what to do: 'You must travel to a watering-place, and then must keep a riding-horse, for it is possible to ride away from bees in the bonnet, and then diversion, diversion, plenty of diversion, you must ensure yourself of having every evening a cheerful game of poker,[1] on the other hand you should not eat much in the evening directly before going to bed, and finally see that the bedroom is well aired—this will surely help.'—'To relieve an anxious conscience?'—'Bosh! Get out with that stuff! An anxious conscience! No such thing exists any more, it is a reminiscence of the childhood of the race. There is no enlightened and cultivated parson who would think of coming out with such a thing—I mean to say, outside the Sunday service, which is a different matter. No, let us never begin here with an anxious conscience, for thus we might soon turn the whole house into a madhouse. I am so minded that if I had in my employ a servant, however excellent in other respects, whom I should be loath to lose and should greatly miss—if I observed that he or she was meddling with the experience of an anxious conscience, I would give unconditional notice to quit my service. That would be the last thing I would tolerate in my house. If it were my own child, he would have to seek other quarters.'—'But, Doctor, this is an awfully anxious dread you have of a thing which you say does not exist, "an anxious conscience"; one might almost think that it is a revenge upon you for wanting to do away with anguish of conscience— this anxious dread of yours is indeed like a revenge!'—And the next kind of Christianity (where in any case there is no question of suffering for the doctrine) is found perhaps rather rarely: a quieter enjoyment of life, observing the requirements of civil righteousness, thinking withal often of God, so that the thought

[1] Literally, the Spanish game of 'ombre', which was still played in S. K.'s time.

of Him is brought in a little along with other things; but without ever having experienced deeply the shock of collision with Christianity, without really observing that Christianity is to the Jew in me a stumbling-block and to the Greek in me is foolishness; and in any case there is no question of suffering for the doctrine.—The common kind of Christianity is: a thoroughly worldly life, avoiding great crimes rather for prudence than for conscience' sake, artfully seeking life's pleasures—and then once in a while a so-called pious mood. This is Christianity . . . in the same sense that a bit of nausea and a slight belly-ache is cholera. 'One may call it cholera any way.' Yes, one may perfectly well do so, and for the sake of precision one may call it Danish, or still more precisely Copenhagen, or still more precisely Christianhaven cholera—and so one may also call this Christianity. That is to say, we off here on the mountain are agreed, or perhaps a single street is agreed, that this is Christianity—and so it is Christianity. What wonder then that people have lost respect for Christianity and the taste for it. For Christianity may, falsely, be made so severe that human nature must revolt against it, rejecting it or repelling it. But it may also be made so lenient or so concocted with sweets that all the efforts that are made to stimulate the appetite and give men a taste for it by proofs and reasons are unavailing, and the thing must end with their being disgusted with it. No, there must be salt in the food. And verily that is provided for in the New Testament. The glad tidings are not to be palmed off upon men by means of proofs and reasons— ignominiously, as when a mother must sit and beg the child to eat the wholesome and excellent food, while it turns up its nose at it and doesn't want to eat. No, the appetite is to be awakened in a different way—and then one will indeed find the glad tidings savoury.

To *suffer* for the doctrine. It is this which changes everything endlessly with respect to becoming or being a Christian, this which imposes endless weight. Or if Christ had preached that kind of Christianity which the parsons preach nowadays, how explain the concern He felt for the disciples and the concern they gave Him, those honest stout-hearted men who verily were willing enough to give up everything in order to take hold and hold fast? But here it was a question of 'following' in the strictest sense. Christ Himself knew that, humanly speaking, He must make these men as unhappy and miserable as a man can be, 'of all men most miserable'—if they were to belong to Him. And not this only, but that He must require them to maintain nevertheless that it was an elect privilege accorded to them, a proof of God's exceeding and especial love towards them. Oh, horror! That this which should be glad tidings, comfort, joy—that it is this which, humanly speaking, makes me of all men most miserable . . . a fate which I can easily avoid by having nothing to do with it! And that in addition to this the requirement is not merely that I shall bear this patiently, but that I shall find joy and blessedness in it—as if one were to require of a man who must endure a bodily torment, not merely that he shall restrain himself from screaming, but that he shall so triumph over himself and the pain that in beholding him it would look as if it were a delight, though the experience was in reality terrible to him and not a clever deceit! Note therefore in Christ's speech with His disciples the thing that again and again was repeated: 'Be not offended in Me; doth this offend you? blessed is he who shall not be offended in Me; these things I have told you beforehand that ye should not be offended; watch and pray, remember what I have said unto you, that when the hour is come ye may not be offended! Ah, it is so narrow and so small a way, and I cannot help you directly. Oh, every moment offence lieth so near, the possibility of offence follows every step! You may come to such a pass that patience is exhausted, faith shattered, and ye revolt against Me—blessed is he who is not offended! And although ye patiently support every suffering—in case your patience is only silent submission, at bottom ye are offended in Me—blessed is he who is not offended in me.' Take a human relationship. Let a lover say to his beloved, 'My dear girl, I give thee thy freedom, we must part; to belong to me would signify (as I can tell thee with certainty beforehand) that thou, humanly speaking, wouldst become as unhappy as possible.' Let us suppose that she replied, 'I will endure everything, for only then am I unhappy when I am parted from thee.'[1] Let us go farther, let us suppose that he replied, 'Very well, but I must require one thing more if thou art to remain with me, that thou must maintain that to be thus unhappy with me is nevertheless the highest happiness.' What then? Would not the girl be fully justified in saying, 'This is madness'? Yes indeed, and if she will not say it, I will say in her behalf,

---

[1] Up to this point the passage reports exactly S. K.'s experience with Regina.

'If such a situation arises in the relationship between human beings, it is madness; and I could wish for nothing better than to have leave to thrash this madness or this badness out of the guilty man.' For as there are kinds of possession which can only be driven out by prayer and much fasting, there is also madness which is only incurred by one's own guilt. But in the relationship between the God-Man and a human being the situation *cannot* be other than this—blessed is he who is not offended!

To *suffer* for the doctrine. 'But there can be no question of that in these times when Christianity has fully triumphed and all are Christians.' I could be tempted to say, 'Woe, woe unto thee, thou hypocrite!' But that I will not do. I prefer to say, 'My good man, you do not yourself believe what you say, you know very well that it is falsehood, and why then such talk, why would you be like the man who stands in full view of everybody with a white stick in his mouth and believes he is invisible?' No, the requirement of suffering for the doctrine is at this instant just as much in force and just as applicable as it was at the beginning. The thing is perfectly simple. Every man who carries out a true act of self-sacrifice will have to suffer for it. If this were not so, true self-denial would be an impossibility; for the self-denial which is rewarded in outward ways is not true self-denial. So Governance takes loving care that if there is an honest man who would deny himself, this may accordingly become true self-denial. On the other hand, false self-denial is to be recognized in the fact that in the first instance it looks like self-denial, but in another way it outwardly pays for itself, and so at bottom is shrewd calculation.

Let us take an example of true self-denial—let it be Luther. He was sternly trained to be able to express that kind of piety which in the Middle Ages was *honoured* and *esteemed* under the name of self-denial—and for this reason was therefore not true self-denial. And it was precisely against this kind of piety Luther inveighed. Now it is possible to think that he had chosen to be, e.g., a highly placed clergyman in order to be rewarded in this way for his self-denial. In such a case it again would not have been true self-denial. But honest Luther saw aright. He bore witness against what the age regarded as true self-denial, he cut himself off from the opportunity of profiting by it, perhaps Governance also helped him in this respect—and here we have true self-denial.

Let such an action take place before us so that we can see exactly how it goes. Thus there is a fairly honest man who feels impelled to bear witness in one way or another for truth against falsehood which is in power just because it is regarded as the truth. He himself understands that this is a danger, but he is willing to expose himself to it. And yet perhaps he has not understood himself entirely. On the other hand, he is entirely convinced of the truth of what he wants to bring out; he is convinced of it to such a degree that (oh, human heart!) he is involuntarily compelled to think that when it is heard it must triumph, must win men. So he speaks it out—but strangely enough he encounters only opposition everywhere, in every way he reaps nothing but ingratitude, not only from those from whom he had expected it, but also from those for whose sake he had thought he ought to bear witness to truth—just as, for example, Moses had his troubles not only with the Egyptians but also from the Jews for whose sake he had exposed himself to all the trials and dangers. Now this man becomes troubled, the experience affects him deeply. So, naturally, he turns for succour thither where he is accustomed to seek it, with Governance. He recounts his distress. What will Governance say in reply? Loving and gentle as Governance always is, it replies, 'My little friend, this in fact is what thou didst desire, thou wouldst practice self-denial, canst thou deny that thou hast got what thou didst bargain for? Here precisely is thine opportunity to practice self-denial.' Let us suppose that he replies, 'Yes, that I understand, now I understand it, but to be frank, I did not quite understand it thus when I decided to act and began it. I feel as if the sea were becoming too high for me.' What will Governance answer? Loving and gentle as it always is, never cruel, it says, 'Yes, yes, my little friend, yet we shall help thee out of this again when thou has humbled thyself under it and learnt humility from this little lesson.' But something else might also come to pass. While Governance makes it clear to the struggler what the situation is, that it belongs precisely to true self-denial, he undergoes a transformation—like the wonder of the child when it suddenly understands, like the blissful wonder of the loving maiden when that which she thought a witness against her being loved she suddenly understands as a witness for it—so too he is lost in wonder. 'For', says he, 'that which I suffered, or that which pained me, was really the fact that in this opposition I saw the proof that I had done the thing badly. But now that thou, loving Governance, dost declare the situation to me and dost declare thyself for me—ah, I desire only to remain apart from all in good understanding with thee.'[1] So here we have an example of true self-denial, which always involves suffering for the good one does. And as it held good 1,800 years ago, so it holds good this year and for 1,800 years to come, that he who inaugurates in this world a good work of self-denial has to suffer for it. But the Christian who does not do this has in one way or another spared himself, shirked his duty, &c. So this he must admit. This I do. But I will neither prate nor dissemble in the pulpit; if I have not attained to suffering for the doctrine, if I never attain it—I admit that this is attributable to me and to my worldly shrewdness. Then, moreover (just as suspected characters have to report themselves to the police bureau), I have to report myself in the presence of Governance concerning this irregularity in my standing as a Christian. Governance will still be willing to deal with me, sheer love and grace and compassion that it is; but it requires that I shall be honest with it.

Christ is the Pattern, and to this corresponds imitation. There is only one true way of being a Christian—to be a disciple. The 'disciple' has this mark among others, that he suffers for the doctrine. Everyone who has not suffered for the doctrine has in one way or another been guilty of using his shrewdness to spare himself. That for this reason he might not dare to call himself a Christian, or that he shall not become blessed, is far from my meaning, God forbid that I should venture to say what would convict me worse than anybody else. But he has to make an admission. And in so far as he is one of those who have undertaken to preach Christianity, he has to consider that by sparing himself he has weakened the impression of Christianity, which has become less recognizable for others, and contributed to confuse the point of view for Christianity. For Christianity did not come into the world in such wise that it was worldly shrewdness and human whimper which meant to win many by abating the price—that is progress in number but retrogression in truth. No, the unconditional (as everybody can understand) cannot come

---

[1] This account of the experience of 'a fairly honest man' is autobiographical in the strictest sense. S. K. has in mind his experience in the 'affair of the *Corsair*'.

in by means of abating the price, for if there is abatement, it is not the unconditional. On the other hand, by abating the price the unconditional is extruded from the world, or (what amounts to the same thing) it so spreads out that it coincides with the conditional.

To suffer for the doctrine, that is done away with. One therefore cannot defend the situation in 'Christendom' by saying, 'There is much imperfection among us, naturally, many weak brethren, many whose Christianity is merely an approximation, even a weak approximation to Christianity, a lot of cockles amongst the wheat.' For then I may ask the speaker, 'Art thou then wheat?' And at all events I dare to say that he who speaks thus is no more a true Christian than I am. Perhaps one will say, 'He is less.' That I will not say. What is the use of such petty human wrangling? But I will say that he is not any more of a Christian, and that I will maintain stubbornly. But then it is confusing to talk in that way: 'there are many among us whose Christianity is merely an approximation'—as if the man who talks thus, and in general the Christianity of 'Christendom', were the true Christianity. That I deny; yet not as though I thought I was the true Christian in contrast with the others. No, as I have said in the book immediately preceding this, 'I belong to the average among us.' I say therefore also (I have indicated it in an earlier book) that my Christianity is not the true Christianity, it is an approximation. Perhaps there are many in this case whose Christianity is an approximation. One ought, however, to be a little careful about this term 'approximation', so as not to extend it so far as to include him whose (shall we say?) Christianity is departure from Christianity. It is so easy to make a mistake when on passing a man along the road to the city one does not notice whether he is going to or from the city.

By construing Christianity as doctrine the situation in Christendom has become sheer confusion, and the definition of what it is to be a Christian has been rendered almost unrecognizable. So Christ as Pattern must be brought to the fore, but not to inspire dread—yet perhaps it is entirely superfluous to be anxious lest one nowadays might be able to alarm anybody with Christianity. But at all events—not to inspire dread, that ought to be learnt from the experience of an earlier time. No, the Pattern must be brought to the fore, for the sake at least of creating some respect for Christianity, to get it made a little bit evident what it is to be a Christian, to get Christianity transferred from learned discussion and doubt and twaddle (the objective) into the subjective sphere, where it belongs, as surely as the Saviour of the world, our Lord Jesus Christ, brought no doctrine into the world and never lectured but as the 'Pattern' required imitation—casting out, however, if possible, by His atonement all anxious dread from men's souls.

THE MORAL

As loudly as here is indicated (I say 'indicated', for in fact I constantly tone down the note to the humble admission), so loudly must the note be struck, if there is to be any seriousness and sense and character and truth in making a protest against the Established Church and wishing to reform it.

In case now anyone among us dares to step out ethically in the role here indicated, appealing moreover as an individual to a direct relationship with God, then I shall instantly (so it is I understand myself at this instant, but I cannot even know whether the next instant I may not be deprived even of the conditions for being able to do it, the next instant, perhaps while I am getting this published),[1] I shall instantly be at his service, by undertaking what before God I shall understand as my task. This task of mine will be to follow him, the Reformer, step by step, never budging from his side, to see if step by step he is in the true character of his role, is actually the Extraordinary. Should it appear that he is this, then my accompaniment will be nothing but bows and reverence before him, the Extraordinary—and verily this I dare say of myself: in this generation he will not find anyone, not a single person, who knows how to bow deeper before the Extraordinary, and this I did not learn in any court, no, higher up, in commerce with the ideals, where one learns to bow infinitely low, lower than any master of ceremonies. But, but . . . if he falls out of his role—that very second I cast

[1] He did not publish it, and perhaps what held him back till it was too late was the consideration that at any instant 'the conditions might be denied him', i.e. that the old Bishop might make the admission he required.

myself upon him, and this I dare say of myself: there is no one in this generation who deals a surer blow than I, when that is my task, or when one falsely represents himself as the Extraordinary. This sure blow I learnt in commerce with the ideals, where one in deep humility learns to hate oneself, but because one had nevertheless the courage to venture to engage with them, one receives as a gift of grace the power to deal this blow.

If on the contrary there is no one in this generation who ventures in the character of this role to assume the task of 'Reformer'—then (unless by that time the Established Church, instead of making admission of the truth that it, Christianity, is only a mildly modified approximation Christianly, will affirm that in a strict sense it is true to Christianity in accordance with the New Testament, and will thereby condemn and nullify itself), then let the Established Church be established and upheld; bungling efforts at reform are more pernicious than the most pernicious establishment, because reformation is the highest thing, and hence bungling at it is the most pernicious thing of all. Grant that the Established Church has its faults, many of them, say what thou wilt—if thou wilt not step forth in *character* as the true Reformer, then thou shalt hold thy tongue about reforming. Oh, of all characterlessness the most appalling!—to want to contrive mendaciously to look like a reformer, or to want to carry out a reform with a little partisanship, by balloting, &c.

No, if there is no such man among us, let us stick to the Established Church; let us enter into ourselves, let each one for himself admit how far behind we are in Christianity, but Thou, O my God, wilt preserve me from making things even worse by wanting mendaciously to carry out a reform.

And let it be said as loudly as possible, and would that

it might if possible be heard everywhere, and would to God that everywhere it is heard it might be heeded: *The evil in our time is not the Established Church with its many faults; no, the evil in our time is precisely this evil lust, this flirting with the will to reform,* this hypocrisy of seeking escape from the consciousness of one's own incapacity by the diversion of wishing to reform the Church, a thing which our time is least of all capable of doing. When the Church needed a reformation, no one reported for the task, there was no thronging to join the movement, all fled back, only one solitary man, the Reformer, was disciplined in all stillness with fear and trembling and much trial of temptation to adventure in God's name the extraordinary task. Now it is a muddle, as if it were on a country dance-floor, with all this wanting to reform; this cannot be God's thought, but is a swaggering device of man, and therefore instead of fear and trembling and much trial of temptation, there is Hurrah! Bravo! acclamation, balloting, a spree, a racket—and a false alarm.

March 1855

This book dates from the time when the old Bishop was still living. It is for this reason kept in remoteness [from practical questions of reform], both because I then understood thus my relation to the Established Church, and because out of consideration for the old Bishop I also was inclined to understand my relation thus.

Now I speak much more decisively, more openly, more truly, without meaning to imply by this that my previous way of speaking was untrue.

THE UNCHANGEABLENESS OF GOD

An Address

by

S. KIERKEGAARD

[Translated by David F. Swenson]

Copenhagen

1855

[Preached May 18, 1851]

DEDICATED

TO THE MEMORY OF

my deceased father

MICHAEL PEDERSEN KIERKEGAARD

formerly a hosier here in town.

August, 1855

PREFACE

This address was delivered in the Church of the Citadel, on the 18th of May, 1851. The text is the first I have used. Later I have often brought it forward; now I again return to it.

S. K.

May 5, 1854.

PRAYER

O THOU who art unchangeable, whom nothing changes! Thou who art unchangeable in love, precisely for our welfare not submitting to any change: may we too will our welfare, submitting ourselves to the discipline of Thy unchangeableness, so that we may, in unconditional obedience, find our rest and remain at rest in Thy unchangeableness. Not art Thou like a man; if he is to preserve only some degree of constancy he must not permit himself too much to be moved, nor by too many things. Thou on the contrary art moved, and moved in infinite love, by all things. Even that which we human beings call an insignificant trifle, and pass by unmoved, the need of a sparrow, even this moves Thee; and what we so often scarcely notice, a human sigh, this moves Thee, O Infinite Love! But nothing changes Thee, O Thou who art unchangeable! O Thou who in infinite love dost submit to be moved, may this our prayer also move Thee to add Thy blessing, in order that there may be wrought such a change in him who prays as to bring him into conformity with Thy unchangeable will, Thou who art unchangeable!

TEXT

The Epistle of James 1 : 17–21

EVERY good gift and every perfect gift is from above, coming down from the Father of lights, with whom can be no variation, neither shadow that is cast by turning. Of His own will He brought us forth by the word of truth, that we should be a kind of first-fruits of His creatures. Ye know this, my beloved brethren. But let every man be swift to hear, slow to speak, slow to wrath: for the wrath of man worketh not the righteousness of God. Wherefore putting away all filthiness and overflowing of wickedness, receive with meekness the implanted word, which is able to save your souls.

My hearer, you have listened to the reading of the text. How near at hand does it not seem now to turn our thoughts in the opposite direction, to the mutability of temporal and earthly things, to the changeableness of men. How depressing and wearisome to the spirit that all things are corruptible, that men are changeable, you, my hearer, and I! How sad that the change is so often for the worse! Poor human consolation, but yet a consolation, that there is still another change to which the changeable is subject, namely that it has an end!

And yet, if we were to speak in this manner, especially in this spirit of dejection, and hence not in the spirit of an earnest consideration of corruptibility, of human inconstancy, then we would not only fail to keep close to the text, but would depart from it, aye, even alter it. For the text speaks of the opposite, of the unchangeableness of God. The spirit of the text is unmixed joy and gladness. The words of the Apostle, coming as it were from the lofty silences of the highest mountain peaks, are uplifted above the mutabilities of the earthly life; he speaks of the unchangeablensss of God, and of nothing else. He speaks of a 'father of lights', who dwells above, with whom there is no variableness, not even the shadow of any change. He speaks of 'good and perfect gifts' that come to us from above, from this father, who as the father of 'lights' or light is infinitely well equipped to make sure that what comes from Him really is a good and perfect gift; and as a father He has no other ambition, nor any other thought, than invariably to send good and perfect gifts. And therefore, my beloved brethren, let every man be 'swift to hear'; not swift to listen to all sorts of loose talk, but swift to direct his attention upward, from whence comes invariably only good news. Let him be 'slow to speak'; for our ordinary human talk, especially in relation to these things, and especially that which comes first over our lips, serves most frequently only to make the good and perfect gifts less good and perfect. Let him be 'slow to wrath'; lest when the gifts do not seem to us good and perfect we become angry, and thus cause that which was good and perfect and intended for our welfare to become by our own fault ruinous to us—this is what the wrath of man is able to accomplish, and the 'wrath of man worketh not the righteousness of God'. 'Wherefore put aside all filthiness and overflowing of wickedness'—as when we cleanse and decorate the house and bedeck our persons, festively awaiting the visit, that we may worthily receive the good and perfect gifts. 'And receive with meekness the implanted word, which is able to save your souls.' With meekness! In truth, were it not the Apostle speaking, and did we not immediately obey the injunction to be 'slow to speak, slow to wrath', we might well be tempted to say: This is a very strange mode of speech; are we then altogether fools, that we need an admonition to be meek in relation to one who desires only our welfare?—it is as if it were meant to mock us, in this context to make use of the word 'meekness'. For suppose someone were about to strike me unjustly, and another stood by, and said admonishingly: 'Try to endure this treatment with meekness'— that would be straightforward speech. But imagine the friendliest of beings, one who is love itself; he has selected a gift for me, and the gift is good and perfect, as love itself; he comes to me and proposes to bestow this gift upon me—and then another man stands by and says admonishingly: 'See that you accept this treatment meekly!' And yet, so it is with us human beings. A pagan, and only a human being, the simple sage of antiquity, complains that whenever he proposed to take away from a man some folly or other, and so help him to a better insight, thus bestowing a benefit upon him, he had often experienced that the other became so angry that he even wished to bite him, as the simple sage said jestingly in earnest. Ah, and what has God not had to endure these six thousand years, what does He not endure from morning until night from each of mankind's many millions —for we are sometimes most wrath when He most intends our welfare. Indeed, if we men truly understood what conduces to our welfare, and in the deepest sense truly willed our own welfare, then there would be no need to admonish us to be meek in this connexion. But we human beings (and who has not verified this in his own experience) are in our relationship to God as children. And hence there is need of an admonition to be meek in connexion with our reception of the good and perfect—so thoroughly is the Apostle convinced that all good and perfect gifts come from Him who is eternally unchangeable.

Different viewpoints! The merely human tendency (as paganism indeed gives evidence) is to speak less about God, and to speak almost exclusively and with sadness about the mutability of human affairs. The Apostle, on the other hand, desires only and alone to speak of God's unchangeableness. Thus so far as the Apostle is concerned. For him the thought of God's unchangeableness is one of pure and unmixed comfort, peace, joy, happiness. And this is indeed eternally true. But let us not forget that the Apostle's joy has its explanation in the fact that the Apostle is the Apostle, that he has already long since wholly yielded himself in unconditional obedience to God's unchangeableness. He does not stand at the beginning, but rather at the end of the way, the narrow but good way which he had chosen in renunciation of everything, pursuing it invariably and without a backward look, hasting towards eternity with stronger and ever stronger strides. But we on the contrary, who are still beginners, and subject to discipline, for us the unchangeableness of God must have also another aspect; and if we forget this, we readily run in danger of taking the lofty serenity of the Apostle in vain.

Let us then speak, if possible to the promotion both of a wholesome fear and of a genuine peace, of Thee, who art unchangeable, or about Thy unchangeableness.

God is unchangeable. In His omnipotence He created this visible world—and made Himself invisible. He clothed Himself in the visible world as in a garment; He changes it as one who shifts a garment—Himself unchanged. Thus in the world of sensible things. In the world of events He is present everywhere in every moment; in a truer sense than we can say of the most watchful human justice that it is present everywhere, God is omnipresent, though never seen by any mortal; present everywhere, in the least event as well as in the greatest, in that which can scarcely be called an event and in that which is the only event, in the death of a sparrow and in the birth of the Saviour of mankind. In each moment every actuality is a possibility in His almighty hand; He holds all in readiness, in every instant prepared to change everything: the opinions of men, their judgements, human greatness and human abasement; He changes all, Himself unchanged. When everything seems stable (for it is only in appearance that the external world is for a time unchanged, in reality it is always in flux) and in the overturn of all things, He remains equally unchanged; no change touches Him, not even the shadow of a change; in unaltered clearness He, the father of lights, remains eternally unchanged. In unaltered clearness— aye, this is precisely why He is unchanged, because He is pure clearness, a clarity which betrays no trace of dimness, and which no dimness can come near. With us men it is not so. We are not in this manner clear, and precisely for this reason we are subject to change: now something becomes clearer in us, now something is dimmed, and we are changed; now changes take place about us, and the shadow of these changes glides over us to alter us; now there falls upon us from the surroundings an altering light, while under all this we are again changed within ourselves.

This thought *is terrifying, all fear and trembling*. This aspect of it is in general perhaps less often emphasized ; we complain of men and their mutability, and of the mutability of all temporal things, but God is unchangeable, this is our consolation, an entirely comforting thought: so speaks even frivolity. Aye, God is in very truth unchangeable.

But first and foremost, do you also have an understanding with God? Do you earnestly consider and sincerely strive to understand—and this is God's eternally unchangeable will for you as for every human being, that you should sincerely strive to attain this understanding—what God's will for you may be? Or do you live your life in such a fashion that this thought has never so much as entered your mind? How terrifying then that He is eternally unchangeable! For with this immutable will you must nevertheless some time, sooner or later, come into collision— this immutable will, which desired that you should consider this because it desired your welfare; this immutable will, which cannot but crush you if you come into hostile collision with it.

In the second place, you who have some degree of understanding with God, do you also have a good understanding with Him? Is your will unconditionally His will, your wishes, each one of them, His commandments, your thoughts, first and last, His thoughts? If not, how terrifying that God is unchangeable, everlastingly, eternally, unchangeable! Consider but in this connexion what it means to be at odds with merely a human being. But perhaps you are the stronger, and console yourself with the thought that the other will doubtless be compelled to change his attitude. But now if he happens to be the stronger—well, perhaps you think to have more endurance. But suppose it is an entire contemporary generation with which you are at odds; and yet, in that case you will perhaps say to yourself: seventy years is no eternity. But when the will is that of one eternally unchangeable—if you are at odds with this will it means an eternity: how terrifying!

Imagine a wayfarer. He has been brought to a standstill at the foot of a mountain, tremendous, impassable. It is this mountain . . . no, it is not his destiny to cross it, but he has set his heart upon the crossing; for his wishes, his longings, his desires, his very soul, which has an easier mode of conveyance, are already on the other side; it only remains for him to follow. Imagine him coming to be seventy years old; but the mountain still stands there, unchanged, impassable. Let him become twice seventy years; but the mountain stands there unalterably blocking his way, unchanged, impassable. Under all this he undergoes changes, perhaps; he dies away from his longings, his wishes, his desires; he now scarcely recognizes himself. And so a new generation finds him, altered, sitting at the foot of the mountain, which still stands there, unchanged, impassable. Suppose it to have happened a thousand years ago: the altered wayfarer is long since dead, and only a legend keeps his memory alive; it is the only thing that remains—aye, and also the mountain, unchanged, impassable. And now think of Him who is eternally unchangeable, for whom a thousand years are but as one day—ah, even this is too much to say, they are for Him as an instant, as if they did not even exist—consider then, if you have in the most distant manner a will to walk a different path than that which He wills for you: how terrifying!

True enough, if your will, if my will, if the will of all these many thousands happens to be not so entirely in harmony with God's will: things nevertheless take their course as best they may in the hurly-burly of the so-called actual world; it is as if God did not pay any attention. It is rather as if a just man—if there were such a man!—contemplating this world, a world which, as the Scriptures say, is dominated by evil, must needs feel disheartened because God does not seem to make Himself felt. But do you believe on that account that God has undergone any change? Or is the fact that God does not seem to make Himself felt any the less a terrifying fact, as long as it is nevertheless certain that He is eternally unchangeable? To me it does not seem so. Consider the matter, and then tell me which is the more terrible to contemplate: the picture of one who is infinitely the stronger, who grows tired of letting himself be mocked, and rises in his might to crush the refractory spirits—a sight terrible indeed, and so represented when we say that God is not mocked, pointing to the times when His annihilating punishments were visited upon the human race—but is this really the most terrifying sight? Is not this other sight still more terrifying: one infinitely powerful, who—eternally unchanged!—sits quite still and sees everything, without altering a feature, almost as if He did not exist; while all the time, as the just man must needs complain, lies achieve success and win to power, violence and wrong gain the victory, to such an extent as even to tempt a better man to think that if he hopes to accomplish anything for the good he must in part use the same means; so that it is as if God were being mocked, God the infinitely powerful, the eternally unchangeable, who none the less is neither mocked nor changed—is not this the most terrifying sight? For why, do you think, is He so quiet? Because He knows with Himself that He is eternally unchangeable. Anyone not eternally sure of Himself could not keep so still, but would rise in His strength. Only one who is eternally immutable can be in this manner so still.

He gives men time, and He can afford to give them time, since

He has eternity and is eternally unchangeable. He gives time, and that with premeditation. And then there comes an accounting in eternity, where nothing is forgotten, not even a single one of the improper words that were spoken; and He is eternally unchanged. And yet, it may be also an expression for His mercy that men are thus afforded time, time for conversion and betterment. But how fearful if the time is not used for this purpose! For in that case the folly and frivolity in us would rather have Him straightway ready with His punishment, instead of thus giving men time, seeming to take no cognizance of the wrong, and yet remaining eternally unchanged. Ask one experienced in bringing up children—and in relation to God we are all more or less as children; ask one who has had to do with transgressors— and each one of us has at least once in his life gone astray, and goes astray for a longer or a shorter time, at longer or shorter intervals: you will find Him ready to confirm the observation that for the frivolous it is a great help, or rather, that it is a preventive of frivolity (and who dares wholly acquit himself of frivolity!) when the punishment follows if possible instantly upon the transgression, so that the memory of the frivolous may acquire the habit of associating the punishment immediately with the guilt. Indeed, if transgression and punishment were so bound up with one another that, as in a double-barrelled shooting weapon, the pressure on a spring caused the punishment to follow instantly upon the seizure of the forbidden fruit, or immediately upon the commitment of the transgression—then I think that frivolity might take heed. But the longer the interval between guilt and punishment (which when truly understood is an expression for the gravity of the case) the greater the temptation to frivolity; as if the whole might perhaps be forgotten, or as if justice itself might alter and acquire different ideas with the passage of time, or as if at least it would be so long since the wrong was committed that it will become impossible to make an unaltered presentation of it before the bar of justice. Thus frivolity changes, and by no means for the better. It comes to feel itself secure; and when it has become secure it becomes more daring; and so the years pass, punishment is withheld, forgetfulness intervenes, and again the punishment is withheld, but new transgressions do not fail, and the old evil becomes still more malignant. And then finally all is over; death rolls down the curtain—and to all this (it was only frivolity!) there was an eternally unchangeable witness: is this also frivolity? One eternally unchangeable, and it is with this witness that you must make your reckoning. In the instant that the minute-hand of time showed seventy years, and the man died, during all that time the clock of eternity has scarcely moved perceptibly: to such a degree is everything present for the eternal, and for Him who is unchangeable.

And therefore, whoever you may be, take time to consider what I say to myself, that for God there is nothing significant and nothing insignificant, that in a certain sense the significant is for Him insignificant, and in another sense even the least significant is for Him infinitely significant. If then your will is not in harmony with His will, consider that you will never be able to evade Him. Be grateful to Him if through the use of mildness or of severity He teaches you to bring your will into agreement with His—how fearful if He makes no move to arrest your course, how fearful if in the case of any human being it comes to pass that He almost defiantly relies either upon the notion that God does not exist, or upon His having been changed, or even upon His being too great to take note of what we call trifles! For the truth is that God both exists and is eternally unchangeable; and His infinite greatness consists precisely in seeing even the least thing, and remembering even the least thing. Aye, and if you do not will as He wills, that He remembers it unchanged for an eternity!

There is thus sheer fear and trembling, for us frivolous and inconstant human beings, in this thought of God's unchangeableness. Oh, consider it well! Whether God makes Himself immediately felt or not, He is eternally unchangeable. He is eternally unchangeable, consider this, if as we say you have any matter outstanding with Him; He is unchangeable. You have perhaps promised Him something, obligated yourself in a sacred pledge ... but in the course of time you have undergone a change, and now you rarely think of God—now that you have grown older, have you perhaps found more important things to think about? Or perhaps you now have different notions about God, and think that He does not concern Himself with the trifles of your life, regarding such beliefs as childishness. In any case you have just about forgotten what you promised Him; and thereupon you have proceeded to forget that you promised Him anything; and finally, you have forgotten, forgotten—aye, forgotten that He forgets nothing, since He is eternally unchangeable, forgotten that it is precisely the inverted childishness of mature years to imagine that anything is insignificant for God, or that God forgets anything, He who is eternally unchangeable!

In human relationships we so often complain of inconstancy, one party accuses the other of having changed. But even in the relationship between man and man, it is sometimes ·the case that the constancy of one party may come to seem like a tormenting affliction for the other. A man may, for example, have talked to another person about himself. What he said may have been merely a little childish, pardonably so. But perhaps, too, the matter was more serious than this: the poor foolish vain heart was tempted to speak in lofty tones of its enthusiasm, of the constancy of its feelings, and of its purposes in this world. The other man listened calmly; he did not even smile, or interrupt the speech; he let him speak on to the end, listened and kept silence; only he promised, as he was asked to do, not to forget what had been said. Then some time elapsed, and the first man had long since forgotten all this; only the other had not forgotten. Aye, let us suppose something still stranger: he had permitted himself to be moved inwardly by the thoughts that the first man had expressed under the influence of his mood, when he poured out, so to speak, his momentary feeling; he had in sincere endeavour shaped his life in accordance with these ideas. What torment in this unchanged remembrance by one who showed only too clearly that he had retained in his memory every last detail of what had been said in that moment!

And now consider Him, who is eternally unchangeable—and this human heart! O this human heart, what is not hidden in your secret recesses, unknown to others—and that is the least of it—but sometimes almost unknown to the individual himself! When a man has lived a few years it is almost as if it were a burial-plot, this human heart! There they lie buried in forgetfulness, promises, intentions, resolutions, entire plans and fragments of plans, and God knows what—aye, so say we men, for we rarely think about what we say; we say: there lies God knows what. And this we say half in a spirit of frivolity, and half weary of life—and it is so fearfully true that God does know what to the last detail, knows what you have forgotten, knows what for your recollection has suffered alteration, knows it all unchanged. He does not remember it merely as having happened some time ago, nay, He remembers it as if it were to-day. He knows whether, in connexion with any of these wishes, intentions, resolutions, something so to speak was said to Him about it—and He is eternally unchanged and eternally unchangeable. Oh, if the remembrance that another human being carries about with him may seem as it were a burden to you—well, this remembrance is after all not always so entirely trustworthy, and in any case it cannot endure for an eternity: some time I may expect to be freed from this other man and his remembrance. But an omniscient witness and an eternally unchangeable remembrance, one from which you can never free yourself, least of all in eternity: how fearful! No, in a manner eternally unchanged, everything is for God eternally present, always equally before Him. No shadow of variation, neither that of morning nor of evening, neither that of youth nor of old age, neither that of forgetfulness nor of excuse, changes Him; for Him there is no shadow. If we human beings are mere shadows, as is sometimes said, He is eternal clearness in eternal unchangeableness. If we are shadows that glide away—my soul, look well to thyself; for whether you will it or not, you go to meet eternity, to meet Him, and He is eternal clearness. Hence it is not so much that He keeps a reckoning, as that He is Himself the reckoning. It is said that we must render up an account, as if we perhaps had a long time to prepare for it, and also perhaps as if it were likely to be cluttered up with such an enormous mass of detail as to make it impossible to get the reckoning finished: O my soul, the account is every moment complete! For the unchangeable clearness of God is the reckoning, complete to the last detail, preserved by Him who is eternally unchangeable, and who has forgotten nothing of the things that I have forgotten, and who does not, as I do, remember some things otherwise than they really were.

There is thus sheer fear and trembling in this thought of the unchangeableness of God, almost as if it were far, far beyond the power of any human being to sustain a relationship to such an unchangeable power; aye, as if this thought must drive a man to such unrest and anxiety of mind as to bring him to the verge of despair.

But then it is also true that *there is rest and happiness in this thought*. It is really true that when, wearied with all this human inconstancy, this temporal and earthly mutability, and wearied also of your own inconstancy, you might wish to find a place where rest may be found for your weary head, your weary thoughts, your weary spirit, so that you might rest and find complete repose: Oh, in the unchangeableness of God there is rest! When you therefore permit this unchangeableness to serve you according to His will, for your own welfare, your eternal welfare; when you submit yourself to discipline, so that your selfish will (and it is from this that the change chiefly comes, more than from the outside) dies away, the sooner the better—and there is no help for it, you must whether willing or resisting, for think how vain it is for your will to be at odds with an eternal immutability; be therefore as the child when it profoundly feels that it has over against itself a will in relation to which nothing avails except obedience—when you submit to be disciplined by His unchangeable will, so as to renounce inconstancy and changeableness and caprice and self-will: then you will steadily rest more and more securely, and more and more blessedly, in the unchangeableness of God. For that the thought of God's unchangeableness is a blessed thought—who can doubt it? But take heed that you become of such a mind that you can rest happily in this immutability! Oh, as one is wont to speak who has a happy home, so speaks such an individual. He says: my home is eternally secure, I rest in the unchangeableness of God. This is a rest that no one can disturb for you except yourself; if you could become completely obedient in invariable obedience, you would each and every moment, with the same necessity as that by which a heavy body sinks to the earth or a light body moves upward, freely rest in God.

And as for the rest, let all things change as they do. If the scene of your activity is on a larger stage, you will experience the mutability of all things in greater measure; but even on a lesser stage, or on the smallest stage of all, you will still experience the same, perhaps quite as painfully. You will learn how men change, how you yourself change; sometimes it will even seem to you as if God Himself changed, all of which belongs to the upbringing. On this subject of the mutability of all things one older than I would be able to speak in better fashion, while perhaps what I could say might seem to someone very young as if it were new. But this we shall not further expound, leaving it rather for the manifold experiences of life to unfold for each one in particular, in a manner intended especially for him, that which all other men have experienced before him. Sometimes the changes will be such as to call to mind the saying that variety is a pleasure—an indescribable pleasure! There will also come times when you will have occasion to discover for yourself a saying which the language has suppressed, and you will say to yourself: 'Change is not pleasant—how could I ever have said that variety is a pleasure!' When this experience comes to you, you will have especial occasion (though you will surely not forget this in the first case either) to seek Him who is unchangeable.

My hearer, this hour is now soon past, and the discourse. Unless you yourself will it otherwise, this hour and its discourse will soon be forgotten. And unless you yourself will it otherwise, the thought of God's unchangeableness will also soon be forgotten in the midst of life's changes. But for this He will surely not be responsible, He who is unchangeable! But if you do not make yourself guilty of forgetfulness with respect to it, you will in this thought have found a sufficiency for your entire life, aye, for eternity.

Imagine a solitary wayfarer, a desert wanderer. Almost burned by the heat of the sun, languishing with thirst, he finds a spring. O refreshing coolness! Now God be praised, he says—and yet it was merely a spring he found; what then must not he say who found God! and yet he too must say: 'God be praised, I have found God—now I am well provided for. Your faithful coolness, O beloved well-spring, is not subject to any change. In the cold of winter, if winter visited this place, you would not become colder, but would preserve the same coolness unchanged, for the waters of the spring do not freeze! In the midday heat of the summer sun you preserve precisely the same coolness, for the waters of the spring do not become lukewarm!' There is nothing untrue in what he says, no false exaggeration in his eulogy. (And he who chooses a spring as subject for his eulogy chooses in my opinion no ungrateful theme, as anyone may better understand the more he knows what the desert signifies, and solitude.) However, the life of our wanderer took a turn otherwise than he had thought; he lost touch with the spring, and went astray in the wide world. Many years later he returned to the same place. His first thought was of the spring—but it was not, it had run dry. For a moment he stood silent in grief. Then he gathered himself together and said: 'No, I will not retract a single word of all that I said in your praise; it was all true. And if I praised your refreshing coolness while you were still in being, O beloved well-spring, let me now also praise it when you have vanished, in order that there may be some proof of unchangeableness in a human breast. Nor can I say that you deceived me; had I found you, I am convinced that your coolness would have been quite unchanged—and more you had not promised.'

But Thou O God, who art unchangeable, Thou art always and invariably to be found, and always to be found unchanged. Whether in life or in death, no one journeys so far afield that Thou art not to·be found by Him, that Thou art not there, Thou who art everywhere. It is not so with the well-springs of earth, for they are to be found only in special places. And besides—overwhelming security!—Thou dost not remain, like the spring, in a single place, but Thou dost follow the traveller on his way. Ah, and no one ever wanders so far astray that he cannot find the way back to Thee, Thou who art not merely as a spring that may be found —how poor and inadequate a description of what Thou art!— but rather as a spring that itself seeks out the thirsty traveller, the errant wanderer: who has ever heard the like of any spring! Thus Thou art unchangeably always and everywhere to be found. And whenever any human being comes to Thee, of whatever age, at whatever time of the day, in whatever state: if he comes in sincerity he always finds Thy love equally warm, like the spring's unchanged coolness, O Thou who art unchangeable! Amen!

INDEX

*Since the words listed below are most of them key words which recur on con-
secutive pages, the Index indicates only the page where a particular theme begins
or re-begins, without purposing to point to every recurrence of a word.*